THE STRUGGLE FOR EUROPEAN PRIVATE LAW

The European codification project has rapidly gathered pace since the turn of the century. This monograph considers the codification project in light of a series of broader analytical frameworks – comparative, historical and constitutional – which make modern codification phenomena intelligible. This new reading across fields renders the European codification project (currently being promoted through the Common Frame of Reference and the Optional Sales Law Code proposal) vulnerable to constitutionally grounded criticism, traceable to normative considerations of private law authority and legitimacy. Arguing that modern codification phenomena are more complex than positivist, socio-legal and historical approaches have suggested over the past two centuries, the book stages a path-breaking method of analysis of the law-discourse (*nomos*-centred) which questions at once the reduction of private law to legislation and of law to power and, on this basis, redefines the ways in which to counter law's disintegration and crisis in the context of Europeanisation.

Professor Niglia reconstructs the European codification project as a complex structure of government-in-the-making that embodies a set of contingent world views, excludes alternatives, challenges the plurality of private laws and entrenches conflicts that pertain not only to form (codification, de-codification, recodification) but also to dilemmas implicated in determining the substantive orientation of European private law. The book investigates the position of the codifiers and their discontents in the shadow of the codification strategy pursued by the European Commission – noting a new turn in the struggle over the configuration of private law which has taken place since the Savigny-Thibaut dispute of 1814 which this book critically revisits exactly two centuries later. This monograph is particularly aimed at readers interested in exploring the complexities, and interconnections, of the supposedly separate realms of comparative law, European law, private law, legal history, constitutional law, sociology of law and, last but not least, legal theory and jurisprudence.

Volume 50 in the series Modern Studies in European Law

Modern Studies in European Law

Recent titles in this series:

Lawyering Europe: European Law as a Transnational Social Field
Edited by Antoine Vauchez and Bruno de Witte

Services and the EU Citizen
Edited by Frank S Benyon

The Accession of the European Union to the European Convention on Human Rights
Paul Gragl

Normative Patterns and Legal Developments in the Social Dimension of the EU
Edited by Ann Numhauser-Henning and Mia Rönnmar

The European Neighbourhood Policy and the Democratic Values of the EU: A Legal Analysis
Nariné Ghazaryan

EU Security and Justice Law: After Lisbon and Stockholm
Edited by Diego Acosta Arcarazo and Cian C Murphy

EU Environmental Law, Governance and Decision-Making
Maria Lee

Shaping the Single European Market in the Field of Foreign Direct Investment
Philip Strik

Nationalism and Private Law in Europe
Guido Comparato

EU Asylum Procedures and the Right to an Effective Remedy
Marcelle Reneman

The EU Accession to the ECHR
Edited by Vasiliki Kosta, Nikos Skoutaris and Vassilis P Tzevelekos

The European Court of Justice and External Relations: Constitutional Challenges
Edited by Marise Cremona and Anne Thies

For the complete list of titles in this series, see
'Modern Studies in European Law' link at
www.hartpub.co.uk/books/series.asp

The Struggle for European Private Law

A Critique of Codification

Leone Niglia

•HART•
PUBLISHING
OXFORD AND PORTLAND, OREGON
2017

Hart Publishing
An imprint of Bloomsbury Publishing Plc

Hart Publishing Ltd
Kemp House
Chawley Park
Cumnor Hill
Oxford OX2 9PH
UK

Bloomsbury Publishing Plc
50 Bedford Square
London
WC1B 3DP
UK

www.hartpub.co.uk
www.bloomsbury.com

Published in North America (US and Canada) by
Hart Publishing
c/o International Specialized Book Services
920 NE 58th Avenue, Suite 300
Portland, OR 97213-3786
USA

www.isbs.com

First published in hardback, 2015
Paperback edition, 2017

British Library Cataloguing-in-Publication Data
A catalogue record for this book is available from the British Library.

ISBN: HB: 978-1-84946-260-0
PB: 978-1-50991-382-4

Typeset by Compuscript Ltd, Shannon
Printed and bound in Great Britain by
Lightning Source UK Ltd

Ai miei genitori

Preface and Acknowledgements

This book is a companion to *The Transformation of Contract in Europe* (2003) and to the monographic trilogy of essays on European private law (2006–10). As we now face the prospect of private law's unification – beyond harmonization – this book explores the new ways in which private law material is ever more directed to the task of disintegrating Europe's plural law-lifeworld. This is a phenomenon, a fragment of a wider crisis, in which private law equally operates as a counter-movement *vis-à-vis* the forces of disintegration. The book aims at contributing to the task of restoring awareness of European law's present condition and to the much needed refinement of the private law discourse towards engagement and responsibility.

I am grateful to many colleagues for the exchanges which have contributed to the shaping of this book; to avoid the risk of omissions, I do not name them here. I hope that in reading this book they will find places where they will see my silent tribute to them. Thanks to the following institutions for financial support: The British Academy; The Carnegie Trust for the Universities of Scotland; The Italian Ministry of Education and Research; The Leverhulme Trust; The University of Michigan Law School; and to the European University Institute, the University of Heidelberg, the University of London and the University of Modena e Reggio Emilia libraries. Parts of this book were presented at the University of Cambridge, the Heinrich-Heine-University Düsseldorf, Harvard University, the University of Heidelberg, the London School of Economics and Political Science, the University of Michigan, the University of Modena and Reggio Emilia, the University of Queensland, the University of Salerno and Utrecht University; I am grateful to the conveners of those events and to the participants for comments. Thanks to Hart Publishing for placing their trust in this project, much honoured as I am for this volume to be the 50th in the prestigious European law book series. Legislation and cases updated as of January 2014.

Professor Leone Niglia
Summer 2014

Table of Contents

Prologue

AN ARGUMENT

CONVENTIONAL COMPARATIVE AND historical studies portray the arbitrary power of the legislature as the engine of modern codification phenomena. A code[1] is taken to be statute par excellence, that is, legislation (*thesis*) that dominates the production and application of private law in lieu of leaving it in the hands of scholars and judges (*nomos*).[2] In this view, codification internalises the dynamics that lead to the code-output, that is, the struggle

[1] In this book, 'code' means civil code, unless otherwise indicated.

[2] See, eg, RC Van Caenegem, *Judges, Legislators and Professors: Chapters in European Legal History* (Cambridge, Cambridge University Press, 1987) 153 (opposition *nomos* vs *thesis*; commenting on Savigny's position in the 1804 dispute over codification as 'struggle' 'between legislators and professors'); RC Van Caenegem, *A Historical Introduction to Private Law* (Cambridge, Cambridge University Press, 1992, translated by DEL Johnston) 8–9 ('The *Code* was to be conceived first and foremost as a positive legal text, and any doctrinal excess must be avoided; the terms of the statute must not become obscured by theories and lectures. This view accords with the notion of the absolute primacy of statute as a source of law. Doctrinal interpretation, case law (in which the judge is reduced to a passive role as the voice of the statute), and custom are subordinated to the authority of the statute.'; 'Statute, which at certain stages of legal evolution had been wholly eclipsed, was now the source of law *par excellence*'); A Watson, *The Making of the Civil Law* (Cambridge, MA, Harvard University Press, 1981) 168 ('With codification, law becomes basically and primarily statute law, and the code is the private law statute *par excellence*... The systematic and comprehensive nature of the code with supporting legislation makes law statute-oriented to an extent that is otherwise impossible; and the code and supporting legislation provide the skeleton of the whole of private law'). In the words of K Cosack in Hans Planitz (ed), *Die Rechtswissenschaft der Gegenwart in Selbstdarstellungen*, vol I (Leipzig, F Meiner, 1923–25) 16: 'I simply do not believe that contemporary law has emerged from the old law, but I regard it as something new, created by the needs of the present day and the arbitrary power of the legislature' (quoted in, and translated by, R Zimmermann, *Roman Law, Contemporary Law, European Law: The Civilian Tradition Today* (Oxford, Oxford University Press, 2001) 49). Critically, see the reading of P Grossi, *Assolutismo Giuridico e Diritto Privato* (Milan, Giuffrè, 1998) 21 ('Con riguardo all'ampio pluralismo giuridico preesistente la codificazione rappresentò un esproprio: il giuridico, dimensione abbastanza indifferente agli occhi di quel potere politico incompiuto che fu proprio dell'età medievale post-medievale, percepito ora dal lucidissimo potere borghese come prezioso e insostituibile *instrumentum regni*, viene monopolizzato... monopolio del principe ed espropriazione della produzione giuridica dalle mani dei giuristi ... Con il risultato più incredibile e grottesco: il giurista ufficiale, in forza della sua plagiata coscienza, sembra non rendersi conto dell'esproprio subìto e vive soddisfatto, pago di quella briciola che il legislatore gli concede: l'esegesi; che é però soltanto l'elemosina a un povero nullatenente') and of C Varga, *Codification as a Socio-historical Phenomenon* (Budapest, Akadémiai Kiadó, 1991) 281 et seq (the interface between advance of capitalism, state bureaucracy and codification, drawing on Max Weber) and 290 (codification seen as the product of 'the new establishment', which 'permitted' 'the formation of a superstructure reflecting the needs of the economic structure').

(*Kodifikationsstreit*) of the legislator against scholars and judges.[3] The canonical description of the *Code civil* as doing away with pre-revolutionary legal particularism – including 65 general customs, over 300 local customs, Roman law modified by local conditions, decisions of local *Parlements*, supplemented by canon law and by Roman law qua *ratio scripta*, opinions of writers and inputs by courts[4] – through the one-off emanation of a 'single body of law, called the Code Civil' on 21 March 1804 marks the birth of this vocabulary.[5] This was followed by over two centuries of various combinations of nationalist and rationalist conceptual constructs that have further elaborated upon this vocabulary by depicting modern codes as contributing to the making of state sovereignty in *that* way.[6] This book sees more structure. A critical reading of this conventional view examines the concrete significance of the broader range of actors that operate in codification contexts. It is argued that codes have no inherent truth when divorced from the jurisprudential forces that surround them.[7] The jurisprudential forces, alongside the legislature, are the key engines of codification. Codes are hybrid objects, both statute and jurisprudence; they are not just the product of 'the will of the

[3] Van Canaegem (n 2) 153.

[4] For this synthesis of the state of the art of the law in France around the end of the eighteenth century, see J-L Halperin, *The French Civil Code* (UCL Press, 2005, translated by Tony Weir) 2.

[5] See Law of 21 March 1804 (*Loi du 30 Ventôse an XII* (code qua 'table rase des sources de l'Ancien droit'). See AFJ Thibaut, *Über die Notwendigkeit eines allgemeinen bürgerlichen Rechts für Deutschland* (Heidelberg, Mohr und Zimmer, 1814), reprinted in Hans Hattenbauer, *Thibaut und Savigny. Ihre Programmatisches Schriften* (Munich, Verlag Franz Vahlen, 1973) 68 (arguing for the necessity of a code to be adopted by all German governments based on the consideration that the existing law is contradictory, divisive and bars real knowledge of the law for judges and lawyers).

[6] The writings that instigated the *Kodifikationsstreit* (Thibaut (n 5); FC von Savigny, *Vom Beruf unserer Zeit für Gesetzgebung und Rechtswissenschaft* (Heidelberg, Mohr und Zimmer, 1814; translated as *Of the Vocation of Our Age for Legislation and Jurisprudence* (London, Littlewood & Co, 1831, translated by Abraham Hayward) no doubt have fundamentally contributed to the construction of this powerful narrative, for they shared the nationalist ideals of the time, although they offered remarkably conflicting conceptions of codification, with Thibaut holding the rationalist belief of a code based on 'clear, unequivocal and exhaustive' provisions (my translation; see Thibaut (n 5): 'Man kann und muss an jede Gesetzgebung zwey Forderungen machen: dass sie formell und materiell vollkommen sey; also dass sie ihre Bestimmungen klar, unzweydeutig und erfchoepfend aufstelle, und dass sie die buercherlichen Einrichtungen weise und zweckmaessig, ganz nach ben Beduerfnissen der Unterthanen, anordne', now in Hans Hattenbauer (ed), *Thibaut und Savigny. Ihre Programmatichen Schriften* (2nd edn, Munich, Verlag Franz Vahlen, 2002) 41) towards providing for a 'wise government', whilst Savigny famously adopted a historicised view of codification that led him to believe that legal thought of the time was not yet mature for the move towards codification. These narratives were then taken up in other countries, from Italy to Spain to Switzerland, by writers who re-deployed them in idiosyncratic jurisprudential contexts (for details, see P Caroni, 'Il codice rinviato. Resistenze europee all'elaborazione e alla diffusione del modello codicistico' in P Cappellini and B Sordi (eds), *Codici. Una riflessione di fine millennio* (Milan, Giuffrè, 2002) 263).

[7] In this book, by 'jurisprudence' or 'jurisprudential forces', I mean both scholars and judges, for judges co-determine the success or failure of codes at the post-enactment stage, whilst at times even participating in the elaboration of code-texts (eg, judicial resistance vis-a-vis the project of legal unification of the monarchy during the *Ancien Régime*, according to the reconstruction of Caroni (n 6) 289, n 66; 'divided' opinion among the top judges of the *tribunal de cassation* on the 1801 draft code on divorce and equality in succession according to the reconstruction of JL Halpérin, *The French Civil Code* (London and New York, UCL Press, 2006; translated by T Weir) at 12). As commonplace in comparative and historical studies on codification, I conflate the role of lawyers sitting in committees charged with the drafting of civil codes with that of 'scholarship'.

legislator', but epistemic material. The emphasis of conventionalism on the absolute, monopolising role of the national legislature in codification episodes has led to the view that the law, once codified, would become somehow insulated from jurisprudential resistance and nuances in interpretation. But the truths of any description of, and conception of, the codification phenomenon must lie in looking at the role played by the surrounding community of interpreters. At this level, one discovers at times jurisprudential forces that massively produce the legal material around which codes are made and implemented. However, concurrently, one also discovers jurisprudential forces that resist and that even manage to subvert and sabotage codes.[8] This contingency contributes to the understanding of whether draft codes are enacted, and why enacted codes succeed or fail. This perspective, it is submitted, can provide a critical insight into what the current European codification process[9] is really about.

* * *

In modern codification episodes of the nineteenth and twentieth centuries, the legislature has never acted in splendid isolation, but in tandem with the legal elites. Modern codification has always been a *nomotethic* phenomenon, the product of the joint energies of *thesis* and *nomos* rather than the unilateral superimposition of legislative material over scholars and judges. The activities of scholarship and of judges have powerfully co-determined the making of modern codification (eg, the committees of lawyers appointed with the task of writing codes) and the extent to which codes have actually been implemented on the ground (eg, the 1804 *Code civil des français* could become operational only with the exegetic turn in scholarship and adjudication of the 1840s and 1850s). Coming to the current century, this book portrays the idea of a European civil code as a complex project of re-organisation of the private law realm (the making of a pan-European governmental technique of market ordering geared towards implementing a libertarian ideology) willed by the European Union (EU) legislature *and* by key strands of European private law scholarship. It investigates the details of this encounter, that

[8] For a rising movement of thought away from legislation-centred understandings of the codification phenomenon towards the need for taking the role of scholarship and of adjudication seriously in modern codification phenomena, see, eg, Caroni (n 6) 263 (detailing episodes of scholarly resistances); A Gambaro, 'Codici e diritto giurisprudenziale' in Cappellini and Sordi (n 6) 507 (the code-texts reveal their character only if one learns about their use in the context of the legal community qua 'legal process'); L Niglia, *The Transformation of Contract in Europe* (The Hague, Kluwer Law International, 2003) (codified texts on contract law understood in relation to the role of the communities of scholars and judges). Even the most significant of all sabotage processes, the demise of codification via de-codification, must be explained in jurisprudential terms, rather than just as the product of legislation, given the role played by the jurisprudential forces in making it possible: see ch 2 (taking a critical view of Irti's de-codification thesis in relation to this aspect). Both codification and de-codification are *jurisprudential* processes.

[9] By 'European codification process', I mean the contingent process set in motion by the jurisprudential forces and by the EU legislator and having given rise to the code-text of the Draft Common Frame of Reference and its synthetic version, the Optional Sales Law Code. On the naming of the proposed code as a 'misnomer', see ch 1.

is, it describes the proposed code as a powerful governmental technique of market ordering in-the-making constructed by the jurists. Learning structures legislation and not vice versa. I investigate the argument that behind the European codification move is an attempt on the part of strands of private law scholarship to impose a monistic interpretative private law regime (and, relatedly, willingly or unwillingly, an ideological order) that contrasts starkly with the structures of national private law constellations, organised as they are around the piecemeal governing of conflicts of interests and values (material rights) as they emerge out of the fragmentation of private law (de-codified), via pragmatic techniques aimed at conflict synthesis (including conflicts to which the EU Directives on consumer private law apply). An artificially re-created monistic law is being resurrected that threatens the realm of the living law, which is characterised as pluralist, fragmented and de-codified, and as pragmatic experimentation of synthesising conflicts among material rights. Given the power of the jurists behind the phenomenon, this book explains that the attempt to replace national private (de-codified) law with a European code architecture is contingent less on the vicissitudes of the legislative process (the capacity of the European Commission to win consensus before the European legislative institutions over its agenda for unifying private law via codification) and more on the outcome of the struggles among the jurisprudential forces over an organisation of private law based on monistic (code) *or* pragmatic (balancing) techniques. At stake in the option for a European code is more than just legislative technique (the remaking of the private law harmonisation agenda around a code rather than Directives) and legislative politics (the re-orientation of private law towards market libertarian objectives). Deep down, and concurrently, at stake is the issue of whether or not to sacrifice the civilian experience as reconstituted, over the second half of the twentieth century, around pragmatic techniques. This book alerts scholarship to its social responsibility in taking sides in the context of the new dispute over codification, which is strikingly similar in structure to all of the previous codification disputes. For ever since the first and most celebrated of all, the 1814 *Kodifikationstreit* between Savigny and Thibaut, each codification dispute has been not just about a one-off conflict between the legislator and jurisprudence regarding whether or not to make a code, but a chapter of deeper conflicts among the jurisprudential forces themselves as to the *méthode* around which to organise private law.

STRUCTURE

The book is organised into four chapters. The first offers a 'top-down perspective' of how the proposed code has been constructed in the context of the EU legislative process, while the remaining chapters deal with a 'bottom-up perspective', analysing the meaning of the European codification process from the vantage point of the living law as articulated in the wider, plural European community of interpreters.

Chapter one explains how scholarship and the EU Commission have co-operated in the design of the European code-text (the Draft Common Frame of Reference and its synthetic version, the Optional Sales Law Code),[10] being a classical repetition of the 'nomothetic' (*nomos*-and-*thesis*) phenomenon of codification. They have given birth, once more, to a code-text that, like many of its predecessors in modern times, claims to be universal (that is, in the interests of all), but in actual fact aims both at serving an overarching ideological plan and at disciplining law towards complying with that plan by fettering the course of jurisprudential interpretation as applied to the consumer private law Directives within the multinational private law experience.

Chapter two looks at how the jurisprudential forces (both scholarly and judicial) operate in organising private law, including their engagement with the consumer private law Directives. It explains that the jurisprudential forces have managed to free themselves from the disciplinary constraints of their respective national civil codes – *nomos* gaining autonomy and independence from *thesis* and giving birth to a law that is much less ideologised (that is, ideologically pluralist, built as it is on engaging with the pursuit of synthesising conflicts among material rights) than the nineteenth-century mono-ideological law of the bourgeois codes.

Chapter three critically reads the latest version of the proposed European code-text, the Optional Sales Law Code, as a legislative attempt to chain *nomos* to *thesis* by conjuring up a code-text with an overarching ideological plan at its core, an attempt that has already been met with various points of resistance, which the chapter closely considers. The chapter explains that the codification process is encountering dissent from within, coming from strands of scholarship that criticise the code move by drawing on the acquired values of the national experience of de-codification. From this vantage point, the codification process emerges as an attempt to *re*-codify private law by *re*-chaining *nomos* to *thesis*. Defending national mandatory rules against the 'social dumping' effect of the proposed Optional Sales Law Code, for example, is a way in which scholarship re-articulates the values of de-codified national private law (the defence of a core set of material rights) against the market-orientated ideology of the code.

Chapter four translates the re-codification agenda in the deeper terms of an internal confrontation between the private law jurisprudential forces (scholarly). Re-codification emerges as not just a legislative (chapter three) but also as a jurisprudential attempt to re-chain *nomos* to *thesis*, with the codifiers intending to tame what they have always described as the 'chaos' of the de-codified ways of

[10] See, respectively, the Draft Common Frame of Reference (DCFR): C von Bar and E Clive (eds), *Principles, Definitions and Model Rules of European Private Law. Draft Common Frame of Reference* (Oxford, Oxford University Press, 2009) and the two previous editions without comments and notes: C Von Bar et al (eds), *Principles, Definitions and Model Rules of European Private Law: The Draft Common Frame of Reference* (Münich, Sellier, *Outline Edition*, 2009); C von Bar et al (eds), *Principles, Definitions and Model Rules of European Private Law: The Draft Common Frame of Reference* (Münich, Sellier, *Interim Outline Edition*, 2008); and the *Optional Sales Law Code: Proposal for a Regulation of the European Council and the Parliament for a Common European Sales Law*, 11 October 2011; SEC(2011) 1165 and 165 final.

law. The chapter offers an archaeology of the legal material on which the codifiers base their position that their critics, drawing on different sets of legal material, disagree with and contend. It notes a struggle over the (European) code that pertains to the return of a clash of competing conceptions regarding how to organise private law. On the one hand, *nomothetic*, that is, codified – the 'science of law' and its 'ordering' of private law abstract rights, with rights conceived of as descending from the allegedly coherent and complete code-system, as set out by the act of imperium of the legislator, and orientated to a contingent, 'individualist' ideological agenda.[11] On the other hand, *nomo*-centred, that is, de-codified – judges and scholars co-operating towards synthesising material rights' conflicts as they emerge in the context of the fragmentation of the private law system, according to a pluralistic constitutional plan based on socially orientated values.[12] The chapter also highlights the ideological implications that descend from preferring a particular alternative or, as is sometimes the case instead, from positioning oneself somewhere along the continuum defined by the competing vocabularies. It is submitted that the codification project is contingent on the outcome of these struggles among the jurisprudential forces. This is an aspect taken up once more in the conclusion to the book, where I discuss the problematic of *étatisation* (code as state-like structure) and of authority (code as normative material) implicated in the current codification phenomenon and the extent of responsibility that lies with legal thought in deciding for, or against, a European civil code.

[11] For this conception of modern codes, including its embodiment in the European codification movement, see ch 1. For the deep structures of thought behind this conception, as articulated in the context of the contemporary European codification movement, see ch 4.

[12] For this conception of a de-codified private law as developed in national legal systems, see ch 2.

1

Code

A judge working with a code has . . . been likened to somebody who has been told he could walk about more or less as he liked in a room, but could not go outside. (H Kötz)*

I will forthwith set about drawing up, for the use of the United States . . . a compleat body of proposed law, in the form of Statute law: say, in one word, a Pannomion, a body of Statute law, including a succedaneum to that mass of foreign law, the yoke of which, in the worldless, as well as boundless, and shapeless shape of the common, alias unwritten law, remains still about your necks. (J Bentham)**

I. ADVENT OF THE EUROPEAN CODE PROJECT (1989 TO TODAY)

PROPOSED BY THE European Parliament some 25 years ago[1] on questionable grounds[2] and, ever since, carried forward by the European Commission and strands of European private law scholarship (albeit controversially),[3] the Brussels-led codification project is gathering momentum. For the first time since the pronouncements of the European Parliament, a legislative proposal has

* H Kötz, 'Taking Civil Codes Less Seriously' (1987) 50 *Modern Law Review* 1.

** J Bentham, 'Letter to the President of the United States', 1811 in P Schoefield and J Harris (eds), *Jeremy Bentham, 'Legislator of the World': Writings on Codification, Law, and Education* (Oxford, Clarendon Press, 1998) 5.

[1] European Parliament Resolution on action to bring into line the private law of the Member States Resolution A2-157 [1989] OJ C-158/400 followed by Resolutions A3-0329/94 OJ 1994 C-205, 518; B5-0228, 0229, 0230/2000 OJ 2000 C-377, 326 and A5-0384/2001, OJ 2002 C-140 E, 541, which had envisaged the enactment of a European civil code by 2010.

[2] For a critical perspective see L Mengoni, 'L'Europa dei codici o un codice per l'Europa?' (Rome, Centro di Studi e Ricerche di Diritto Comparato e Straniero, 1993) (commenting on the Resolution of the European Parliament of 26 May 1989 as being ambiguous and not adequately reflected due to support for the idea of a European civil code based on arguments from harmonisation and from unification without accurately distinguishing between them; the European code was held to be 'no realistic alternative').

[3] The proposed Common European Sales Law (CESL) has been criticised not only for lacking a proper legal basis (Article 5 of the Treaty on European Union (TEU) and Articles 114 and 115 of the Treaty on the Functioning of the Euopean Union (TFEU) do not lend themselves to being interpreted as conferring a fully-fledged and explicit constitutional competence to act in the private law field – see S Weatherill, 'Competence and European Private Law' in C Twigg-Flesner (ed), *The Cambridge Companion to European Union Private Law* (Cambridge, Cambridge University Press, 2010)), but also on grounds of proportionality and subsidiarity, and in relation to its content: for analysis, see below, ch 3.

been submitted by the European Commission for the legislative adoption by the EU institutions of a sectorial Optional Code on Sales Law (CESL).[4] This has been presented by the proponents as a first step towards implementing a grander codification design for the whole of Europe.[5] It is more or less an abbreviated version of the Draft Common Frame of Reference (DCFR). The 'code-text' in both versions, extended (DCFR) and shortened (CESL),[6] explicitly claims to be 'complete and self-standing', consciously placing itself within a long-standing tradition that sees a code as a complete and autonomous legislative tool,[7] that is, the re-enactment of a recurring model, a habitual pattern of thought – the *code corpus*[8] – as I describe it with the help of historical examples in the remainder of the book. Today, the European Parliament, inbued with greater legislative powers than those that it enjoyed at the time of its first Resolution of 1989, and the Council of the European Union are considering the legislative proposal for approval or rejection. It appears that negotiations are rather contentious and that the climate reflects that of the vicissitudes of previous legislative proposals such as the Unfair Terms Directive, the Services Directive and the Consumer Rights Directive. But this time one must register the starkly contrasting gravity of the predicament, given that at stake is not a piece of legislation aiming at law's harmonisation (adopting norms leaving a margin of appreciation for national juridical orders), but at law's unification (replacing national juridical orders by a single order).[9] The remainder of the book explains the significance of the highly contested and contestable nature of the legislative proposal under consideration by the European Parliament and the Council of the European Union.

[4] *Proposal for a Regulation of the European Council and the Parliament for a Common European Sales Law* 11 October 2011; SEC (2011) 1165 and 165 *final.*

[5] See L Niglia, 'The Question Concerning the Common Frame of Reference' (2012) 18 *European Law Journal* 736 (work on an 'optional advanced new regime on contract law' is on the way).

[6] The CELS 'code-text' is, notably, the first product of a long-term, pragmatic strategy that aims at implementing more and more of the rules contained in the expansive version of the code-text, the DCFR, via enacting further code-text versions with a wider reach than transborder sales transactions – see Niglia (n 5).

[7] A 'classical definition' has established itself: see, eg, in France, P Rémy, 'Regards sur le code' in *Le Code Civil 1804–2004 Livre du Bicentenaire* (Paris, Dalloz, 2004) 99, 102 (the Code 'ne peut pas être une simple collection de lois: comme l'annonçait la loi du 30 ventose an XII, c'était un corps, un tout cohérent, un systéme de droit civil prétendant à la completude'); in Germany, R Zimmermann, 'Codification: History and Present Significance of an Idea' (1995) 3 *European Review of Private Law* 95; and discussion below, at ch 4. For the label *code corpus*, I draw on Rosario Nicolò, 'Codice Civile' in Francesco Calasso (ed), *Enciclopedia del Diritto* VII (Milan, Giuffrè, 1960) 240, 241 (critically discussing the option of understanding a code in modern times as code '*corpus*, il più completo possibile, di norme precise e analitiche per tutti gli istituti della vita giuridica, ispirate al rigoroso tecnicismo degli iniziati' (emphasis in original)).

[8] It is of a 'European' model that we are talking about. Note F Wieacker, 'Aufstieg, Blüte und Krisis der Kodifikationsidee' in *Festschrift für Gustav Boehmer* (Bonn: Röhrscheid, 1954) 34 (quoted in, and translated by, Zimmermann (n 7) 369), who understands codification as 'a unique creation, hard-won and hard to be defended, of Central and Western Continental legal culture'.

[9] For a reading of the contrast between harmonisation and unification in relation to EU legislation, see M Delmas-Marty (ed), *Critique de l'Integration Normative* (Paris, PUF) at 27 ('L'harmonisation, qui est l'une des modalité d'intégration, consiste en l'adoption d'une norme laissant des marges d'appréciation aus destinataires de la norme.' 'L'unification est la substitution à la pluralite' des ordres juridiques d'un ordre unique'*).*

II. PORTRAYING THE EUROPEAN CODE PROJECT

In sections III and IV below I offer a reading of the proposed European code-text – by which in this chapter I mean its extended version, that is, the DCFR, largely held to be a 'code in all but name'[10] – based on an interrelated, twofold argument.

First, I argue that the proposed code consists of a contingent set of legal materials aimed at disciplining the living law by giving an interpretative advantage to code-based interpretations over and above any sort of conflicting, non-code-based interpretations. The code universalises a certain vocabulary of private law (ideological) and attempts to superimpose it on legal actors. Here, for the purposes of analytical clarity, I am taking some distance from conventionalist accounts that propose a view of the modern codification phenomenon as the necessary product of nationalism or culturalism or combinations thereof, views deployed by scholars when attempting to make sense of the European code-project itself.[11] Instead, in contrast, I understand the 'historicity' of the European code to be less austere, in that it is about the jurists' construction of a heuristic law machine that aims at altering the structures of private law reasoning by shifting them as much as possible away from arm's-length interpretation and towards disciplinary interpretation[12] – that is, a shift away from 'free' interpretation in the hands of scholars and judges to interpretation constrained by a code understood as a 'prison cell'[13] or, to put it another way, as 'Pannomion'.[14]

Second, and at an interconnected level of analysis, I also argue that, in the view of the proponents, the implementation of code-based interpretative disciplining would in turn be bound to profoundly transform the structures of the harmonisation process as currently organised around the Directives, a process that inherently presents a fundamental degree of respect for the plurality of interpretative positions as they play out in the living law. The transformation being pursued is one from harmonisation to unification.[15] Because of the mechanics of disciplinary interpretation set in motion by a code, European code-based material would be disciplinarily superimposed upon legal actors, an eventuality this chapter critically reads and which I discuss further in the remaining chapters. The proposed

[10] The consciousness that a codal instrument is in preparation is everywhere: see a synthesis of the relevant literature and discussion in R Zimmermann, 'The Present State of European Private Law' (2009) 57 *American Journal of Comparative Law* 479 at 491, including references to an author who believes that not to call the DCFR 'code' is a 'clever trick' (M Hesselink, 'The European Commission's Action Plan: Towards a More Coherent European Contract Law?' (2004) 12 *European Review of Private Law* 397, 402) and to another author's work as acknowledging that 'the nebulous term CFR serves as a camouflage' (C von Bar, 'A CFR for European Private Law – Academic Efforts and Political Realities' (2008) 23 *Tulane European and Civil Law Forum* 37, 40).

[11] For illustrations and a critique of such readings as they keep returning in codification debates, see ch 4 below.

[12] 'Disciplinary' in the sense discussed in the remainder of this chapter.

[13] H Wüstendörfer, 'Die deutsche Rechtswissenschaft am Wendepunkt' (1913) 110 *Archiv für die civilistische Praxis* 224 (quoted in Zimmermann (n 7) 379).

[14] See the quotation by Jeremy Bentham in the epigraph.

[15] See, eg, Delmas-Marty (n 9).

code is aimed at changing the patterns of interaction between the supranational and the national level from 'heterarchical' to 'hierarchical', given that, in the view of its proponents, any dissenting national legal actors would be increasingly less able to resist the strategy of legal unification and the ideological agenda behind it.

III. GENEALOGY OF THE EUROPEAN CODE-TEXT: OF CONTINUITY AND DISCONTINUITY IN EUROPEAN LEGAL THOUGHT FROM LANDO'S PRINCIPLES TO THE DCFR

The materials behind the extended version of the proposed European code (the DCFR) emerge out of contingent conditions. It is not a quasi-natural development, a kind of 'inevitable' happening as per some positions that argue that the European code-project, if somehow perfected according to certain preferred standards, will be the best possible private law for Europe. It is instead the cumulative product of the work of certain strands of European private law scholarship. It is their accumulation – at times even chaotic – that has made the code proposal possible.[16] One must start by investigating the contingent structures of scholarship in order to really understand what the European code-project is about. Two periods, preceding and subsequent to the publication of the DCFR, must be distinguished. I argue that although there are elements of continuity between the two 'periods', there are also significant elements of discontinuity. Let me consider each period in turn so as to identify the structures of (dis)continuities that underlie the whole process.

The story of the intellectual engagement of private law scholarship with European integration, ever since its inception, has occupied a considerable number of writings.[17] In my view, if one wishes to capture the gist of this engagement up until the advent of the Common Frame of Reference (CFR), one must consider European private law to have been a scholarly field kept together less by substance and more by form. Its defining features being not debates about (more or less agreed-upon) substantive goals, policies and values, but sustained speculation, centred on a key range of contract and tort rules, aimed at proving that private law consists less of a plurality of national rules and more of common rules. At the core of this perspective is what one can call the 'argument from commonality', the most recent rendition of which is the following:

> It is hoped that the DCFR will promote knowledge of private law in the jurisdictions of the European Union, and in particular will help to show *how much national private laws resemble one another*, and have provided mutual stimulus for development *and indeed how much those laws may be regarded as regional manifestations on an overall common European legacy*.[18]

[16] For more elaboration on this point, see ch 4.
[17] This part and the following are adapted from Niglia (n 5).
[18] DCFR 2009 (full edition) 4 (emphasis added).

The application of the argument from commonality in relation to individual private law rules has demonstrated its very limits. Where unity is asserted, scholars have critically argued instead that diversity operates on the ground. Where harmony is asserted, scholars have critically argued that contestation over goals and policies is the more realistic scenario. Such critical positions have taken the form of arguments from diversity of production regimes *or* from diversity of legal cultures *or* from diversity of the law on the ground as opposed to the law as thought of in mainstream writings on European private law.[19] From this vantage point, had scholarship based the argument from commonality on an attempt at proving 'how much private laws resemble one another' *solely* on the basis of 'identifying' surface similarities of individual rules, I doubt that it would have successfully established itself. There is more structure. The key point of *resemblance* is part and parcel of a deeper work of *assemblage* of private law material. Scholars employ a range of long-established formal doctrinal techniques, chiefly derived from the archive of civilian thought, with a view to creating a *semblance* of Europeaness for private law, less on substantive grounds – where diversity and contestation should have been confronted – and more through manoeuvring formal doctrinal material. Let me discuss this point further.

In orthodox writings on European private law the deployment of three doctrinal techniques reminiscent of past *code corpus* episodes is noticeable. *Systematisation* ('strong')[20] is the first technique, with its undeniable civilian imprint. Overarching concepts and categories, such as obligation or *negozio giuridico*, serve as the conceptual building blocks around which to put private law material in a somewhat orderly fashion. The following statement from the influential *Study Group on a European Civil Code*, which is representative of conventional modes of thinking:

[19] See, respectively, G Teubner, 'Legal Irritants: Good Faith in British Law or How Unifying Law Ends Up in New Divergencies' (1998) 61 *Modern Law Review* 1, 11–32 (diversity of production regimes); P Legrand, 'Against a European Civil Code' (1997) 60 *Modern Law Review* 44 (diversity of legal cultures); L Niglia, 'Taking Comparative Law Seriously – Europe's Private Law and the Poverty of the Orthodoxy', (2006) 54(3) *American Journal of Comparative Law* 401 (diversity of law-in-action in relation to both contract and tort); Zimmermann (n 10) 494, who criticises the belief that, as in Zimmermann's view it is the case of contract law, tort law rules can 'reveal a fundamental legal unity of which the existing legal systems can be regarded as national manifestations'; and referring to the three books (C von Bar, *The Common European Law of Torts* (Oxford, OUP, Volume I, 1998; Volume II, 2000); Cees van Dam, *European Tort Law* (Oxford, OUP, 2006) and Peter Schlechtriem, *Restitution und Bereicherungsaugleich in Europa: Eine Rechtsvergleichende Darstellung* (Tübingen, Mohr Siebeck, Volume I, 2001; Volume II, 2001) as epitomising such opinion.

[20] On 'strong' versus 'weak' forms of systematisation, see below at ch 2. Here I refer to the former: for a re-statement (critical) of the former mode of thought, see Zimmermann (n 7) 371 ('codification is an act of legislation, ie. its validity is based on the intervention of the state'; explaining that this means the 'recording of the rules pertaining to a certain field of law' – and quoting Jeremy Bentham who argued that codification is 'Quite different [from] ordinary legislation' in view of the fact that here 'of the entire field of law . . . some very large portion . . . is to receive an entire new covering all at once': J Bentham, 'Papers Relative to Codification and Public Instruction' in J Bowring (ed), *The Works of Jeremy Bentham, Volume IV* (Edinburgh, Tait, 1843) 518 – alongside with ensuring internal coherence and with having a systematic nature).

> Legal harmonization . . . remains imperfect . . . that deficit can only be remedied when the Community legislator has in view (in the background, at least) an overall system, against which setting the legislator can intervene in social focal points without having to suffer a loss of quality or long-term self-limitation.[21]

Coherence is the second juristic technique that accompanies, reiterates and reinforces systematisation. For legal constructs are meant to be not just systematised, that is, ordered along structured notions and categories, but also coherently organised so as to avoid gaps, ambiguities and inconsistencies towards ensuring the objective of completeness (a comprehensive system of rules). A representative statement in this sense is the one according to which 'there is no point in having components which are incompatible with each other and cannot fit together'.[22] Last but not the least is *neutralism*, that is, the technique based on the argument that there really is no particular substantive agenda behind the whole project, for, in a representative statement:

> [I]t appears to be a natural task of legal science to make inquiries into principles and systems and to develop them into a coherent framework and draft Code, but much less so to take extensive policy decisions.[23]

Overall, agreements on common rules are, in this dominant scholarly view, entirely based on a mere exercise of logic or semantics.

Assemblage of private law material through the three aforementioned techniques has successfully operated in two senses, 'internal' and 'external', so to speak. Internally, lacking consensus on which common rules to choose in particular instances, scholars have found comfort in systematising doctrinal constructs, the generalities of which must have facilitated agreement. And if such a consensus existed at all, the machinery behind neutral doctrinal material must have played a key role in securing it from what appears to concern scholars most, the disarray of policy contestation, let alone loopholes *or* contradictions. Externally, the project has been presented to the wider community of private law scholars as a coherent body of rules no less attractive and authoritative than national clusters of private law rules, whether one seeks best solutions to private law problems *or* whether one claims that the whole body of common rules is 'better' than what national laws can offer.

Certainly, the common-rules vocabulary is one that has achieved a high degree of stability and credibility for both insiders and outsiders. For even those few scholars who, breaking away from conventionalism, have shown sensibility towards the often-conflicting and yet denied substantive issues underlying the whole enterprise have put faith in the formalistic structures of reasoning underly-

[21] Joint Response of the 'Commission on European Contract Law' and of the 'Study Group on a European Civil Code' to the Communication (2002) 2 *European Review of Private Law* 185, 231.

[22] DCFR (outline edition) 18.

[23] S Grundmann, 'The Optional European Code on the Basis of the Acquis Communautaire – Starting Points and Trends' (2004) 10 *European Law Journal* 698, 710.

ing the core argument from commonality.[24] *En bref*, European private law has for a long time consisted of a field shaped more by a formal predicament that produces some commonality effects for those who are caught in it, and less by substantive commitments around which formal structures are then consciously arranged as it the case for reasoning patterns as developed in national private law contexts (the living law), as I describe them in chapter two.

A fundamental shift away from the once entirely formally ordained predicament towards a substantive orientation has taken place with the advent of the (D) CFR, bringing about a new kind of juristic thought.

In other words, the DCFR is a continuation of the path taken by scholarship, as synthesised above. The code-text largely draws on Lando's Principles, as specifically acknowledged by the drafters themselves:[25]

> The former . . . 'Lando Commission' provided the basis for much of Book II and III; it was on their Principles of European Contract Law (PECL) that the Study Group and the Acquis Group built. The Acquis Group concentrated on existing Community Law in the area of general contract law.

The mindset is similar, that is, an assemblage of private law material based on systematisation and coherence at its core. What is different, however, is that substantive concerns have emerged at the core of scholarship in ways that are unprecedented. This change is traceable to the European Commission *nouveau siècle* strategy of shifting from harmonisation to unification (via codification) and of redesigning private law material so as to explicitly orient it towards certain practical policy objectives, an initiative to which scholarship has responded positively, as the pages below indicate. The previous framing around formal reasoning only has now also become substantively orientated. Let me detail how the European private law field has been reframed along these lines, as a result of the activities of the Commission over the past 15 years or so, with the Commission stepping into the scholarly field with more visibility than ever, initiating the CFR process and placing the scholarly work that is at its core under three key, unprecedented sets of constraint. First, the Commission has been funding the enterprise and placing strict deadlines for the delivery of the scholarly work.[26] The most visible rationale for this is that 'things need to be done', the less visible and more important reason

[24] See Manifesto of the 'Study Group on Social Justice in European Private Law' (2004) 6 *European Law Journal* 653: 'Agreement on common rules will symbolise more clearly than any Treaty or Constitution the emergence of a post-national form of governance.'

[25] DCFR 2009 (full edition) 1, a legacy widely acknowledged – see, eg, H Eidenmüller, F Faust, H Grigoleit, N Jansen, G Wagner and R Zimmermann, 'The Common Frame of Reference for European Private Law – Policy Choices and Codification Problems' (2008) 28(4) *Oxford Journal of Legal Studies* 659, 665; DCFR 2009 (full edition) 1.

[26] See Commission Communication, The Way Forward *COM* (2004) 651 final, setting up the CFR 'Network of Excellence'. See, eg, H Beale, 'The European Commission's Common Frame of Reference: A Progress Report' (2006) 2 *European Review of Contract Law* 303, 304 (discussing the details of Commission officials' involvement in the process, including deadline settings; commenting on a point in time in the process at which 'researchers were asked to produce papers at very short notice').

being instead that, here as elsewhere, constraints shape outcomes in processes.[27] Constraints include not only funding and deadline setting but also agenda setting (eg, the decision to place the problem of a wholesale private law harmonisation on the agenda of the EU institutions through the CFR project), policy setting and prioritisations (eg, the decision to demand that scholars amalgamate *acquis* and model rules, and its policy implications, as discussed below) and the framing of action within particular contexts of time (eg, the project has encountered a moment of 'extreme pressure of time dictated by the expiry of the term of office' of the then EU Commission).[28] Second, it has been demanded that 'principles' be introduced alongside and specifically at the beginning of the DCFR, and thus preceding the model rules. Third, the Commission has also demanded that the structure of the DCFR consist of model rules drawn on the *acquis*. Specifically:

> The structure envisaged for the CFR . . . is that it would first set out common fundamental principles of contract law . . . completed by model rules, forming the bulk of the CFR . . .
>
> The CFR will provide . . . fundamental principles and coherent model rules . . . drawing on the *acquis*.[29]

All these constraints read symbiotically indicate a framing act at the origin of the DCFR. What has developed out of the range of Commission-generated constraints, and out of the tensions that have arisen as a result, is something that we can call 'low-intensity formalism'. For *framing* is really about re-centring the established formalistic techniques of systematisation and coherence (high-intensity formalism) away from neutralism and towards instrumental reasons (low-intensity formalism). Below I detail both such instrumental reasons and the way that they have been incorporated into the body of received rules. My argument is that the formalist architecture has been made instrumental to substantive objectives in two complementary ways that meet the Commission-intimated constraints: first, the writing of model rules that incorporate the *acquis* into the received pre-DCFR doctrinal repertoire of common rules (ie, the Lando Commission Principles) (A); and, second, the adding of 'principles' alongside the

[27] The fact that the Commission has effectively managed to obtain the writing of a text (the *Draft*) that conforms to its key demand of amalgamating *acquis and* (certain) principles with the model rules demonstrates the accuracy of findings from studies on negotiations involving the EU institutions, that is, that the ability of EU institutional actors to translate their leadership resources into influence increases with the level of their involvement in intergovernmental negotiations and drafting processes. See, eg, the work of D Beach, *The Dynamics of European Integration* (Houndmills, Basinkstoke, New York, Palgrave Macmillan, 2005); and D Beach, 'EU Institutions and ICG Negotiations – How the Negotiation Process Affects their Ability to Gain Influence in ICGs' in P Meertz and F Cede (eds), *Negotiating European Union* (Houndmills, Basinkstoke, New York, Palgrave Macmillan,, 2004). For details on the high level of involvement of Commission officials in the drafting process leading to the DCFR, through initiation activities, participation in workshops, funding and setting deadlines, see Beale (n 26). Such a level of involvement continues to be sustained in the process concerning the choice of options for adopting a CFR: see, eg, the *Expert Group's Feasibility Study* of 3 May 2011 at www.ec.europa.eu/justice/contract/expert-group/index_ en.htm (demanding a group of experts to write a text based on the DCFR that is 'not only concise but also user-friendly').

[28] Zimmermann (n 10) 493.

[29] See *Commission Communication* (n 26) 17 and 3; DCFR 2009 (full edition) 24.

'model rules' (B). Let me discuss each framing operation in turn before turning to its criticism.

A. The Great Convergence of *Acquis Commun* and *Acquis Communautaire*

Acquis commun and *acquis communautaire* have largely remained independent doctrinal developments for a long time, the first being chosen by those who take a historical view of European private law and the latter being chosen by those who instead cling more on positivistic legal material that focuses on European private law as just law posited via the Directives. This has changed with the CFR. In line with the Commission's intimation to the (D)CFR network of scholars to 'draw on the *acquis*' in writing the model rules, the authors of the DCFR have chosen to conflate the *acquis communautaire* with the received script of model rules as inherited by the Lando Commission (*acquis commun*). Let me explain the meaning of this conflating operation by looking at the set of rules on unfair terms as contained in the Unfair Terms Directive and as incorporated into the DCFR (i) and at further sets of rules contained in Directives and incorporated into the DCFR (including right of cancellation and risk development defence in product liability) (ii).

i. From Directives to Code: The Case of Unfair Terms

In the introduction to the DCFR, the authors offer their understanding of how a key aspect of contract law such as unfair terms in standardised contracts should be regulated on a European-wide basis. In defence of what they call 'minimum intervention' aimed at remedying unfairness in contracting, they argue that:

> [It] must be asked whether it is necessary to make a particular term mandatory or whether a *flexible test* such as fairness would suffice to protect the weaker party. A fairness test *may allow certain terms to be used providing these are clearly brought home to the consumer or other party before the contract is made.* The fairness test thus interferes less with the parties' freedom of contract than making a particular term mandatory would do.[30]

Various of the *acquis*-originated rules taken from the Unfair Terms Directive have been incorporated into the DCFR as model rules in the belief that they are conducive to the 'minimum intervention' rationale. These include, for example, Article II.9:407 on the 'factors' to be considered in assessing unfairness – which the authors of the DCFR comment upon as meaning that standardised consumer terms may be held not to be unfair if the business provides 'a readable print version of the terms prior to the conclusion of the contract.'[31]

[30] DCFR 2009 (full edition) 652 (emphasis added).
[31] ibid.

Seen in light of the *commonality argument*, one must doubt that the conflating of the *acquis* and of the inherited 'European' model rules on unfair terms is really a credible representation of the law on the ground. For this take on the 'fairness test' cannot be held to be the result of a convergence between, on the one hand, national legal regimes and, on the other hand, all national regimes *and* the test of fairness as enshrined in the Unfair Terms Directive. The truth is that the aforementioned DCFR statements and the accompanying model rules are deeply contested. They epitomise a contingent interpretative position that can be located within a range of conflicting views on the issue, as have arisen in the last 15 years or so. The descriptive approach encapsulated in the 'commonality argument' now masks normative considerations, that is, the real choices being made among the many available. In my view, scholars are making substantive choices behind the pretence of 'representing' the law on the ground in the objectifying vocabulary of the commonality argument. Accordingly, conflation is less an objectifying operation aiming at a clearer and better organised law, and more one charged with ideological meaning. Let me briefly refer to the story of the regulatory interface between EU law and the law of unfair terms with a view to exposing how the above DCFR statements articulate a partisan, contestable and contested position in relation to unfair terms – which, I then argue, is also the predicament of other key *acquis*-originated DCFR model rules.

The Unfair Terms Directive 'modernises' contract law, to say it with a word employed by the European Commission, by cutting ties with the long-established model (of Germanic origin) of regulation of standardised contracts revolving around the sanctioning of a selected range of individual terms as unfair. Thus, ever since its enactment, the Directive has set in motion a new mode of regulation whereby judges are required to turn their attention away from the (national) rule book towards 'an overall evaluation of the different interests involved'. This has meant that burdensome terms may be saved from a declaration of unfairness at any time that an overall evaluation of the circumstances surrounding the transaction allows a case against unfairness. Two decisions in which judges have actively engaged with the Directive's test show how such circumstances work in practice. One relevant circumstance may be the information about the relevant term brought to the attention of the consumer before the conclusion of the contract. This information may save the term from unfairness, despite it being substantively burdensome for the consumer by anyone's reasonable assessment, such as in *First National Bank*. Here, a letter sent by the bank to the consumer, in which it was explicitly stated that upon default he would be subject to the obligation of paying post-judicial interests, on top of the contractually owed interests that courts generally impose upon any defaulting party, allowed the bank to escape a judicial declaration of unfairness concerning the relevant pre-formulated contractual term.[32] Another relevant circumstance may be a lower price, as in a German case, *Freiburger*, that happened to reach the Court of Justice of the

[32] *Director General of Fair Trading v First National Bank plc* [2001] UKHL 52.

European Union (CJEU). Here, the fact that the price was lower than it would have been without the inclusion in the contract of a burdensome term for the consumer (to pay for the service before actual delivery) was taken by the CJEU to be a prima facie case for considering the imputed term fair.[33]

Such circumstances, as encapsulated in the Directive's recitals and now in the DCFR,[34] conspire to construct a mode of control that, at bottom, accommodates market competitive imperatives. For it is about targeting the rigid constraints imposed upon entrepreneurs by domestic private law legislation that lends itself to be interpreted in defence of consumers – such as the sort of legislation challenged in *First National Bank* (County Courts Orders prohibiting post-judicial interests) and in *Freiburger* (the Bürgerliches Gesetzbuch (BGB)-based principle that performance on both parties should be contemporaneously perfected).[35] Thus, (un)fairness is re-presented as to be not about cold consideration of individual burdensome terms, as in the classical model developed in Germany and transplanted in many other jurisdictions, but about an overall balancing taking into account the factors enumerated at Article 4(1) Directive (now at Article II.9:407 DCFR). This is the result of a complex legislative process that I have analysed in *The Transformation of Contract in Europe*. Let me summarise here briefly.

The original Proposal of the Commission, containing the circumstantially constructed fairness test, was approved by the then Council of Ministers, thanks to the privileged position of the Commission in the bargaining process – the greater bargaining powers of the Commission entailed in situations of majority, as opposed to unanimity, voting. This was far from a pacific outcome. Indeed, regulatory options on the specific issues raised in the context of the bargaining process – all options directly or indirectly based on the traditional model of regulation focused on assessing the unfairness of terms individually – were strongly defended by some states but altogether dismissed as incompatible with the interest of the Commission in putting forward its own preferred mode of regulation. The reasons for this discord were enumerated by two German scholars, Ulmer and Brandner.[36] One particularly notable reason being their underlying criticism that the then draft directive would be at odds with the Germanic interventionist regime – then based on special legislation (AGBG) and today incorporated into the BGB – aimed at protecting weak contractual parties from the unfairness of terms individually assessed, whatever the circumstances. Despite criticism, the Commission persisted in defending its proposal, interested as it was (and still is) in counteracting any alternative interventionist project aimed at sheltering the

[33] Case C-237/02 *Freiburger Kommunalbauten GmbH Baugesellschaft and Co KG v Ludger Hofstetter and Ulrike Hofstetter* [2004] ECR I-3403.

[34] DCFR 2009 (full edition) 650.

[35] See, respectively, *First National Bank* (n 32) [38] (Lord Steyn *not* being persuaded by counsel's argument that 'it is not legitimate for a court to conclude that fairness requires that a lender must be able to insist on a stipulation designed to avoid the statutory regime under the 1991 Order') and *Freiburger* (n 33) [32] et seq (the latter being a default rule: see ch 2).

[36] See HE Brandner and P Ulmer, 'EG-Richtlinie über missbräuchliche Klauseln in Verbraucherverträgen. Kritische Bemerkungen zum Vorschlag der EG-Kommission' (1991) *Betriebs Berater* 701.

consumer through protectionist standards crystallised in (mandatory) rules. In the Commission's words, as per the preparatory works of the relevant Directive, such an interventionist model of regulation, 'while affording consumers a degree of protection . . . is open to criticism as restricting business activity'; moreover, 'it restricts economic freedom and leads to the risk of higher unemployment following price rises, or to loss of competitiveness'.

Having undertaken various, although unimportant, changes during the decision-making process, the core provisions of the original Commission proposal (and, above all, the controversial 'overall' fairness test anchored to the circumstances) were finally transposed into the Directive as finally approved by the then Council of Ministers in the spring of 1993. Ever since, opposition towards the directive's contentious test of fairness has not at all halted. Indeed, it has even increased, creating a situation that the Commission in the recitals to the then Proposal for a Directive on Consumer Rights labels, appropriately, 'legal fragmentation'.

* * *

The above indicates that Article II.9:403 DCFR, a fragment of a broader incorporation in the DCFR of the text of the Unfair Terms Directive, is a highly contested rule.[37] And the DCFR statements such as those quoted above give full support to the Commission project. For to hold that contractual terms potentially unfair can nevertheless be used 'providing these are clearly brought home to the consumer or other party before the contract is made' means to encapsulate in the unifying common rules vocabulary authorities such as *First National Bank* (yet without citing it). By setting in motion the incorporation of the *acquis* in the received body of model rules (ie, Lando's Principles), the Commission has basically called for an unprecedented expansion in the scope of the common rules scholarly project, instantiating a reformulation of the model rules so as to make them channel the Commission-generated substantive agenda (as encapsulated in the Directives).

ii. From Directives to Code: Further Cases

Let me now argue that the incorporation of the fairness test is only representative of what the DCFR also purports to achieve in relation to other key *acquis*-originated regulatory areas, such as the right of cancellation (Doorstep Directive/Article II.5:101 et seq DCFR) and risk development defence (Product Liability Directive/Article VI.3:204 DCFR). Here, one must note the same discursive patterns, that is, the incorporation of the *acquis* (almost) verbatim,[38] and an

[37] DCFR 2009 (full edition) 634 ('The unfairness term in the present Article . . . *is modelled on* Directive 93/13/EEC Art 3'; 'the list of factors to be taken into account when assessing the unfairness of a contract term is *based on* Directive 93/13/EEC Art 4(1)').

[38] The similarity, if not identity, between the DCFR and corresponding Directives' texts is clear and is explicitly acknowledged by the authors of the DCFR (full version): eg, at 348 (cancellation in Doorstep Directive/Art II.5:101 et seq DCFR) and at 634 (good faith in Unfair Terms Directive/Article II.9:403).

explanation that supports such incorporation on similar 'minimum intervention' grounds. This can be seen at two interconnected levels.

First, certain strands of contemporary economic analysis of law (trespassed from the US to continental Europe – particularly Germany)[39] that predicate the need to justify interferences with freedom of contract on efficiency grounds, towards remedying market failures as a result of information gaps, are studiously redeployed and applied to various (incorporated) *acquis* rules such as the right of cancellation and pre-contractual information duties.[40] The DCFR draws heavily on these strands of thought, as one can see from the following passages:

> [T]he right to withdraw gives the consumer . . . a 'cooling off period' for acquiring additional information and for further consideration whether he or she wants to continue with the contract . . . [r]ules which might be said to promote market efficiency (at least when compared to some more traditional approaches) are those on information duties. There is a public value in better-informed decision making across the board. Interferences with freedom of contract may be justified on the ground that they can serve to promote economic welfare if there is reason to think that because of some market failure (such as that caused by inequality of information) the agreement is less than fully efficient. Consumer protection rules, for example, can be seen not only as protective for the benefit of typically weaker parties but also as favourable to general welfare because they may lead to more competition and thus to a better functioning of markets. This holds true in particular for information duties, where consumers' lack of information about either the characteristics of the goods sold or the terms being offered leads to forms of market failure. Rules in relation to the making of a contract of a particular type or in a particular situation, require one party (typically a business) to provide the other (typically a consumer) with specified information about its nature, terms and effect, where such information is needed for a well-informed decision . . . can be justified as promoting efficiency in the relevant market.[41]

Second, and more specifically, this 'market failure' line of argumentation is deployed with a view to craft consumer protection rules that only serve the overarching aim of leading to a 'more competitive market'. Thus, as I am about to discuss in the following section, 'efficiency' is explicitly presented as one and the same thing with the promotion of contractual and market freedoms,[42] rather than as an argument that may help 'rationalise' any kind of legal intervention, whether 'enhancing' or 'limiting' contractual freedom and competitiveness. This is a line

[39] H Micklitz, 'The Visible Hand of European Regulatory Private Law' in 28 *Yearbook of European Law* (2009), 3, at 13–14.

[40] *cf*, eg, T Wilhelmsson, 'The Variety of Welfarism in European Contract Law' (2004) 10 *European Law Journal* 712, 726 (information duties and cancellation rights as contained in Directives on consumer contract law seen as fundamentally biased towards a freedom of choice ideology, aimed at conjuring up a market-rational contract law centred on choice-driven actors, and explaining this information-based philosophy as the dominant pattern in EU consumer contract law). An example of Germanic law-and-economic literature is H Eidenmüller's *Effizienz als Rechtsprinzip. Möglichkeiten und Grenzen der ökonomischen Analyse des Rechts* (3rd edn, Tübingen, Mohr Siebeck 2005).

[41] See DCFR respectively at 75 and at 96–97 (outline version) and at 61–62 (full version) (emphasis added).

[42] DCFR (full edition) at 38.

of argument relied upon when, for instance, the authors of the DCFR apply a pro-market interpretation of pre-contractual rules on information duties and of liability for products.

Thus, the authors of the DCFR put forward a regime of product liability, borrowed from the Product Liability Directive, that empowers producers to avoid liability by relying on the 'risk development defence', with a view to encouraging the 'minimisation of insurance costs' and to merely safeguarding the values of 'industrial innovation and technical progress'.[43] This is illustrative of a logic that permeates the whole body of DCFR rules, leading as it does to the enumeration of a 'list' of market-friendly rules for both consumer and commercial transactions. In section III.B below, I will consider how, for example, the DCFR puts forward rules that protect the provider of services from liability for non-performance or misperformance in cases in which it would have been too costly for the provider to prevent the damage, or makes the duty to provide pre-contractual information conditional on similar cost considerations. Together with the explicit DCFR preference for 'corrective' over 'distributive' considerations,[44] all of the above demonstrates the endorsement of the Commission's strategy to favour a 'market-orientated' qua competitive-ridden private law;[45] in other words, an assemblage of substantively orientated formal techniques incorporating the command that there are circumstances in which the law requires that established domestic consumer protectionist standards be altogether relaxed.

B. Advent of the Principles

> Model rules, with comments and notes, bring together rules derived largely from the legal systems of the Member States . . . Principles *explain* the main *underlying value judgements*. The word 'principles' surfaces occasionally in the Commission communi-

[43] On such strands of economic analyses, see DCFR (outline version) 16 and on product liability specifically, see DCFR 2009 (full edition) 3522 (discussing the UK state of the art of the directive-generated law of risk development defence and mentioning scholars favouring and criticising the argument for minimising costs).

[44] See DCFR (outline version) 24. On the conceptual link between, on the one hand, 'corrective justice' and market-facilitating contract law policy instruments and, on the other hand, between 'distributive justice' and more progressive forms in which to organise contract law (internally and externally redistributive etc), see Wilhelmsson (n 40) 716 et seq.

[45] On market competitiveness as the driving ideological force behind the Commission agenda of private law reform, see, eg, 'Manifesto' (n 24) at 655–56 (discussing the 'technocratic' approach to contract law in the EU as one narrowly focused on removing impediments to cross-border trade with little consideration for social aspects); Wilhelmsson (n 40) 726 et seq (considering the private consumer law Directives to be predominantly geared towards market facilitating objectives); L Niglia, *The Transformation of Contract in Europe* (The Hague, Kluwer Law International, 2003) (reconstructing the Unfair Terms Directive as instrumental to the promotion of market competitiveness); H Micklitz, 'The Concept of Competitive Contract Law' (2005) 23 *Penn State International Law Review* 549; Norbert Reich, 'Balancing in Private Law and the Imperatives of the Public Interest', in R Brownsword, H Micklitz, L Niglia and S Weatherill (eds), *The Foundations of European Private Law* (Oxford, Hart Publishing, 2011) 221.

> cations . . . with the prefix 'fundamental' attached. That suggests that it may have been meant to denote essentially abstract *basic values*.[46]

In this way the Commission demanded that 'principles' be introduced alongside the model rules, which represents a further reframing of the pre-DCFR script of common rules on which the scholarly unification project is based, for 'principles' are taken to be 'basic values' rather than just another way in which to name the common rules. To really understand the role of the 'principles' in the (D)CFR project, we need to place the whole enterprise in the context of the Commission's regulatory activities as they have unfolded over the past few decades. The introduction of principled reasoning alongside the model rules can be shown to be just *another* vital way for furthering the Commission-generated substantive agenda in two senses. Let me consider each of them in turn (section III.B.i) before discussing the way in which adjudication is meant to work so as to further principled reasoning (section III.B.ii).

i. The Power of Principled Reasoning

Not every 'principle' matters to the DCFR – only a selected few. Principled reasoning is aimed at restructuring interpretation along the lines of the four 'underlying principles' contained in the latest version of the DCFR: freedom, security, justice and efficiency. An ideological matrix lurks behind the chosen four principles for two reasons. First, the DCFR has dropped 11 principles that were contained in the previous edition, some being key 'social principles'[47] such as the protection of human rights, solidarity and social responsibility; the protection of consumers and others in need of protection; the preservation of cultural and linguistic plurality; the protection of reasonable reliance; and the *proper* allocation of responsibility for the creation of risks. Second, 'efficiency' not only recalls the key rationale around which the Commission has developed its project of private law marketisation, but it is the key principle around which the other three revolve. In the words of the DCFR: 'At one level, *freedom*, *security* and *justice* are ends in themselves. People have fought and died for them. Efficiency is less dramatic. In the context of private law, however, *these values* are best regarded not as ends in themselves but *as means to an end – the promotion of welfare*, the empowering of people to pursue their legitimate aims and fulfil their potential.'[48] Then, in explaining the 'meaning' of 'efficiency': 'The rules in the DCFR are in general intended to be such as will promote economic welfare; and this is a criterion against which any legislative intervention should be checked.'[49] If, in this understanding, efficiency means welfare, with welfare (qua the twin aim of keeping

[46] DCFR (full version) 1 and 5 (emphasis added).

[47] Notably, insiders to the DCFR project understand the principles to be more or less 'social' in the way that I describe them in the narrative: see, eg, M Hesselink. 'If You Don't Like Our Principles We Have Others' in Brownsword et al (n 45) 59.

[48] DCFR 2009 (full edition) 37 (emphasis added).

[49] ibid 61.

interventionism at a minimum whilst maximising market competitiveness) being the overarching end goal, then we understand the very language that the authors of the DCFR are adopting, sculpting as they are the values underlying the Commission-originated project into their own work. The programme of minimum intervention spelled out at the beginning of the DCFR, in the stated conviction that the values and principles of 'freedom' and 'efficiency' are 'interchangeable',[50] only aims at defining a legal hermeneutical horizon within which private law actors are supposed to operate. *En bref*, principled reasoning is far from vague and indeterminate,[51] in that it is a proxy for implementing the welfare efficiency, minimum intervention rationale.

Setting out a mode of principled reasoning at the very outset of the DCFR serves the purpose of complementing and reinforcing the operation of conflation of *acquis commun* and *acquis communautaire* as a tool for better furthering the overarching strategy of welfare efficiency. This is because it allows the authors of the DCFR to mould *general* private law rules (as opposed to the *acquis*-imported consumer law rules) so as to accommodate the welfare-efficiency policy through devising a body of *non-consumer* rules in parallel to the *acquis* rules. Whilst drafting model rules is about a passive reception of already-existing rules (ie, those of the *acquis*), principled reasoning is about creating 'new' model rules altogether, towards complementing and expanding the *acquis* rules for the sake of the welfare-efficiency agenda. This can be noted in at least two senses. First, the DCFR makes explicit the overlapping function of principles *and* model rules. Let me recall two key statements:

> Principles explain the main underlying value judgements . . .
>
> The model rules of course build on such . . . principles in any event, whether they are stated or not.[52]

The judge, we are told, in determining liability, should take into account the potential costs entailed in preventing any damage caused by the service provider, which may make the provider not liable, *or*, another example, the costs entailed in acquiring information on the part of who should have disclosed it.[53] These are illustrations of such principled reasoning incorporated into two of the DCFR model rules that place welfare efficiency above potentially competing values.

[50] ibid, respectively, at 38 et seq and at 59 et seq ('The promotion of freedom overlaps with the promotion of efficiency', an argument which precludes the relevance of any efficiency-based interpretation that may 'limit' freedom).

[51] Contrast Eidenmüller et al (n 25) 676 et seq.

[52] See DCFR 2009 (full edition) 1 and 5 (emphasis added).

[53] See, respectively, Article IV.C – 2:105 (providing for the obligation on the service provider to 'perform the service with the case and skill which a reasonable service provider would exercise under the circumstances' and, at Article IV.C. – 2:105(4)(b), that 'in determining the care and skill the client is entitled to expect, regard is to be had, among other things, to . . . if damage has occurred, the costs of any precautions which would have prevented that damage or similar damage from occurring') and Article II – 7:205(3)(b) ('In determining whether good faith and fair dealing required a party to disclose particular information, regard should be had to all the circumstances, including . . . the cost to the party of acquiring the relevant information').

Hence, protecting the value of fair dealings, with the service provider having to respect mandatory quality standards, *or* commanding information disclosure, are issues subordinated to the 'welfare-efficiency' consideration of the costs involved for the service provider in doing that. Further examples follow in which the Draft draws on a number of model rules to emphasise how they all directly channel welfare-efficiency objectives. They include model rules that provide for:[54]

> 'stipulated payments for non-performance' [at para. III. – 3:712, which, in the view of the authors of the DCFR] 'could be said to be more favorable to market efficiency than rules which regard penalty clauses as completely unenforceable'; [recovery for] 'damages for pure economic loss' [(held to be] 'preferable from the point of view of efficiency to the denial of such recovery, as happens under some systems'); 'prescriptions' [in Book III, Chapter 7, which are]) 'designed to promote efficiency by encouraging the prompt making of claims before evidence becomes stale and expensive to provide and by freeing assets which might otherwise be held against the possibility of old claims being made'; 'withholding performance and terminating the contractual relationship in cases of anticipated non-performance' [at III 3:401 and III 3:504, seen as] 'designed to promote efficiency by not requiring the creditor to wait until non-performance actually happens'). [Further model rules] 'promote efficiency by discouraging the providing of unwanted performance' [at paras. III 3:301(2), IV. C – 2:111 and IV.D – 6:101] 'deny(ing) effect to contractual prohibitions on the alienation of assets' (this being) 'designed to promote general efficiency by favouring the free circulation of goods or other assets' [(at paras. III. – 5:108 and VII. – 1:301, which is also the case of] 'rules on acquisition in good faith or by continuous possession' [at paras. VII. – 3:101 and VIII. – 4:101, and noting how] '[a] core aim of the rules in Book IX on proprietary security in moveable assets is the facilitation of economic activity and economic welfare by enabling credit to be obtained on favourable terms against the provision of proprietary security.' [A further set of model rules is about promoting efficiency less for] 'wider public purposes'[the case of the model rules just mentioned, and more] 'for the purposes of the parties who might use the rules'. [Thus, model rules that provide for] 'the absence of any need or consideration for the conclusion of an effective contract' [at para. II 4:101, as well as] 'the recognition that there can be binding unilateral contracts' [and that contracts can confer rights on third parties, all are believed] 'to promote efficiency (and freedom) by making it easier for the parties to achieve the legal results they want in the way they want without the need to resort to legal devices or distortions' [respectively at paras. II – 1:103 and at paras. I – 9:301 to paras. II. – 9:303]. [(A similar objective would be achieved thanks to the fact that] 'voidable contracts can be avoided by simple notice, without any need for courts procedures' [(at para. II – 7:209, and that] 'contractual relationships can be terminated in the same way if there has been a fundamental non-performance of the other party's obligations' [at para. III 3:507].

ii. Principled Reasoning and Adjudication

The deployment of principled reasoning in the DCFR text is made in as centralised form as possible, in two senses, each of which reinforces the welfare-efficiency strategy.

[54] See DCFR 2009 (full edition) 62 and 60.

First, principled reasoning is deployed *within* the body of the individual model rules rather than leaving it to the discretion of judges. Principled reasoning is thus supposed to operate not on its own, so to speak, but through the model rules. And it is worked out in a way that fully accommodates the Commission-generated agenda, the noted model rules on cost-effectiveness in relation to service contracts and to information-giving obligations being only illustrations among the many.[55]

Second, in cases in which the individual model rules do not indicate the sort of principled reasoning that should be made (ie, how to implement welfare efficiency in specific instances), the judge is then supposed to act out of principled reasoning, but only with a view to implementing welfare efficiency. For we are told that only the four welfare-efficiency principles are legal ('underlying'), the rest of them being instead placed outside the legal realm for being 'political' ('overarching'). In other words, either the model rules explicitly implement welfare-efficiency *or*, where there is a vacuum, the judge is supposed to be constrained to implement welfare efficiency. Here all comes full circle. Principled reasoning is intended to be instrumental, and therefore limited, to a welfare-efficiency strategy; it is ultimately intended to be about commanding less judicial discretion and more a defined obligation for the judge to act within the principled constraints.

One cannot really underestimate the importance of constructing judicial power this way, for that construction is a device for empowering judges to superimpose welfare-efficiency interpretations upon the body of 'protectionist' domestic laws that would otherwise remain in place in situations in which there are no model rules that do the job for the judge. An example is a (relatively speaking) indeterminate model rule such as the one providing for tort liability for 'legally relevant damage', which is understood as 'the loss or injury that results from a violation of an interest worthy of legal protection'.[56] In such a case, the judge is nevertheless empowered to go against the grain of established domestic practices if he is interested in heads of liability unknown to, or prohibited under, domestic law through widening liability to make it cover pure economic loss.[57] Seen in this light, the judge is equipped with wider interpretative powers than those derived from (relatively speaking) detailed model rules, which reinforces the strategy of counteracting protectionist rules at odd with welfare efficiency. In fact, and to return to the last example, the DCFR authors explicitly argue that this is the case of the denial of liability for pure economic loss as it is practised in many domestic systems.[58]

[55] ibid.

[56] See Articles VI.1:101 and VI.2:101(1)(c) DCFR 2009 (full edition), and at 3087: 'what we have here is not a general clause in the strict sense, but rather a provision whose component elements are later filled out with more precise content. That does not exclude the prospect that, alongside others with sharply drawn contours, the following Articles may contain rules which have deliberately been left open and flexible. VI.2:101 (meaning of legally relevant damage) and VI.4:101 (general rule on causation) provide examples of this'.

[57] DCFR 2009 (full edition) 62: 'The allowance of damages for pure economic loss seems to be preferable from the point of view of efficiency to the denial of such recovery as happens under some systems' and 'It is difficult to see any justification for distinguishing between pure economic loss and loss caused by damage to property or injury to the person'.

[58] ibid.

En bref, the DCFR-dictated judicial empowerment is the flipside of a principled private law regulatory project[59] motivated out of the vital concern, underlying the Commission-generated agenda, to dismantle domestic protectionist standards.[60] In this sense, the disregard for domestic legislation in *First National Bank*, as a way to further the Directive-generated strategy of releasing banks from legislative-based restriction on post-judicial interests for borrowers in default, must be an ideal-typical decision for the authors of the DCFR.[61]

iii. A Pyramidal Formation

The framing act has produced a pyramid-like composition. At its apex is the welfare-efficiency principle to which the remaining three 'underlying' principles are ancillary; then the model rules follow that implement welfare efficiency, with the support of the commentary. Systematisation and coherence are everywhere, working as a conceptual *trait d'union* ensuring that principles and model rules are held together hierarchically and that they are correlated to each other so as to avoid gaps, ambiguities and inconsistencies. In other words, we are presented with a 'system' allegedly capable of 'producing results' that flaw coherently from the combined application of the chosen principles and model rules. Thus, statements abound that illustrate such a neo-pandectistic attitude, alongside a neo-exegetic attitude cherishing textual clarity. For example:

> [E]very attempt was made to achieve . . . a clear and *coherent* structure. The terminology should be precise and should be used consistently . . .
>
> The text should be well-organised, accessible and readable.
>
> It should be as simple as . . . consistent with the need to convey the intended meaning.
>
> It should not contain irrational, redundant, or contradictory provisions.
>
> *[C]oncepts used* . . . should be capable of *fitting together coherently* in model rules, whatever the content of those model rules.
>
> If the definitions are essential for the model rules, it is also true that the model rules are essential for the definitions. There would be little value in a set of definitions which was internally incoherent. The definitions can be seen as components which can be used in the making of rules and sets of rules, but there is no point in having components which are incompatible with each other and cannot fit together.[62]

[59] Eidenmüller et al (n 25) 676 et seq see the DCFR critically as setting the stage for judicial arbitrariness and loss of legal certainty, rather than in the context that I am discussing here. A reading of the previous DCFR edition, without commentary, may well have led to the belief that the DCFR is all about allowing as wide judicial discretion as possible (see Eidenmüller et al (n 25) 676 et seq). In the fully edited edition, the commentary in great details defines the interpretative boundaries in line with the principle of welfare efficiency.

[60] This being an attempt at profoundly altering the traditional patterns of cooperation between domestic scholars and judges that, on the continent, are at the roots of domestic resistance and avoidance vis-a-vis the directives: see L Niglia, 'The Non-Europeanization of Private Law' (2001) 4 *European Review of Private Law* 575.

[61] As discussed above.

[62] DCFR 2009 (full edition), respectively, at 15 and 10 (emphasis added).

The old assemblage of doctrinal formations comprised amorphous doctrinal formations based on aseptic systematisation and coherence techniques. The new assemblage consists of a focal point made of substantive values, re-engineered as 'legal principles', around which the doctrinal material revolves – a new version of legal material that 're-compacts' the private law field,[63] as established in the work of the Lando Commission. Let us call it the *second assemblage* in the history of beyond-the-state juristic thought of the last three decades. For the deployment of systematisation and coherence typical of the first assemblage is now coupled by practical substantive objectives – those encapsulated in model rules and in principled reasoning and instrumental to the minimum-interventionist agenda coined by the Commission and shared by the DCFR scholars.[64]

IV. FUNCTION OF THE EUROPEAN CODE-TEXT. THE RETURN OF CODE-BASED UNIVERSALISATION AND DISCIPLINING

Like previous modern codes based on the model of the *code corpus*, the proposed European code is about furthering universalisation and discipline. Universalisation prepares the terrain for disciplining – it would be useless without disciplining. Let me discuss each point in turn, emphasising the impact of any move towards code discipline on the harmonisation process, that is, the codifiers' objective of placing private law under hierarchical structures of interpretation and away from free interpretation, as is the case today.

A. The Proposed Code as a Device for Law's Universalisation

It is typical of modern codes to embody universality. One way to articulate universality is to claim that the code-law is the embodiment of the general public interest rather than partisan and sectarian. The universality of the individual qua 'subject of law' in nineteenth-century codes is an illustration. The currently proposed code is no different. A long-standing partisan and contested ideological agenda, engineered by the Commission, has now been transposed into the DCFR as if it were of some kind of universal value (ideology). The objectifying talk whereby all rules are the same, that is, the argument from commonality, is key to this operation (vocabulary). Thus, to return to the examples given above, we are told that judging the *overall* fairness of contractual terms, rather than individually, *or* exempting from liability the provider of services due to the high costs

[63] On 'field impacting', see D Kennedy, 'Thoughts on Coherence, Social Values and National Tradition in Private Law' in M Hesselink (ed), *The Politics of a European Civil Code* (The Hague, Kluwer Law International, 2006); and D Kennedy (ed), *Legal Reasoning. Collected Essays* (Aurora, CO, The Davies Group, Publishers, 2008), as discussed in the remainder of this chapter.

[64] That the *code corpus* is a model understood to incorporate substantive values is acknowledged in comparative and historical studies: see, eg, the historical perspective of F Wieacker, *A History of Private Law in Europe* (Oxford, Clarendon Press, 1995).

otherwise involved in avoiding damages is less about attempting to legitimise a partisan project and more about just 'deriving' model rules from Member States' legal traditions. This presents the script as a sort of 'better rendition' of the 'existing (national) law(s)' in a spirit of 'objective' and 'authoritative' scholarship. Note the employment of the vocabulary of 'underlying principles', that is:

> The perspective is thoroughly European and the fundamental basis of the work has been scholarly research and impartial thought and argument based on that research. Model rules, with comments and notes, bring together rules derived largely from the legal systems of the Member States and the overarching Community law. Principles explain the main underlying value judgements. Definitions bring to the defined terms and concepts the shared experience and ideas of jurists from thirty jurisdictions.[65]

Here the talk of 'principles' that 'explain the main underlying value judgements', as opposed to, more realistically, 'underlying values', indicates the attempt at somehow masking the pursuit of partisan market libertarian values under the cover of formal categories ('principles'), re-enacting the long-standing private law individualistic vocabulary borrowed from the nineteenth-century bourgeois codes. The model rules are traceable to an allegedly overarching, at once 'shared' and 'principled', private law order – as if the value choices underlying the DCFR were 'good law for all'. Let me quote again:

> Model rules, with comments and notes, bring together rules derived largely from the legal systems of the Member States . . . Principles *explain* the main *underlying value judgements*. The word 'principles' surfaces occasionally in the Commission communications . . . with the prefix 'fundamental' attached. That suggests that it may have been meant to denote essentially abstract *basic values*.[66]

This universalising operation is questionable in at least two senses. First, fundamental 'transparency' requirements are missing. For, rather than disclosing the underlying policy choices, proposing them to the public square and advising on the best arrangement of legal material that would serve their implementation, DCFR scholars do the opposite – they opt for a partisan ideological position and universalise it by employing legal narratives grounded on (supposedly) universal legal material (the 'argument from commonality') *and* values (the 'argument of principles as values').

Second, there is an inherent radicality in this universalising operation that must be acknowledged in all its dangerous potential. The whole enterprise is worrying less for creating 'general private law rules' by extending consumer law rules to business transactions (through conflation or principled reasoning) *or* by making other similar kinds of generalisations that are not entirely convincing on pragmatic grounds,[67] and more for its strategic use of comparative law material for the

[65] See DCFR 2009 (full edition) 1 (emphasis added).

[66] ibid 1 and 5 (emphasis added).

[67] These are worrying issues that scholars rightly have critically addressed: see Nils Jansen and Reinhard Zimmermann, '"Restating the Acquis Communautaire?" A Critical Evaluation of the Principles of the Existing EC Contract Law' [2008] *Modern Law Review* 505 et seq.

universalising purpose, in the sense that an approach whereby 'all-private-law-is-the-same' is unabashedly applied to every single area of private law, irrespective of diversity and contestation on the ground.[68]

B. The Proposed Code as a Device for Law's Disciplining

The authors of the DCFR are not just interested in an academic rendition of the model rules in universal terms. Tools for implementation of the chosen model rules matter no less to them. Thus, below, I explain that the authors have framed their version of universal law in a code-like structure, with the objective of definitively overcoming law's fragmentation through the deployment of the kind of discipline typically associated with codification strategies. Let me refer briefly to the three sets of model rules originated in directives and now incorporated into the DCFR with a view to preparing for my chief argument about 'disciplining'. They are the test of fairness, the right of withdrawal *and* the risk development defence. At the time of writing, each such rule presents us with problems in legislative implementation and judicial enforcement, all acknowledged by the Commission as situations of 'legal fragmentation'.[69] The *living law* of the three sets of directives' rules is characterised by a continuum ranging from full compliance to non-compliance to part compliance (depending on which country one considers). Behind such diverse compliance scenarios lie episodes of contestation over goals and policies – more or less protectionist for consumers – which the insiders, respectively, see as less or more conducive to market competitiveness. Contestation revolves around legal issues such as whether or not: (1) to test the *overall* unfairness of contractual terms rather than that of terms individually; (2) to allow the risk development defence for avoiding product liability; and (3) to allow the extension of the right of cancellation from consumers to guarantors *and* loan takers in linked contracts.[70] Below, I argue that a European code encapsulating a universalised version of the law in a code-like fashion is about setting the stage for a mechanism bound to alter the living law, aimed as it is at subverting its pluralistic structures. All such alterations in the way in which the law is practised on the ground are sought after at once under the spell of legal necessity and pursuant to the Commission-generated project. The codifying strategy is to make the law shift

[68] For the legal comparative counter-discourse based on elements of diversity and contestation, and on the many guises in which comparative law is being emasculated on the altar of universalism, see Teubner (n 19) (diversity of production regimes); Legrand (n 19) (diversity of legal cultures); Niglia (n 19) (diversity of law-in-action).

[69] See recitals to 'Proposal for a Directive of the Parliament and of the Council on Consumer Contractual Rights' (Brussels, 3 September 2009).

[70] Representative writings that expose all such conflicts are Mathias W Reimann, 'Product Liability in a Global Context: The Hollow Victory of the European Model' (2003) 2 *European Review of Private Law* 128 (on product liability); Reich (n 45) (on right of cancellation in the contentious *Heininger* and post-*Heininger* sagas in relation to the right of cancellation *and* on unfair terms); Niglia (n 45) (on unfair terms).

away from an authority entirely contingent on the choices of domestic legal actors, ranging from compliance to non-compliance, to a new disciplinary authority superimposed upon them and leaving them little, if any, choice; law's structures would be changed so as to accommodate the Commission-backed market-orientated agenda; a new kind of authority, entirely disciplinary, would replace the current living law's *fiat* based on policy diversity and contestation, and its implicit plural authority. Let me now explain in more detail the ways in which the codifiers are pursuing the establishment of a disciplinary discourse.

i. The Present Situation – Post-Nationality in Legal Reasoning

As a result of the continuous enactment of the private consumer law directives and of their incorporation in domestic laws, judges and scholars operate in truly post-national conditions. Legal reasoning is neither entirely domestic nor entirely European, lying as it does somewhere in between, for the articulation of legal arguments must sound 'persuasive' at once for legal actors within and outside domestic systems. One way in which this kind of post-national legal consciousness has been restated is the so-called 'comparative law interpretation':

> [W]hen a national judge is faced with a uniform law, he must not simply deploy his trusty old national rules of construction but modify them so as to arrive at an internationally acceptable result which promotes legal uniformity . . . the judge must look to the foreign rules which formed the basis of the provisions to be applied, he must take account of how courts and writers abroad interpret it, and he must make good any gaps in it with general principles of law which he has educed from the relevant national legal systems.[71]

The CJEU is obviously the main vehicle for this kind of *persuasive authority*,[72] but domestic courts are no less so. Thus, in one instance, the *Bundesgerichtshof* was inclined to the view that clause 5 of the disputed contract was not an unfair term under German law. However, it considered that having regard to the wide variety of rules applying in the Member States, this assessment was not free from doubt. It therefore decided to stay the proceedings and to refer the question to the Court for a preliminary ruling.[73]

Below, I argue that the plan of the codifiers is to obtain approval of a code/CFR that would in turn be bound to strengthen the authority of the incorporated *acquis* (the Directives) in a disciplinary mode. For it would re-orient law's reasoning structures of persuasion, as presently utilised by jurists and judges in relation

[71] Konrad E Zweigert and Hein Kotz, *An Introduction to Comparative Law*, translated by Tony Weir (Oxford, Clarendon Press, 1998) 21; and *Freiburger* (n 33) [14].

[72] 'For the Member States of the Common Market the Court of Justice of the European Communities is the leading example: it has already used the method of comparative legal interpretation in a large number of decisions with great success': Zweigert and Koetz (n 71) 21 and referring to the works of Bleckmann, Daig, Martiny and Pescatore.

[73] See *Freiburger* (n 33) [14].

to the consumer law *acquis*, from 'attracting adherence' to 'obliging' it – to put it in Glenn's words.[74]

ii. Disciplining Adjudication and Scholarship

a. Codification and Grammaticalism

The remaking of the European doctrinal repertoire undertaken via the DCFR is about creating an 'official' legal grammar, in a similar fashion to what civil codes typically do.[75] Indeed, the DCFR has been held to be a misnomer for a true codification project, a 'code in the making'.[76] Indicators in support of this view include the following (not in order of importance): first, the incorporation of the DCFR into a 'regulation establishing a European Civil Code' is one of the officially recognised options in the CFR materials. Second, the Commission held that, whatever its form (binding or not), the legislative instrument of incorporation 'should be comprehensive and self-standing, in the sense that references to national law should be as much as possible reduced'. Notably, these are two characteristics key to the 'identity' of codes (in the sense of *code corpus*) in the modern age.[77] Third, the *Feasibility Study* of the *Expert Group* – which is option-neutral (written on an 'as if' basis) – produced a code-like 'self-standing and comprehensive' text that will arguably be the basis for an optional instrument such as the CESL or for a toolbox or for both.[78] Fourth, law and economics studies on private law in the EU federative context consider an optional instrument to be a 'centralising' mode of regulation *inter alia* for lowering both transactions costs and barriers to trade.[79] In brief, an all-encompassing ('comprehensive') and original ('self-standing') set of code-like rules is what the whole CFR enterprise aims at.[80] From this vantage point, it all comes full circle, as modern history teaches us that all codes (under-

[74] P Glenn, 'Persuasive Authority' (1987) 32 *McGill Law Journal* 261, 263 (persuasive authority is 'authority that attracts adherence as opposed to obliging it'; AM Slaughter, 'A Typology of Transjudicial Communication' (1994–95) 29 *University of Richmond Law Review* 99 (referring to Glenn's understanding as making intelligible the work of courts operating in the context of Europeanisation). On persuasive authority, see also Zweigert and Koetz (n 71) 21.

[75] Legrand (n 19) 54–55 (a code provides 'an officialised construction of reality' and it also is a coherent 'language' with the effect of excluding alternative views of justice).

[76] In the sense of it being a *code corpus*: see fn 10 above.

[77] For the *code corpus* position whereby codes are 'comprehensive frameworks for society by providing systematic and exhaustive legislation of whole areas of law' and are 'promulgated to allow for a fresh start of the legal system, abrogating all previous sources of law', see, eg, J Basedow, 'Transjurisdictional Codifications' (2009) 83 *Tulane Law Review* 973, 975; R Zimmermann (n 7) 95 (focusing on comprehensiveness); P Caroni, 'Kodifikation' in A Erler and E Kaufmann (eds), *Handwoerterbuch zur Deutchen Rechtsgeschichte* (Berlin, Erich Schmidt Verlag, 1978) 907 et seq.

[78] M Hesselink, 'A Toolbox for Judges' (2011) 17 *European Law Journal* 441, 443.

[79] W Kerber and S Grundmann, 'An Optional European Contract Law Code: Advantages and Disadvantages' (2006) 21 *European Journal of Law and Economics* 215, 232 (arguing that 'an appropriately designed optional code . . . can be capable of combining important advantages of centralization . . . with crucial advantages of decentralisation').

[80] Scholars largely agree that 'draft common of reference' is a misnomer: see, eg, von Bar (n 10) 40; S Weatherill, 'The Multi-level Structure of Private Law: Introduction' in Brownsword et al (n 45) 319 (DCFR seen as a 'code-in-the-waiting').

stood as *code corpus*) are 'frames of reference' *and* all frames of reference are 'codes'. For code-based restructuring projects, led by legislatures, orient the private law field so as to make it gravitate towards contingent perceptions of legal necessity – thus fundamentally reshaping the structures of legal reasoning of the insiders, from judges to scholars. It is to such dynamics that we must turn our attention now, before making sense of the DCFR in their light, that is, as a project that attempts to re-enact the *code corpus* technique. The *code corpus* dynamics can be summarised using a two-step argument.

First, whenever successful, the implementation of the technique of the *code corpus* marks the triumph of the textual attitude for a significant and lengthy time, as for example had been the case of the French and Italian examples in the second half of the nineteenth century and beyond.[81] It leads to the production of a mass of interpretative patterns revolving around the codified text rather than other 'sources' (eg, scholarship) of and/or grounds for (eg, policy) reasoning. An interpretative consciousness develops that revolves around attentiveness to the text, understood to be all-encompassing and all-generating, that is, prompting 'correct' solutions for any and all cases. Interpreters act, and justify their job, on this narrow grammaticalist basis, rather than on policy or value or other non-grammatical grounds (*grammaticalism*).[82] Highly rationalised academic commentaries on the canonical code text, adopting a grammaticalist type of interpretative approach, only strengthen the legislative project.[83] The private law field then becomes 'highly impacted',[84] given that grammaticalist-based interpretative utterances become key to the success and prestige of scholarly argumentation and judicial opinions.

Second, whenever a *code corpus* is successfully implemented, such impacting processes in turn discipline law's application, for they exacerbate the work of those who, for whatever reason, wish to further decisions other than those dictated by the requirements of the 'impacted field'. Dissenters have the extra burden of having to argue against code-based grammatical interpretative patterns (offering counter-grammaticalist arguments themselves based on grammatical

[81] On France, see M Lasser, 'Judicial (Self-)Portraits: Judicial Discourses in the French Legal System' (1995) 104 *Yale Law Journal* 1325; on Italy, see Niglia (n 45) 52 et seq.

[82] For 'grammaticalism' understood in this way, I am borrowing from Lasser (n 81) 1327, n 3 (arguing that a grammatical reading 'assumes that a text's vocabulary and syntax (ie, its grammar) can mechanically generate the proper reading of that text' and critically noting the many decades that it took in post-codification France for insiders to unveil the actual choices being made under the cover of grammaticalism). On the role that 'systematisation' plays in reinforcing what I call 'grammaticalism', insofar as it 'ossifies' the code-shaped patterns of interpretation, see C-W Canaris, *Systemdenken and Systembegriff in der Jurisprudenz* (Berlin, Duncker und Humblot, 1983) as referred to in N Jansen and R Michaels, 'Private Law and the State' (2007) 71 *Rabels Zeitschrift*, at 395–96: 'Systematic thinking with a codified legal order . . . aims at finding and, at best, developing an authoritatively imposed system within the . . . codifications *tend to ossify the systematic assumptions of the times of their enactment*' (emphasis added).

[83] On the general role of 'dense academic commentary' in strengthening law-in-action, see Kennedy (n 63).

[84] I am borrowing the terminology of fields being less or more 'impacted' and I am adapting to the context of my analysis the related argument about 'more work' (in what I call 'highly impacted fields') from Kennedy (n 63) 13 et seq.

reasoning). This represents an extra burden that does not exist in 'lowly impacted fields' with no such unified legal grammar – and in which legal actors base their arguments on policy or value considerations, or indeed any chosen authority and argumentative structure that, in their view, is conducive to sustaining their own interpretative positioning on individual issues.[85] Doctrinal and judicial controversies develop within the grammaticalist horizon rather than in direct relation to the actual choices inevitably being made. Below I will give some examples taken from past centuries.

Synthesising what happened after the enactment of the *Code civil des français*, Van Canaegem argued that jurists such as Merlin de Douai, Jacques de Maleville and Zachariae, following the enactment of the *Code civil* , all 'lawyers educated under the ancient regime who devoted their studies to the new codes . . . continued to make use of the sources from which the *Code Civil* had drawn so much, Roman and customary law', *but* that their work was only transitional, for: 'After them, the legal scene was dominated by true exegetes.' 'The codes now existed . . . [j]udges had only to respect them strictly; authors had merely to interpret the articles of the codes faithfully. It was out of the question now for case law or scholarship to attempt to innovate or play a creative role . . . [l]aw had merged with statute.' In a representative statement by the jurist-exegete *Laurent*: 'Statute, even if it were a thousand times absurd, would still have to be followed to the letter, because the text is clear and formal.'[86] In post-BGB Germany, a 'conservative and text-orientated approach' prevailed in the work of 'the traditional middle-class lawyers' for at least half of the nineteenth century, something that also occurred in Italy in the decades following the 1942 Italian Civil Code.[87] Further, two concrete examples of exegetically and formalistically constructed judicial decisions that survived for decades despite well-founded, policy-orientated criticism are, first, the more than a century that it took for strict liability in accidents caused by industrial machinery and transport to be established in French courtrooms, a process delayed by the need to overcome the textual hurdle of 'liability by fault' contained in Articles 1382, 1383 and 1384 of the *French Code Civil*, which notably happened in definitive form with the *Jand'heur* decision of the *Chambers Réunies* of the Cour de cassation in February 1930, more than 120 years later. Second, the more than five decades that it took for Italian courts to make the drafter of standardised contracts responsible for burdensome terms, despite its double signature of the contract, an additional formality provided for in Articles 1341–42 Italian Civil Code and judicially applied so as to rescue the drafter from any liability,

[85] We owe to Pierre Legrand ((n 19) 55) the confirmation of the dichotomy exegesis/critique, which I am discussing in strictly legal historical and comparative terms, in the interdisciplinary language of anthropology and sociology, relying on the works of Barthes, Bourdieu, Goody, Lewellyn and Ong and inter alia noting how 'exegetical loyalty denies that critique can perform a dynamic contrapuntal function in the face of established dogma'. Note, however, my criticism of the culturalist tenet in the remainder of this book.

[86] All citations taken from RC Van Caenegem, *A Historical Introduction to Private Law* (Cambridge University Press, 1992, translated by DEL Johnston) 147 et seq.

[87] ibid 158 (on Germany); Niglia (n 45) (on Italy).

despite policy-based protestation from dissenting scholars that a pro-adherent interpretation could and should have been adopted.[88]

b. Codification and Grammaticalism Today

The promoters of the DCFR project aim at re-enacting past codification experiences in which the *code corpus* organisational technique has been successfully implemented. It is expected that, pushed within the boundaries of the newly codified grammar, the work of the jurist or of the judge will face key changes in interpretative terms; that law's reasoning structures of persuasive authority will be put under pressure, in a similar fashion to what typically happens when legislatures embrace and implement the strategy of codified grammaticalism. In other words, according to this plan, judges and scholars educated in the current, 'pre-codification' (ie, pre-CFR) environment, in which domestic and European legal sources compete for standing – constituting what I have called an unregimented 'living law' – will have to confront the descent of code-centred, disciplinary grammaticalism, which, if all goes according to plan, will lead to an empowerment of legal actors who embrace interpretative grammaticalism based on a CFR code over those who dissent. The project is one of the 'normalisation' of private law via the 'disempowerment' of any potentially dissenting position. As I discuss in more detail in chapter three, there are already actors who, due to their interest in relying on interpretative material left outside a CFR code (that is, the so-called 'optional code'), see themselves potentially disempowered. Thus, there are scholars who understand the proposal of an *optional legislative instrument* to be about marginalising mandatory standards as currently encapsulated in domestic laws and who accordingly criticise it for bringing about 'social dumping' in private law.[89] They argue that an optional instrument amounts to outright 'deregulation', in the sense that 'fewer mandatory rules' would apply than is the case under the existing law based on domestic mandatory rules. Their argument stems from the background consideration that, once a 'comprehensive and self-standing' (optional) code is enacted, anyone who wishes to position themselves against any of the code-based rules and principles will operate at a disadvantage. Code-minded scholars and

[88] For details on strict liability in France and the drafter's liability in Italy, see, respectively, Zweigert and Koetz (n 71) 659 et seq; and Niglia (n 45). The disciplinary character of code structures remains key to understanding European and non-European, past and present codification phenomena: see, eg, B Fauvarque-Cosson, 'Faut-il un Code Civil Européen?' (2002) 3 *Revue Trimestrielle de Droit Civil* 463, 480: 'Le débat sur le Code civil européen nous renvoie l'image idéale et fortement symbolique d'un droit unifié. Pour nous autres Francais, il se rattache en outré a la forte tradition codificatrice laissée en heritage par les Romains et reprise par Napoléon'; and, on codification as 'a tool to establish political power over the population by creating legal dependence and asserting centralised control', despite the rhetoric of promoting republicanism and egalitarian values liberalism, see also MC Mirrow, 'The Power of Codification in Latin America. Simon Bolivar and the Code Napoleon' (2000) 8 *Tulane Journal of International and Comparative Law* 83, 88.

[89] See, eg, M. Hesselink, 'An Optional Instrument on EU Contract Law: Could it Increase Legal Certainty and Foster Cross-Border Trade?' *European Parliament, Policy Department, PE 425.642*, at 16–17; Kerber and Grundmann (n 79); JW Rutgers, 'An Optional Instrument and Social Dumping' (2006) 2 *European Review of Contract Law* 199.

judges will be able to 'powerfully' counter-argue that the optional code is 'comprehensive and self-contained'[90] and, as to substance, that it *sufficiently* protects contractors. A similar kind of opposition vis-a-vis an optional code comes from the English Law Society's consideration that cross-border contracts and their performance can be linked to different areas of law, such as tort law and property law, areas which would still need to be governed by the laws of Member States.[91] Here, the target of criticism is the position of the codifiers whereby it would be realistic to think that cross-border disputes (to which an *OI*-optional code would arguably apply) can be entirely placed under the aegis of the optional code (*independently of* domestic laws). Again, these are critical concerns that stem from the consideration that reliance on any interpretative material placed outside the *OI*-optional code would be hard.

The codifiers expect a reversal of reasoning patterns to happen, with the domestic jurist and judge having to embark on the employment of a considerable array of extra arguments so as to challenge the applicability of a CFR code to disputes, rather than only arguing on the substance of the issues in dispute on the basis of their own domestic laws, eventually resisting European law. For non-compliance patterns towards European (private) secondary law, as things stand, show exactly this – as symbolised by one Supreme Court, which famously and defiantly held that 'it is up to the national court' to adjudicate, on a matter explicitly regulated by the Unfair Terms Directive, on an exclusive basis.[92] The codifiers expect a CFR code to alter the burdens of argumentation. The minimal burden of simply rejecting European law in defence of national law, as today, would be replaced by the onerous burden of having to counteract any sort of CFR-based, grammaticalist interpretation. It will no longer be the case of dealing with the product of the 'arbitrary command' of the EU institutions, as in the classical critical works of diverse authors such as Brandner, Legrand and Ulmer,[93] all relying on the authority *imperio rationis* of one's own legal system. The codifiers expect that it will no longer be the case that the Directives are perceived as presumptively weak on doctrinal grounds *and*, correspondingly, that domestic grammatical readings and orderings are presumptively held to be more authoritative than the Directives. The reference to the DCFR by Advocate General Trstenjak in *Martin* only anticipates the stronger, 'official-text' kind of interpretative authority to come for an

[90] For this argument in relation to an optional instrument on European contract law, drawing on the experience of the Principles of European Insurance Contract, see Basedow (n 77) 995–96.

[91] See the Law Society (UK) at http://international.lawsociety.org.uk/files/LSEW_FINAL_Contract-Law-Response_5_12_10_0.pdf. Further concerns along similar lines of argument have been raised by the UK Law Commission: see www.justice.gov.uk/lawcommission/docs/Work_of_Law_Com_2011-2015.pdf at para 2.52: 'The adoption of a European OI would have potentially dramatic consequences . . . the OI may deviate from English contract law in some long settled areas.'

[92] BGH, 7 July 1998, 1998 *Der Betriebs-Berater* 1864: 'it is for the German courts to determine whether the term in question is subject to review in respect of its subject matter, and the ECJ, pursuant to Article 177 of the EC Treaty, has no say in this area'. The UK Supreme Court also resisted referring the bank charges case to the CJEU, holding that the interpretation of UK Regulations implementing the Unfair Terms Directive, is a matter for domestic law only: *Office of Fair Trading v Abbey National plc and others* [2009] UKSC 6.

[93] See, respectively, Legrand (n 19); Brandner and Ulmer (n 36).

acquis encapsulated in a CFR code.[94] *En bref*, we are talking of the strategy of instantiating a shift away from 'lowly impacted' towards 'highly impacted' field-making and of the resulting constraints falling upon any dissenting voice.[95] To put it another way, in the view of the codifiers, if a CFR code were to be enacted, *disciplined interpretation* would be bound to replace the existing patterns of *interpretative pluralism.*

The codifiers expect the *code corpus* to work towards concretising their agenda in a second sense, that is, in terms of policy preferences. As one learns from past codification patterns in which the *code corpus* technique has been successfully implemented, codes have been effective tools for policy reform. They are meant, through grammaticalism, to implement policy choices, by legislative imposition 'from the top', on the community of scholars and judges – thus redistributing powers from judges and scholars to the legislature, as a way of overcoming the typical conservativism of lawyers vis-a-vis attempts at policy innovation.[96] From this vantage point, codification is about making the legislature see its preferred policies enter law's structures with as little scrutiny as possible from the legal community of interpreters at large. Historically, this is why patterns of resistance towards change through codification projects must (also) be traceable to policy-orientated reasons, as raised by vigilant members of the legal community who happened to think differently. Thus, Savigny's opposition to the project of a Germanic civil code, in his *Vom Beruf unserer Zeit für Gesetzgebung und Rechtswissenschaft*, has been explained as being motivated by political conservativism vis-a-vis the ideas of the French Revolution as incorporated into the Napoleonic Code, and Carter's opposition to a New York Civil Code in the second half of the nineteenth century has been equally explained on policy ground, that is, in terms of a defence of the interests of the business community vis-a-vis intrusive legislation.[97]

Seen in this light, the *DCFR* aims at re-enacting a strategy typical of these past codification efforts – the turning of policy into grammar for the purpose of superimposing policy material through grammaticalism.[98] Accordingly, the redistribution of law-making powers entailed in a European code, that is, the empowerment of legal actors who embrace code-based interpretative grammaticalism over those who dissent, aims at shifting key policy decisions away from (domestic) judges and scholars towards the (EU) legislature. The codifiers expect the body of Commission-generated policy claims, as incorporated into the model rules and attached commentary, to become the 'unproblematic decoding of the text'.[99] The

[94] Advocate General Opinion, Case C-227/08 *Eva Martin Martin v EDP Editores* [7 May 2009], at para 51.

[95] See Kennedy (n 63).

[96] See van Caenegem (n 86) 12 (modern codifications seen as instruments of social reform); M Reimann, 'The Historical School Against Codification: Savigny, Carter, and the Defeat of the New York Civil Code' (1989) 37 *American Journal of Comparative Law* 95, 119.

[97] Reimann (n 96) 115.

[98] See Lasser (n 81) 1408 (on dependency of policy on grammar).

[99] I borrow from P de Man, *The Resistance to Theory* (Minneapolis, MN, University of Minnesota Press, 1986) 14 et seq as reconstructed in Lasser (n 81) 1327.

text itself would be represented as mechanically capable of generating 'the proper meaning', becoming the powerful interpretative terrain for translating the policy choices that lag behind a CFR code in the everydayness of law enforcement.[100]

V. ON THE NEED TO EXPLORE THE CODIFICATION PHENOMENON FROM THE PERSPECTIVE OF THE WIDER RANGE OF JURISPRUDENTIAL FORCES

As has typically been the case of modern codification episodes whenever the goal of the codifiers has been to enact a *code corpus*, the proposed European code emerges as a powerful technical apparatus deployed by the EU legislature and its legal brethren for the purpose of disciplining interpretation, so as to make it instrumentally revolve around a range of preferred substantive objectives – a 'total' ('complete') market ordering governmental technique. Under the cover of 'universalisation' lies the strategy of shaping the market order according to a partisan vision of the common good. Today, the universalisation of market libertarianism, yesterday, the universalisation of the bourgeois ideal of a free market (*Code civil*; *BGB*).[101] As in the past, under the cover of pursuing a rationalisation of the legal process lies the strategy of disciplining interpretation,[102] but there is now a need to explore further dimensions. Let me explain.

There has clearly never been such thing as a homogeneous world of legal science allegedly entirely committed to the codification enterprise in codification episodes from the *Code civil* onwards. Whoever believes in that kind of world would incur the same kind of positivistic 'error' as depicting codification as just an act of the sovereign, for it would mistake legal change for a holistic movement, this time jurisprudential rather than legislative. The world of private law is more complex than that. In modern codification episodes, there have always been currents of thought that oppose codification either in its entirety or, less rigidly, through opposing the specific ways in which the codification move is being organised and arguing in favour of weaker codification models. Arguments viewing the code as legislation based on principles rather than the *code corpus* in twentieth-century Italy and Germany exemplify this critical position that is not entirely opposed to codifying the law.[103] Another example is the position, put forward immediately after the enactment of the BGB, that the new code should be considered 'merely' 'restatement' rather than *code corpus* and that it should not bar attempts to pursue 'justice beyond the positive law' against 'the high priests of legal scholarship' (the Pandectist scholars) and their pretended truth whereby the code is undoubtedly 'comprehensive, systematic, precise, highly technical . . . a

[100] Lasser (n 81) 1327.

[101] On bourgeois codes, see G Tarello, *Storia della Cultura Giuridica Moderna. Assolutismo e Codificazione del Diritto* (Bologna, Il Mulino, 1976); Wieacker (n 64) and the discussion below in ch 4.

[102] For critical considerations on rationalisation qua legal certainty as a key factor in shaping the codification movement, see ch 4.

[103] For discussion, see below, ch 4 (referring to disputes in Germany and Italy over the code-form, including the position whereby 'legislation by principles' would be preferable).

'prison cell' for legal scholarship'.[104] Moreover, opposition and resistance patterns can arise at any stage in the codification process. Examples prior to the start of the official stage of drafting a code include: Savigny, who opposed the codification of German private law in 1814 for its attempt to conceptualise the law as a set of abstract rules of reason not really embedded in the community, as in his view it should have been the case; scholars and judges who opposed the codification of French private law during the *Ancien Régime*; and the jurists who opposed the attempts at codification in Lombardy by Maria Theresa and Joseph II, in Piedmont by Charles Albert and in the Stato Pontificio during the nineteenth century.[105] Examples during the drafting process include: the case of divergent views on whether codification should be 'strong' or 'weak' at the drafting stage of the *Code civil* as embodied in the *Cambacérès* code-projects, reputed to have been closer to revolutionary principles than the *Portalis* project; and the criticism of the Second Commission set up in 1990 vis-à-vis the 1888 First Draft of the BGB, which centred on the Draft being 'abstract and pedantic . . . out of touch with reality . . . lacking a drop of socialist oil', all features which were then retained nevertheless.[106] Following the enactment of a code, examples of opposition and resistance patterns include: the emergence of strands of scholarship that silently opposed the *Code civil* by ignoring it for a few decades after its enactment, continuing to interpret private law according to Roman law; and the fact that, in the two decades after enactment, the BGB may have been passively applied by scholars and judges in exegetic mode, but the Imperial Court itself did not refrain from engaging in more liberal interpretations in some decisions.[107] Once enacted, the codes themselves were framed as more or less 'complete' bodies of rules, that is, less or more reliant on 'external sources' such as *ius commune*, depending on the kinds of compromises between, on the one hand, feudal and local interests, and, on the other hand, the centralised ethos of the codification enterprise, as achieved in each historical episode among the conflicting jurisprudential forces – the case of the Prussian *Allegemeines Landrecht* (entering in force in 1794) and of the Spanish Civil Code of 1889.[108] Overall, one can list the names of writers who defended

[104] For this synthesis, I am drawing on R Zimmermann, *Roman Law, Contemporary Law, European Law: The Civilian Tradition Today* (Oxford University Press, 2001) 55, citing the work of F Wieacker.

[105] For the last three episodes, see Pio Caroni, 'Il codice rinviato. Resistenze europee all'elaborazione e alla diffusione del modello codicistico' in P Cappellini and B Sordi (eds), *Codici. Una riflessione di fine millennio* (Milan, Giuffrè, 2002) 263, 289, n 66 (recounting resistance coming from the *ceto forense*).

[106] On France, see the discussion below in ch 4. On Germany, see Zimmermann (n 104) 54 (First Draft published in 1888 'condemned for being too abstract and pedantic', 'denounced as a pandectist textbook cast in statutory form', 'out of touch with reality' and 'lacking even a drop of socialist oil'; most of these features were basically retained in the last version of the code, despite the fact that the 'criticism was heeded by the Second Commission set up in 1890').

[107] Respectively J Gordley 'The Myths of the French Civil Code' (1994) 42 *American Journal of Comparative Law* 459; Zimmermann (n 104) 5: 'It is widely believed today that the first two decades under the BGB were marked by an exaggerated statutory positivism displayed, particularly, by the Imperial Court: a kind of "école de l'exégèse" engaging in a "legal game of chess" [in the words of Josef Partsch in his *Vom Brumdes römischen Rechts in der heutigen Universität*) but then offering a more nuanced version of this story that points to episodes of judicial activism on the part of the Imperial Court'. See for further discussion Zimmermann (n 104) at 57 et seq.

[108] Caroni (n 105) 280 et seq.

feudal interests and were against codification, and of those who openly defended the bourgeois codification movement – among the former, Justus Môser, August Wilhelm Rehberg and Carl Ludwig von Haller;[109] the latter being obviously represented by Thibaut and his followers. In the nineteenth century, everywhere from Germany to Italy to Switzerland, the constitutional context (monarchic and feudal) could be relied upon as a ground for resisting or placing limits on the reception of codification ideas.[110] I refer to a republican constitutional context held to be needed for the implementation of a project such as codification, which tended to be 'liberal and democratic' as opposed to monarchic and feudal, albeit with the exception of Switzerland, which was traditionally republican, but where opposition to the code arose in defence of local democracy by the Cantons.[111] What is remarkable is the ways in which legal narratives mixed up with social, political and constitutional arguments in the work of jurists, and determined the relevant interpretative tendencies and patterns vis-à-vis the codification idea, for example, the case of the Spanish reception of the Savignian ideas in Catalonia in the nineteenth century where the interest in defending the economic and political autonomy of local authorities was furthered by reliance on arguments borrowed from the Germanic historical school.[112] On this basis, one must admit that any code is always, at least partly, non-code; that no code is ever really 'realised', despite pretences to totality and perfection typical of many historical code-projects; that what is *code corpus* according to some is not to others (eg, criticism of French social scholars during the second half of the nineteenth century vis-à-vis the *Code civil*),[113] and that, what matters above all is that the contending jurisprudential

[109] For discussion, see ibid (with relevant bibliography) 292 et seq.

[110] For discussion see ibid 280 et seq.

[111] ibid 298 et seq.

[112] ibid 284 (for discussion and references).

[113] As I argue in the remainder of this book, there is no objective rendition of what a code 'is', but only contingent discourses (contested and contestable) coming from the insiders to the codification phenomena that determine what interpretative communities hold it to be, at times contentiously rather than consensually, alongside contingent discourses coming from external observers and regarding what they understand and/or evaluate a code to be. The popularity of the objective rendition is traceable to the ever highly regarded positivistic belief in the code as powerful legislative object, as *code corpus* and, as such, allegedly 'perfect' in its being instrumental to the rationalising activities of the legislature (allegedly centralising, unifying, ordering and bettering the law). Communities of legal actors at times have managed to construct a strong consensus around the idea of the *code corpus*, with the code then happening to be perceived as complete, coherent, self-standing, system – see, eg, J-L Halpérin, 'Le regard de l'historien' in *Le Code civil 1804-2004 Livre du Bicentenaire* (Dalloz, Paris, 2004) 43, 46: 'Loi du 30 Ventôse an XII a précisément instauré "un seul corps de lois" . . . les lois qui composent le Code civil appareissent au premier abord former un ensemble des plus homogènes don't l'objectif était d'assurer l'unité du droit civile français en faisant table rase des sources de l'Ancien droit, comme l'ordonne l'article 7 de la même loi', and code believed to be 'système'; P Remy, 'Regards sur le code', *Livre du Bicentenaire*, 99, 100: 'c'était un corps, un tout coherent, un systéme de droit civil prétendant à la completude'. Also, as I discuss later, *code corpus* understood as the conviction that a code consists of a complete body of internally coherent and gapless rules has notably been the target of criticism of socially orientated scholarship (notably but not only in France) who then reconstructed the 'entity' as internally incoherent and ideologically biased, an example of how the perceptions of the insiders are what really matters in any attempt at 'defining' a code (for an analysis in English of this kind of critique, see Marie-Claude Belleau 'The "Juristes Inquiets": Legal Classicism and Criticism in Early Twentieth-Century France' (1987) 2 *Utah Law Review* 379). The classical 'definition' of a code in terms of *code*

forces put forward 'descriptions' of what a code 'is' that are far from 'objective' and are only part and parcel of an engagement in support of, or critique of, the code form.[114]

In other words, one needs to investigate the features of the wider private law world if we are to understand the codification phenomenon, which means studying the legal forces that work in favour of the codification move or against it, and any variations thereof within that continuum. 'Enactment' of a code and its 'implementation' are only umbrella terms which obscure the ways in which these forces operate.[115] Put simply, and to make an extreme point, in no time in modernity (nineteenth and twentieth centuries) can it be said that a code-text has been either 'accepted' by the entire legal community of interpreters[116] or 'resisted' by them.[117] Only complexes of pro-code interpretations of the law that may then lead to enacting a contingent code-text, or to not enacting any code at all, and complexes of post-enactment interpretations that may then lead to successfully implementing code rules or not or only partly so (for certain institutions and norms rather than for others).[118] It all depends on the 'outputs' of the interplay of the conflicting jurisprudential forces. Anything that happens under the phenomenon 'codification' must be measured against that background – for example, the enactment of a code significantly imbalances the interpretative game in favour of

corpus (for a recent restatement, critically, see Zimmermann (n 7)) is a perspective that fails to take into account the 'meaning' of a code understood as contingent form. I consider this approach, as opposed to the objectifying approach that considers a code to be *code corpus* or not (the 'code proper' argument), to make really intelligible the historical episodes of codification (see below, ch 2) as well as the European project of codification as discussed in this chapter and as in chs 3 and 4. To this one must add the many competing views on code reforms ('recodification' *sensu lato*): for example, contrast S Patti, *Diritto Privato e Codificatione europea* (Milan, Giuffrè, 2007) 171 et seq (the Germanic 2002 recodification reform as informed by a new rationality that reduces the space of private autonomy and increases that of mandatory rules; as distant from traditional liberal orientation of the BGB, of the Directives and of the norms incorporating them in the BGB; 2002 German reform as a model for European codification project) with H-W Micklitz, 'The Expulsion of the Concept of Protection from the Consumer Law and the Return of the Social Elements in the Civil Law: A Bittersweet Polemic European University Institute Working Papers 2012/03 at http://hdl.handle.net/1814/20374 (critical account of an individualistic vocabulary insofar as it underlies the substance of the German recodification process, also seen as anticipation of European developments). In favour of recodification in France, referring explicitly to the German 2002 reform and the 1992 Dutch code, is P Rémy 'Regards sur le code' in *Le Code Civil 1804–2004 Livre du Bicentenaire*, 99, 118.

[114] For further discussion, see below, ch 4.

[115] For a focus on the social and political side to these tensions, see, eg, Caroni (n 105); C Varga, *Codification as a Socio-historical Phenomenon* (Budapest, Akadémiai Kiadó, 1991).

[116] Contrast the strong theory of 'acceptance' in N Jansen, *The Making of Legal Authority: Non-legislative Codifications in Historical and Comparative Perspective* (Oxford, Oxford University Press, 2010) 44 (proposing 'the concept of a legal text's authority', including codes, in the following terms: as 'the abstract authority of a text giving expression to a legal norm consists in the legal profession accepting it as an ultimate source of the law, without requiring further legal reasons to do so. Of course, there may be political, prudential, moral, or other reasons for recognising such a text as legal authority. But such reasons are not part of the legal system').

[117] See Caroni (n 105).

[118] For example, Zimmermann (n 104) 56 et seq identifies tort law cases (paras 823 I, 823 II and 826 BGB) in which the Imperial Court was not positivistic in the early years of the BGB in relation to certain institutions and norms, but acknowledges that that Court was so in relation to other areas such as 'the protection of a person's personality' (at 79).

the forces sympathetic to codification, as it 'normalises' the position of the codifiers, so it places an extra burden of interpretation on the opposing forces who have to do the 'extra work' of furthering their viewpoints. Managing to enact arm's-length interpretation, and the time-length for doing that, depends on the strength of the non-codifying forces, as occurred in the case of product liability in France and of standard form terms in Italy as discussed above, where it took decades for the jurisprudential forces to do the extra work of interpretation required to see their viewpoints succeed in conditions of interpreting under the shadow of the code. *En bref*, each codification episode in its various stages, from drafting to implementing, marks the flipside of complex combinations of relative strengths and weaknesses of any of the underlying jurisprudential forces. Codification is dynamic and never static, for there is never a code-text but always interpretations of it and perspectives about it. Understanding a code is about engaging with, and capturing, these perspectives.[119] The description of the traits of a *code corpus* is always just one 'view of the cathedral', taken from the vantage point of its proponents, that demands an understanding of the position of those who criticise it for really grasping the totality of the phenomenon.

On this analytical basis, there is need to understand better the jurisprudential forces that surround the new codification project, covering the wider range of forces that operate outside the 'European private law school' that has produced the code-text currently considered before the EU legislative institutions as a result of the proposed draft for an Optional Sales Code (a synthetical version of the DCFR), and unveiling the conflicting formal and substantive viewpoints about how to organise private law as they come from the wider community of private law interpreters. This is what the remainder of the book purports to do. It starts with a description of such jurisprudential forces, whose 'DNA' lies in having shifted away from the code-form over the course of the twentieth century. It then moves on to consider the clashes between the opposing jurisprudential forces (the codifiers and the opponents to codification), arguing that it is at this level of analysis that one can make really intelligible the codification process underway. That is, a major attempt to re-codify private law[120] and to reverse the de-codification

[119] On the relationship between 'understanding' this way on the part of the insiders and creating an 'effect of authority' around the code-text, see the Epilogue to this volume.

[120] For a conscious understanding of the European codification process as an option, however problematic, for remedying the 'problems' entailed in the 'de-codification process' within domestic private law, see the representative essays of P Rémy 'Regards sur le code' in *Le Code Civil 1804-2004 Livre du Bicentenaire* (Paris, Dalloz, 2004) 99, at 118 (there are two ways to overcome decodification – the recodification of French civil law or the European codification of private law – for a European code would confirm 'le caractère cyclique de codifications – la loi de l'éternel retour de la codification, comme enterprise de mise en ordre et d'intelligence du droit par l'écriture'; reference to the German law for the modernisation of the law of obligations of 2002 entered into force on 1 January 2002 as a recodification model; recodification of French law is problematic as it would 'exige surtout une volonté politique exceptionnelle . . .' for 'l'esprit politique du temps, qui oscille horizontalement entre le "traitement du social" e la "gouvernance", ne se prête pas à la construction d'une cathédral de droit civil'; the European civil code 'a révolté la plus grande et la meilleure part de la doctrine française'); and of G Alpa and M Andenas, *I Fondamenti del Diritto Privato Europeo* (Milan, Giuffrè, 2005) 121 (overview of recodification debates in France, Germany, Italy and arguing '[l]'interrogativo ricorrente esprime un dilemma

process, an attempt rooted in strands of scholarship committed to the idea of a *code corpus* that, if successful, is bound to alter the value structures of private law towards abandoning the welfarist paradigm and embracing market libertarianism.

inquietante: correggere il codice o attendere la codificazione europea?' at 121; '[a]lla fine del Novecento si è tuttavia prepotentemente imposta l'esigenza di rinnovare il testo del codice, non potendo essere considerata più sufficiente l'interpretazione correttiva, adeguatrice e creativa dei giudici' at 112; citing F Ghestin, *Traité de droit civil. Introduction générale* (Paris, Librairie Générale de Droit et de Jurisprudence, 1994) as holding that the two options of recodifying the French civil law of obligations and the European codification project are compatible at 121).

2

Jurisprudence

> [N]ous n'avons plus en réalitè, et malgré les apparences, un droit civil codifié! . . . *Nous n'avons plus de Code civil*! (F Larnaude, 2004)*
>
> Sur ce corps, le temps a passé, retranchant ici, ajoutant là; hors du Code, d'autres lois civiles ont proliféré, elles-même recueillies par d'autres Codes; le Code est-il encore le corps des lois civile? Avons-nous encore un Code? (P Rémy, 2004)**
>
> Mon Code est perdu (Napoléon)***

I. INTRODUCTION

ANALYSIS OF THE jurisprudential forces and their movements is required in order to fully understand what is really at stake in the project of a European code. At the national level, jurisprudential movements (scholars and judges)[1] have managed to liberate themselves from the disciplinary constraints of the national codes, having abandoned code-based disciplinary interpretation and embraced 'arm's-length interpretation'.[2] Remarkably, this approach also characterises the interpretative engagements of national legal actors supranationally with the Directives, in the context of the private law harmonisation process. The new codification move effectively attempts to straitjacket jurisprudence once more, transforming it from arm's length into a disciplinary mode – albeit this time in the name of a European rather than national codification project. This is the very meaning of the attempt to replace harmonisation by codification. This reading goes beyond conventional understandings whereby the codification struggle is understood to take place between code (European) and

* F Larnaude, 'Le Code Civil et la nécessité de sa Revision' in *Le Code Civil 1804–2004 Livre du Bicentenaire* (Paris, Dalloz, 2004) 908–09 (emphasis in original).

** P Rémy, 'Regards sur le code' in *Le Code Civil 1804–2004 Livre du Bicentenaire* (Paris, Dalloz, 2004) 99, 100.

*** Attributed to Napoléon.

[1] In this book I adopt 'jurisprudence' as being inclusive of scholarship and adjudication, understood as historical forces, unless otherwise indicated: for details, see ch 4.

[2] By 'arm's length', I mean interpretation not subjected to the disciplinary constraints typically associated with the making and implementation of a *code corpus*, as I have discussed above in ch 1.

codes (national),[3] arguing that it is instead a struggle between the legislature and jurisprudence.[4] This argument is put forward in two chapters. In this chapter, I investigate the aforementioned dimension, which in my view is largely neglected in conventional narratives on the European codification project, that is, the story of the movement of jurisprudence away from the code-ideology as established in nation states during the age of codification, a story that has taken place mostly over the second half of the past century, first nationally and then in European mode in the context of the EU harmonisation project.[5] In the following chapter (chapter three), I then investigate how, as is typically the case in modern codification processes, the present codification movement, through the usual engagement of the community of legal interpreters, has been impacting on the living structures of jurisprudence at the pre-code enactment stage. In scholarly circles one can note a series of polemical predicaments that epitomise the structures of that impact.

* * *

In the preceding chapter, I have considered the many weaknesses of the European code-project as traceable to the consideration that the codification strategy aims at centralising law anew at the undue sacrifice of the plurality of interpretative positions on private law that emerge from the impact of the Directives on national legal traditions. Specifically, an anti-pluralist ethos emerges in the code-project via the re-proposition of a register of code-based interpretation that, as in many of the past applications of code-based rules in private law disputes,[6] is bound to obstruct the coupling of law with well-grounded, widely established arguments of substantive justice that challenge code-based interpretative positions – the examples being the development of the law of unfair terms and of product liability as discussed in chapter one, signifying situations in which the law became alienated from the aspiration to achieve the objectives of justice considered to be appropriate

[3] For a critical analysis of this conventional understanding, see R Michaels, 'Code vs Code. Nationalist and Internationalist Images of the Code Civil in the French Resistance to a European Codification' (2012) 8 *European Review of Contract Law* 277 (emphasising, in both cultural and political terms, the conflicting images of the civil code held in French scholarship and in turn projected onto the idea of a European code itself). Note P Legrand, 'Against a European Civil Code' (1997) 60 *Modern Law Review* 44 (criticising a European civil code for being about superimposing the civilian understanding of private law, understood in cultural terms, onto the common law, thus drawing on a conception of continental law systems as just code-based). Contrast L Niglia, *The Transformation of Contract in Europe* (The Hague, Kluwer Law International, 2003) (codes in the contemporary nation states France, Germany and Italy understood as among the many reference points of the interpretative work of scholars and judges, with interpretation happening in relation to many more factors than just code-based rules).

[4] Let me recall that this is a first-step argument leading to ch 4, where I argue that, in the final analysis, struggles among the jurisprudential forces themselves lie behind modern codification phenomena, including the present European codification project.

[5] A credible starting point in time for the European chapter of this story is 1985, as in that year Directives started to be enacted that encroached upon private law (ie, the Product Liability and the Doorstep Directives).

[6] See above, ch 1 and, for a historical and critical contextualisation of the *code corpus* vs *code open* argument, see ch 4.

in the circumstances. Further to this point, closer consideration of the dynamics of private law jurisprudence makes it possible to explore further the anti-pluralist ethos of the proposed codification project, insofar as it sheds light on a problematic incompatibility between the living jurisprudence throughout Europe (which comprises individual national jurisdictions whilst enjoying a 'European character' whenever it engages with interpreting the Directives) and the disciplinary project of a pan-European code. I argue that, according to the strategy of the codifiers, to opt for a European code means to set in motion a mechanism that works towards dismantling those jurisprudential structures and, as a result, sacrificing the values of constitutional authority attached to them. A *code corpus* is the tool that the codifiers deploy towards diverting jurisprudence away from arm's-length interpretation, creating a powerful, fixed interpretative 'ultimate reference point on authority'[7] bound to replace the contingent points of authority emerging out of the living structures of private law jurisprudence. If successfully implemented, the code is bound to de-constitutionalise and to re-constitutionalise private law this way, I argue, considering that the (monistic) 'culture' of economic market fundamentalism is being superimposed on the (plural) 'culture' of the many and often conflicting constitutional values underneath national constitutional private law systems.[8] The critique taken at this further level makes the original point that, on closer inspection, in danger is not just jurisdictional diversity, that is, the survival of individual jurisdictions in relation to private law matters (as argued in chapter one), but the survival of a European kind of jurisprudential diversity (both state-based and post-state), that is, the possibility for jurisprudence (scholarship and adjudication) itself to survive in the shape that it currently has – as a constitutional force for the (re-)creation of private law, as developed over the last decades nationally and, I argue in this book, in the context of Europeanisation as a transformed private law phenomenon that is no longer just national. This is the argument that I will make in the following pages.

* * *

In chapter one I have considered the Common Frame of Reference (CFR) initiative, as engineered over the course of the last 15 years, as a code-project that

[7] RC Van Caenegem, *Judges, Legislators and Professors: Chapters in European Legal History* (Cambridge University Press 1987) 41 ('the ultimate reference point on authority is different' as, quoting Konrad E Zweigert and Hein Kotz, *An Introduction to Comparative Law*, translated by Tony Weir (Oxford, Clarendon Press, 1998), 'the common law tends to the independence of casuistry . . . while the continental law tends to the coherence of a system'); H Eidenmüller, F Faust, H Grigoleit, N Jansen, G Wagner and R Zimmermann, 'The Common Frame of Reference for European Private Law – Policy Choices and Codification Problems' (2008) 28(4) *Oxford Journal of Legal Studies* 659, 660 (noting that 'the establishment of an authoritative European reference text promises to constitute a significant step forward').

[8] On welfarism as embodying a variety of conflicting values, see, eg, T Wilhelmsson, 'Varieties of Welfarism' (2004) 10 *European Law Journal* 712; D Kennedy, 'A Transnational Genealogy of Proportionality in Private Law' in R Brownsword, H-W Micklitz, L Niglia and S Weatherill (eds), *The Foundations of European Private Law* (Oxford, Hart Publishing, 2011) 185.

threatens to alter the mechanics of interpretation, arranged in post-grammaticalist (post-codification) mode, as they have been operating among scholars and judges during the second half of the past century and up until today. The code-project is really about attempting to turn the clock back to the times of code-grammaticalism, when, in crucial private law fields as, for example, unfair terms in standardised contracts *or* tort law as applicable to product liability, enactment of a code meant to regiment interpretation by displacing any of the dissenting voices.[9] From this vantage point, it is a codification project that, ironically (considering that its stated objective is to aim at replacing national civil codes, either partly or entirely), if successfully implemented, is bound to restore the (grammaticalist) interpretative style that the application of national codes unleashed, rather than overcoming them as the unifying rhetoric might suggest. This is because it would re-establish (albeit in European mode) modes of interpretation that have been largely left behind pursuant to the sequential shifting away from grammaticalism that this book will recount – from codification (in the nineteenth century)[10] to de-codification (in the twentieth century) – towards re-codification (the twenty-first century).[11] I have also argued that what really matters to the proponents of the code strategy is not just structure but also substance – substantive objectives pursued through structural re-arrangements; in other words, to entrench a range of preferred policies through the re-establishment of code-based grammaticalism. The project of remaking the existing structures of private law is related to such dual concerns.

The code-critique that I have proposed up to now becomes all the more compelling if one sees it, as I argue one should, against a set of deeper structures that underlie the interpretative private law operations. I am thinking of constitutional structures. It is the purpose of this chapter and the next to bring to the reader's attention those very structures and, on this basis, to re-articulate the code-critique in deeper terms. My critique will become a constitutional code-critique, a three-step argument complementing the critique in Chapter One of the reborn *code corpus* model understood as interpretative machinery. For ease of exposition, I will deal with the first two steps of my argument in this chapter, while leaving the third step of the argument to the following chapter.

First, I consider how modernity conditions as developed during the twentieth century have transformed private law.[12] They have made of it a truly instrumental

[9] See above, ch 1 (discussing code-based grammaticalism and detailing rules on standardised terms and on product liability contained in the DCFR as being at odds with the corresponding protectionist rules in the nation state).

[10] Understood as *code corpus*: see above, ch 1 (section IV).

[11] On *decodificazione*, here referred to as 'de-codification', see N Irti, *L'etá della decodificazione* (4th edn, Milan, Giuffrè, 1999), and, before, N Irti, 'L'etá della decodificazione' in *Diritto e Societá* (1978), at 613; on 're-codification' in its dual manifestation ('weak' versus 'strong'), see below.

[12] Cf J Habermas, *Between Facts and Norms: Contribution to a Discourse Theory of Law and Democracy* (translated by W. Rehg; Cambridge, MA, MIT Press, 1996) 84 et seq (drawing on the work of Ludwig Raiser with a view to recounting 'the welfare-state materialization of private law') and 194–95 (welfare-state materialised law); L Raiser, *Die Aufgabe des Privatrechts* (Kronberg/Ts, Athenaeum, 1977) 98 et seq.

qua politicised field[13] as a result of the plurality of social forces taking control of the ivory tower of (state) legislative (and administrative) power. Private law has overcome the closure of nineteenth-century legal science around 'heavenly concepts' (*Pandektenwissenschaft*) in that it has become open to the interplay of the contingent strategies furthered by, and corresponding to, the needs and aspirations of the plurality of societal forces and constituencies – rather than merely formal engagement with the making of, and reinforcement of, centralised state power structures as occurred with the enactment of, and the implementation of, the civil codes in nineteenth-century France, Germany, Italy and other continental countries.[14] During the course of the twentieth century, the raison d'etre of private law became about reframing law around the needs and aspirations of the broader societal spectrum of actors. In this sense, one can talk of a process of politicisation (instrumentalising law to social interests) and, relatedly, of pluralisation (instrumentalising law to the plurality of often conflicting social interests).[15] Private law has become a major tool for governing such conflicts – politicisation has taken an active (making choices about how to resolve the conflicts) rather than a passive role (as if inert in relation to the ongoing and unresolved conflicts). I then consider a process in parallel to, and coterminus with, the first, that is, how the broader societal processes of politicisation and pluralisation[16] as channelled through the legislative branch have equally transformed jurisprudence[17] from 'professional' into 'constitutional' (co-development of legislative and jurisprudential patterns). I consider a process of *jurisprudential constitutionalisation* that has developed by way of an active engagement on the part of scholars and judges in the governing of the relevant conflicts. That is, the jurisprudential forces have been actively 'synthesising' the conflicts between individuals and groups around a

[13] Strictly speaking, politicisation has taken place with the nationalisation of private law and the reduction of *Recht/Diritto/Droit* to *Gesetz/Legge/Loi*, but here I am taking a more positive understanding, that is, I look at a deeper politicisation in the context of which the body politic as a whole, rather than just as centralised state power, happened to become the theatre of law's instrumentalisation, as I discuss in the remainder of this chapter.

[14] See the remainder of the chapter and, eg, Habermas (n 12) 25 et seq (pluralisation; internally differentiated and pluralised life-worlds); F Wieacker, *A History of Private Law in Europe* (Oxford, Clarendon Press, 1995) 431 et seq ('dissolution of internal unity of private law'; 'fragmentation' and private law); G Teubner, *Constitutional Fragments* (Oxford, Oxford University Press, 2012), as discussed at n 21 below.

[15] On pluralisation and materialisation, see, eg, Habermas (n 12) 84 et seq (drawing on Raiser to recount 'the welfare-state materialization of private law'); Wieacker (n 14) 431 et seq ('dissolution of internal unity of private law'; 'fragmentation' and private law; the rise of 'social law'). See also G Gurvitch, *L'idée du droit sociale* (Aalen, Scientia Verlag Aalen, 1932, reprint of 1972).

[16] For the link between pluralisation of interest groups and the formation of corresponding pluralities of values, see Habermas (n 12) 84 et seq; for a converging view on pluralisation notably held on distinct theoretical grounds, see Niklas Luhmann, *Theory of Society*, vol 1 (translated by Rhodes Barrett; Stanford, Stanford University Press, 2012) 298 ('selection criteria . . . are geared throughout to instability, and this means that new "inviolate levels" have to be inserted – semantically, in the form of the nineteenth-century conceptuality of value; structurally in the form of the autopoietic autonomy of functional systems').

[17] For a historical excursus of the changes in the structures of jurisprudence from pre-modernity (early modernity) to modernity see G Tarello, *Storia della Cultura Giuridica Moderna. Assolutismo e Codificazione del Diritto* (Bologna, Il Mulino, 1976).

solid core set of material rights – with the consequence that code-based classical contractual, tortious and property rights (formal) as bequeathed from nineteenth-century jurisprudential operations have been replaced by a set of de-codified contractual, tortious and property 'social' rights, 'constitutional' for being based on the ethos of welfarist materialisation. The re-imagining and reconstructing of the place of civil codes in the private law 'system' of the nation state has been a key step in this process, I argue, with a repositioning of the code from 'central' to 'peripheral' as described in a line of writings that I recount under the label 'de-codification'.

Second, and focusing on the jurisprudential side of things (that is, looking at both scholarship and adjudication as constituting the living 'jurisprudence'), I consider that Europeanisation has continued this dual process of (legislative) politicisation and of (jurisprudential) constitutionalisation, bringing about the formation of a European-wide 'jurisprudential pluralism' centred on the plurality of constitutional private law traditions as 're-constituted' (qua 're-created') via their three decades-long engagement with the EU Directives. By 're-creation', I understand Europe's private law as working in plural mode less for being based on a plurality of national systems and more for consisting of a plurality of interpretative positions built through the patterns of interaction between European and national law. The core set of 'social' private law rights have been adjusted towards including the Directive-based law coming from the EU. I argue that a new European-wide private law jurisprudence has been emerging that represents the living law that orthodox European legal thought behind the codification project neglects to take account of.

Third, in chapter three, I develop further the analysis of this chapter. I consider how the new codification project is about attempting to block off the constitutional practices of jurisprudential synthesisation, as a result of the project's aim at dismantling the heritage of material rights and of replacing them with a list of neo-classical 'formal rights' instrumental to a new constitutional regime (market libertarian). Two processes in my view make this agenda intelligible – *de-constitutionalisation* and *re-constitutionalisation*, capturing as they do the real meaning of the new codification movement, which will then both enable and demand the consideration of the implications of the codification project for the wider Europe that I will undertake in the final pages of chapter three.

II. DEVELOPMENT OF A PLURALIST PRIVATE LAW OUT OF CLASSICAL JURISPRUDENCE

In this section, I discuss what in my view it really means for contemporary private law to be 'plural'.[18] My focus is on the developments in the private law field from

[18] For further theoretical, historical and normative explanations of what is meant by 'plural', see L Niglia (ed), *Pluralism and European Private Law* (Oxford, Hart Publishing, 2013).

post-war times up until today.[19] I aim at giving a synthetic account of how private law has transformed from classical[20] (monist) into contemporary (pluralist), with a special emphasis on the work of judges and scholars.

A. Turning Points in History: Politicisation Processes in the Twentieth Century

The remarkable period to look at in order to understand the twin processes of politicisation and pluralisation as affecting contemporary private law is, I think, the second half of the twentieth century.[21] This section focuses on a series of pro-

[19] The argument has been made that law was 'plural' well before the twentieth century. For example, in relation to medieval and to early modern law, in the sense of the concept of *Rechtsvielfalt* as developed in the work of P Oestmann (ed), *Gewohnheit. Gebot. Gesetz. Normativität in Geschichte und Gegenwart* (Tuebingen, Mohr Siebeck, 2011); and P Oestmann, *Rechtsvielfalt vor Gericht. Rechtsanwendung und Partikluarrecht im Alten Reich* (Frankfurt, Klostermann, 2002), as discussed in N Jansen, *The Making of Legal Authority: Non-legislative Codifications in Historical and Comparative Perspective* (Oxford, Oxford University Press, 2010) 11 et seq; and N Jansen, 'Legal Pluralism in Europe' in Niglia (n 18) 109 (a concept 'commonly used in the context of medieval and early modern law' which 'refers to a coexistence of potentially conflicting legal norms, legal systems and legal authorities of different kinds'). See also Pia Letto-Vanamo, 'Fragmentation and Coherence of Law – A Historical Approach' in P Letto-Vanamo and J Smits (eds) *Coherence and Fragmentation in European Private Law* (Münich, Sellier Europa Publisher, 2012) 151, 163 et seq; N Jansen *The Making of Legal Authority. Non-Legislative Codifications in Historical and Comparative Perspective* (Oxford, OUP, 2010) at 44 ('lawyers have often found themselves arguing on the basis of legal systems that were characterised by plural, fragmented and conflicting legal authorities and by organically changing rules of recognition'). I am here qualifying this argument, considering that the constitutionalisation which I am discussing here as a major source of pluralism is a contingent product of late modernity (twentieth century) rather than the whole of modernity starting from the sixteenth century or so. It is inevitable that historians look at developments in their *longue durée*, but there are discontinuities produced by politicisation and pluralisation that must be taken seriously. From this vantage point, it is right to hold that 'the validity or authority' of pre-modern law 'is not easy to understand . . . or to explain in terms of modern law': Letto-Vanamo 'Fragmentation', 159.

[20] On 'classical' private law in the nineteenth century, see, eg, Wieacker (n 14), but note my own understanding in this book of the *code corpus* as developing in the period 1850–1950 rather than just the Nineteenth Century.

[21] For a recent re-exploration (in the vocabulary of constitutional law that, however, in my view overlaps with what I am saying in the narrative, evidencing developments in parallel in constitutional and private law of the nation state) of what I call 'politicisation', see Teubner (n 14) 24–27; and in relation to 'pluralisation', see Teubner (n 14) 5–6 (also discussing 'fragmentation'). For an analysis of similar phenomena from a writer with a different theoretical colour, see Habermas (n 12) 25 et seq. Some understand pluralisation as equivalent to 'fragmentation': see Teubner (n 14) 6 (claiming that 'Since the time of its nation-state beginnings, constitutionalism has been faced with the unresolved question of whether or how the constitution should also govern non-state areas of society. Are the economic, scientific, education, medical, and other social activities to be subjected to the normative parameters of the state constitution? Or should social institutions develop their own constitutions autonomously? (at 5); pointing to 'The problematics of societal constitutionalism . . . caused . . . by the fragmentations of the social whole and the autonomisation of the fragments during the heyday of the nation state' (at 6); arguing that 'Liberal constitutions could conceal the question in the shadow of constitutionally-protected individual freedoms. In sharp contrast, the totalitarian political system of the 20th century attempted to eliminate the autonomy of social sub-areas completely, thus concealing the question of independent societal constitutions by subjecting all areas of society to the state's authority. The welfare states of the late 20th century . . . achieved a peculiar balance between a state constitutionalism, which progressively extended its principles to social spheres, and a constitutional pluralism, in which the state in fact respected a certain autonomy of social sub-constitutions' (at 6). See also Teubner (n 14) 5–6

cesses in this period that have redesigned the structure of private law (vocabularies) as bequeathed from the nineteenth century, constituting a movement away from the nineteenth-century great transformation of law into a 'system'.[22] Such processes of 'new politicisation'[23] as developed in the second half of the past century include the success of national constitutional projects in relation to horizontal relations qua 'constitutionalisation' of private law; the 'de-codification' of private law; and the deployment of special laws as a means to protect status positions behind specific agglomerations of social interests. Before recounting each process, let me explain, *en bref*, how their combined impact has profoundly changed the structure of continental private law.[24]

I see the central characteristic of the politicisation of private law to have been, in post-war times and up until today, the making of the welfare state and related value requirements (the balancing of market-orientated efficiency and solidarity-based considerations)[25] understood as co-determinative of the substance of contract, tort and property laws. Limiting freedom of contract via mandatory rules or via informational and cooperation duties are examples of the living law that developed as the paradigm of 'welfare state materialisation' replaced that of 'bourgeois formal law' (from 'formal' to 'material' rights).[26] This is what is commonly referred to in private law literature as the project of law's 'materialisation' or 'socialisation'.[27] It is a time in which (a contingent set of) values gained centre stage in public discourse, as opposed to times in which values (even those that were de facto given predominance) took a back seat when juridical discourse developed a tendency towards a categorical, a-contextual and technical kind of legal reasoning as characteristic of nineteenth-century classical legal thought.[28] I

(considering 'the constitutional question of whether to subject economic, scientific, education et al societal activities' to the 'normative parameters of the state constitution' or let them 'develop their own constitutions autonomously', and criticising those who consider the current globalisation to be responsible for fragmentation). One need not subscribe to the theory of societal sub-constitutions to understand pluralisation as fragmentation.

[22] See, eg, Wieacker (n 14) 341 et seq (Pandectistic thought; methodic construction of a systematic science of law). For these transformative processes as traceable back to the eighteenth century, see Tarello (n 17).

[23] Tarello (n 17) 16 (on 'tecnicizzazione e depoliticizzazione delle attivita' giuridiche professionali' in shift from the eighteenth to the nineteenth centuries and the converse process of 'detecnicizzazione della scienza giuridica e di responsabilizzazione, in senso politico, del ceto giuridico' as characterising, in the view of Tarello, the times in which he was writing (the 1970s). By 'politicisation', I mean a description of the processes of 'detecnicizzazione' and of 'responsabilizzazione in senso politico' as happening at both the legislative and jurisprudential (judicial and scholarly) levels.

[24] I say continental private law to distinguish it from European private law qua Europeanisation inclusive of the common law. For the deep similarities between the materiality of English law and of continental laws, see Niglia (n 3) in relation to contract law.

[25] *cf* Wilhelmsson (n 8) 715 ('the welfare state is characterised by a continuous balancing between market-oriented efficiency and solidarity-based interventions of the state').

[26] Habermas (n 12) 194–95. Materialisation is a substantive paradigm that involves changes in consciousness (vocabularies), as I describe them in Niglia (n 3) and in this book.

[27] On the 'materialisation' of private law, see above, n 14.

[28] See Tarello (n 17) 5 et seq ('tecnicizzazione della scienza giuridica' in the nineteenth century). In keeping with my view on the *code corpus* as 'classical' in this book, I mean the period 1850–1950 rather than just the Nineteenth Century. .

understand it all to have happened along the following line of events (stretching back to the nineteenth century),[29] not necessarily in order of importance or of causal relationship – industrialisation; social interdependence; pluralisation of values; interdependency of units, from parties to associations to social and economic organisations (plurality of social forces 'entering history'; plurality of claims and values 'entering' the law), each generating their own preferred (project of) type of law; and 'constitutionalisation' as regulating the 'inner order' of social formations including private law social formations.[30] These events were related more or less this way.

One must consider the increasing background awareness of the 'divergence between unity and diversity in constitutionalism',[31] 'a diversity which became even greater with the emergence of parties, associations and social organisations since the industrialisation of the nineteenth century', and that: 'In the course of the 20th century, this discrepancy changed the constitution into a politico-strategic manoeuvring instrument by very different, often antagonistic, social and political groups.'[32] This has been a process in which social corporatism took centre stage[33] and in which the law became a vehicle for both regulating and constitutionalising (whilst, in any case, respecting to a great degree the autonomy of) social formations.[34] If the nineteenth-century 'bourgeois-enlightenment codification'[35] and corresponding constitutionalisation had marked the triumph of individualism and the 'elimination' of recognition and protection for 'intermediate bodies, communities or natural societies',[36] post-war constitutionalism and private law's architecture has been characterised by recognition and protection of intermediate bodies such as parties, associations and social organisations.

In connection with these pluralisation processes in which private law absorbed the demands for recognition of organisational interests and values coming out of 'civil society', private law politicised, alongside constitutional law,[37] in the further

[29] I am thinking of the work of jurists such as F Geny, *Méthode d'interprétation et sources en droit privé positif. Essai Critique* (2nd edn, Paris, LGD, 1919); and R Saleilles, *Étude sur la théorie générale de l'obligation d'après le premier Code civil pour l'Empire Allemand* (3rd edition, Paris, LGD, 1914; 1st edition, 1889); ibid, *De la déclaration de volonté: Contribution à l'étude de l'acte juridique dans le Code civil allemand* (Paris, 1901); ibid, *De la personnalité juridique: Histoire et théorie* (Paris, 1910).

[30] See Teubner (n 14) 24 et seq ('the policy of the welfare state is not merely to regulate social activities but to constitutionalize the inner order of autonomous social sectors').

[31] T Vesting, 'Constitutionalism or Legal Theory' in C Joerges et al (eds), *Transnational Governance and Constitutionalism* (Oxford, Hart Publishing, 2004) 29, 35.

[32] ibid 35.

[33] PF Kjaer, 'The Structural Transformation of Embeddedness' in C Joerges and J Falke (eds), *Karl Polanyi, Globalisation and the Potential of Law in Transnational Markets* (Oxford, Hart Publishing, 2011) 85, 91 (discussing the unfolding of 'complex corporatist regimes'). For a recent description of these developments in relation to constitutionalist aspects, see Teubner (n 14) 24 et seq.

[34] Teubner (n 14) 24.

[35] Tarello (n 17) 27 ('codici borghesi-illuministi').

[36] ibid (discussing scholarly writings on codes and constitutions that focus their attention on corporativist/communitarian perspectives).

[37] Similar to, and thus sharing ground with, the parallel phenomenon of 'constitutional pluralism': *cf*, eg, N Walker, 'The Idea of Constitutional Pluralism' (2002) 65 *Modern Law Review* 317.

sense of taking on itself the role of both regulating and constitutionalising[38] the multitude of interests underlying such processes, insofar as they were relevant to its sphere of operation alongside that of constitutionalism. This has occurred through the issuing of special legislation with a fragmentation impact on the code-system, as I will explain in the remainder of the chapter. From this vantage point, politicisation stands for both the incorporation of interests and values in the body of private law (passive politicisation *qua* reception) and for the pluralist governing of them (active politicisation qua engagement).[39] Co-determination rights for labour unions or protectionist standards in contracts pre-formulated by businesses (sometimes associations of) are good illustrations of active politicisation.[40] Thus, once the plurality of social forces took over the ivory tower of sovereign legislative and administrative power – which one must think of as a true 'counter-movement' vis-a-vis the commodification process entailed in the 'movement' of modernity[41] – (private) law became the object of value-laden choices made by the then newly prevailing forces, with the legal elite organising a law made instrumental to the complex and conflicting requirements of state interventionism.[42] It is in these conditions that what is known as the project of 'materialisation' of private law took place. Techniques and modes of thought were employed that implemented this substantive agenda, giving birth to the new paradigm, understood as the 'formalisation' of materialised rights in that rights incorporated social values, with the insertion of social values in the classical fabric of private law, such as in the case of freedom of contract being limited by mandatory rules or of information duties being imposed upon contractors; of property rights more or less heavily limited via the doctrine of abuse of rights (*abuso del diritto*); and of strict liability as opposed to the classical liability by fault.[43] It is in this context that special legislation became a primary instrument for the materialisation of private law, channelling the demands for protection entailed in the variety of fragmented societal interests. Private law contributed to the work of constitutional law

[38] Teubner (n 14) 24.

[39] On plurality versus pluralism, see Niglia (n 18).

[40] See respectively Teubner (n 14) 24 and Niglia (n 3).

[41] For recent critical analyses on the role and nature of such 'movements' and 'counter-movements', see Joerges and Falke (n 33).

[42] The list of writings on this would be impossible to compile, but see, eg, the treatment of the 'socialisation' of private law by Gurvitch (n 15) and by F Wieacker *Das Sozialmodell der klassischen Privatrechtsgesetzbuecher und die Entwicklung der modernen Gesellschaft* (Karlsruhe, CF Mueller, 1953); Wieacker (n 14) 431 et seq (new legitimation of private law lies with the legal consciousness of the social state and private law's harmonisation with social law; functionally, economic and social processes are not guided by direct intervention of the state or by the private autonomy of economic actors, but through the cooperation of social groups or compromise mediated by public powers).

[43] See, eg, Kennedy (n 8) 211 et seq; MW Hesselink, *CFR and Social Justice: A Short Study for the European Parliament on the Values Underlying the Draft Common Frame of Reference for European Private Law: What Roles for Fairness and Social Justice?* (Munich, Sellier, 2008) 13–14; Niglia (n 3) (including historical aspects of materialisation). See also in general D Kennedy, 'Comment on Rudolf Wietholter's "Materialization and Proceduralization in Modern Law" and "Proceduralization of the Category of Law"' in C Joerges and D Trubek (eds), *Critical Legal Thought: An American-German Debate* (Baden-Baden, Nomos Verlagsgesellschaft, 1988).

towards 'constitutionalising the inner order of autonomous social sectors'.[44] However, this was the leitmotif that was implemented via a 'variety of capitalistic' forms of regulation. Sometimes it did so by taking on itself functional activities such as health services or education. Sometimes it left it to the market to operate 'freely', but it acted by civilising market relations – from labour relation (co-determination) to standardised contracting (intervening to limit abuse of private power) to tort liability (placing liability on the cheapest cost avoider). From this vantage point, it has become a key feature of private law to revolve around clashes and struggles among interests and ideas all related to the deep structures of politicisation and pluralisation.[45] Plurality and conflicts are two sides of the same coin. The resolution of conflicts via decisionist structures built via cooperation between the workings of governmental activities orientated to interventionism (legislation – *thesis*) and of the legal elites (jurisprudence – *nomos*)[46] has been the genius of private law as developed within the nation state over the second half of the twentieth century and up until today. Let me now focus on such structures.

B. Into Politicisation I: Of Agency and Techniques (the Legislative Branch)

Looking at politicisation and pluralisation in some more detail, and in particular at the agents driving it and the chosen techniques, one must certainly acknowledge that it has been the legislative process that has acted as a major institutional vehicle towards entrenching the changes under scrutiny. It is to this process that I wish to pay attention now (section B), before considering the no less fundamental role played by the other agents, jurists and judges, to which I dedicate section C.

In my view, the legislative branch has played its role through the following intertwined key structures: i) special legislation; and ii) de-codification. Let me discuss each in turn.

[44] Teubner (n 14) 24 on the distinction between welfare states taking on functional tasks themselves or engaging in political coordination as the dual reaction towards avoiding the failures of liberal constitutionalism and totalitarian regimes. In relation to private law, see Niglia (n 3) (contrasting Italy, characterised by an interventionist approach, with Germany, characterised by a coordinating approach, enabling but limiting market processes, in contract law settings).

[45] On the theoretical notion of struggles in the context of plural(ist) scenarios, *cf* R Michaels, 'Why We Have No Theory of European Private Law Pluralism' in Niglia (n 18) 139, 155 (arguing that, as '"social" ideas struggle with more market liberal ones' in Nordic countries, scholarship loses sight of the underlying struggles when it reasons in term of 'homogeneity'), inter alia drawing on the work of R Goksor, 'Jurisprudence on Protection of Weaker Parties in European Contract Law from a Swedish and Nordic Perspective' (2006) 6 *Chicago-Kent Journal of International & Comparative Law* 184; Niglia (n 3) (arguing how scholarship tends to lose sight of the dimension of struggles and conflicts as they operate both supranationally and infra-nationally in relation to the making and implementation of the Unfair Terms Directive).

[46] See Niglia (n 3) and below, ch 4.

i. Special Legislation

Legislatures enacted special laws (in as diverse areas as tenancy, unfair terms and labour law) aimed at targeting specific sets of social interests so as to give them a special kind of protection vis-à-vis the operations of market processes, according to a model of either functional interventionism or of regulation by coordination.[47] The Gesetz zur Regelung des Rechts der Allgemeinen Geschäftsbedingungen (AGB-Gesetz–AGBG) (which since 2002 has been incorporated into the BGB) is a model example of the latter kind – the interests of weak contractual parties, as a result of the imposition on them of unilaterally drafted standardised contracts, were protected by rules first developed in the courtrooms and then incorporated into the AGBG. The *Loi Scrivener* is a model example of the former.[48] Each piece of special legislation represents an 'autonomous' place for the protection of specific interests – a microcosm of rules and principles understood to be independent of the macrocosm of the code-system (*code corpus*) and indeed in opposition to it, given that each micro-system presents an autonomous logic entirely contingent on the fragmented (aiming at the protection of specific interests) kind of interventionism engineered via welfare politics. In the understanding of authoritative scholarship, each piece of legislation forms a world of its own in a landscape in which the code is held to be no longer capable of offering a meta-rationality (understood as systematic in the 'classical' sense) for administering the interpretation of the rules contained in special legislation.[49] The interpretation of each micro-system must be about strictly implementing the command of the legislature as one can evince it from considering each micro-system on its own.[50] One major claim at the basis of the making of special legislation of this kind has been that 'the rapid changes in the political, social and technological conditions of our time have led to detailed special legislation designed to further specific social objectives which are alien to the basic philosophy of the codes'.[51] To put it in socio-legal terms, the narrative is one of 'functional differentiation'.

The 'prediction' in the late 1980s was that 'this legislation will gradually supersede the codes and transform them into bodies of mere residual law to be resorted to only if no more specific provision can be found'.[52] This is a rendition of the

[47] See above at fn 44.
[48] Niglia (n 3).
[49] Irti, *L'etá della decodificazione* (n 11) 44 et seq and 71 et seq.
[50] ibid 97 et seq (defending the view that the interpreter should apply exegesis when decoding the pieces of special legislation).
[51] H Kötz, 'Taking Civil Codes Less Seriously' (1987) 50 *Modern Law Review* 1, 13.
[52] ibid 12–13 and referring to Irti, *L'etá della decodificazione* (n 11) and Irti, *Diritto e societá* (n 11) 613 et seq, but note that the opinion that special legislation had already superseded codes had been stated a decade earlier by Natalino Irti (let alone that it was a feature of earlier times, that is, the late nineteenth century and of the first half of the twentieth century: see, for example, Louis Josserand in the late 1930s in his 'La reconstruction d'un droit de classe' *Dalloz*, 1937, chron., 1 et seq; Pio Caroni 'Codificare su due versanti: quello civile e quello penale. Riflessioni sul mito del codice-guida' in E Tavilla (ed), *Giuseppe Luosi, giurista italiano ed europeo. Traduzioni, tradizioni e tradimenti della codificazione. A 200 anni dalla traduzione in italiano del Code Napoléon (1806–2006)*(Atti del Convegno

process that came from an authoritative voice of the German private law world and that emphasised the value of arguments that about a decade earlier had been coined by Irti, who placed them under the catchword 'de-codificazione'.

ii. The Eclipse of Codes – An Age of De-codification

By 'de-codification', I refer to a phenomenon that has been taking place in continental jurisdictions since at least the second half of the past century.[53] It revolves around the continual enactment of special laws in matters of private law, in areas such as tenancy, unfair terms and labour relations, and it emerges as an analytical category for capturing the impact of this mass of special legislative acts on the deep structures of code-based private law. It has been a way to reconstruct the enactment of special laws, an interpretative perspective adopted in scholarly writings that has in turn created a new consciousness, both scholarly and judicial,

Internazionale di Studi, Mirandola-Modena, 19–20 October 2006 (2009)), 337 at 348–49 (noting the need to acknowledge the role of social legislation alongside the codes).

[53] Irti, *L'etá della decodificazione* (n 11) 29 et seq associates the start of the de-codification phenomenon with 1 January 1948, when the Italian Constitution entered in force. On the French debate on themes surrounding the de-codification phenomenon, see contributions to *Le Code Civil 1804–2004 Livre du Bicentenaire* (Paris, Dalloz, 2004). This is a lively debate out of which the following notions emerge: *decodification, un pullulement de petis codes, spéciaux, parcellaires; éclatement; fragmentation; dispersion; mutation; prolifération des sources internationals.* On Germany, see, eg, the synthesis in Kötz (n 51); and R Zimmermann, 'Codification: The Civilian Experience Reconsidered on the Eve of a Common European Sales Law' (2012) 8(4) *European Review of Contract Law* 367. For an example of the complexity of the phenomenon, see F Larnaude, 'Le Code Civil et la nécessité de sa Revision' in *Le Code civil 1804–1904 Livre du Centenaire* (Paris, Dalloz, 2004) 901: 'La France, qui avait voulu une législation claire, complète, suffisamment précise, harmonieusement agencée, n'a plus qu'un droit civil fragmentaire, fait de pieces et de morceaux, compliqué, et déparé par de trop nombreuses lacunes' (at 909), and recounting writings demanding revision of the code by one jurisconsulte économiste (Rossi) in 1837, 'un autre jurisconsulte économiste' (Batbie) in 1866 and by the jurist Acollas, and referring to 'lois nouvelles . . . restées en dehors . . . viennent embarasser . . . le magistrate, l'avocat, le practicies' introducing 'des contradictions' and noting that 'la jurisprudence . . . a fait . . . de textes du Code civil un véritable trompe-l-oeil', for 'Le practiciens, le tribunaux modifient incessantement le Code' and: 'Le Code civil a des parties mortes, il a des obscurities, génératrices de controverses sans fin, et malgré la jurisprudence, malgré le lois nouvelles, il n'est plus en harmonie avec les conditions actuelles de la société . . . des régles que tout le monde met de côté, mais que religieusement les commentateurs expliquent et développent avec abundance . . . byzantinisme' (at 909–12); 'l'idée de la revision est ancienne' (at 907) and arguing for the need for a revision 'pourrait faire rentrer dans le Code civil des réglementations qui le mettraient plus en harmonie aver les besoins, les sentiments, la justice du présent' and then citing Saleilles's work *Introduction à l'étude du droit civil allemande*: 'L'économie sociale du monde s'est modifiée, il faut que le droit centenaire du Code civil . . . se modifie aussi, qu'il la suive dans ses transformations', then arguing that: 'En particulier dans la famille et dans le droit ouvrier, le Code civil est incontestablement arriéré à la fois et profondément insuffisant. Ni la puissance paternelle, ni l'autorité maritale ne sont aujourd'hui en fait ce qu'elles pareisset être à lire les articles du Code. Et quant au droit ouvrier, à cette législation de classe que s'est imposée malgré toutes les résistances, et qui n'a pas dit son dernier mot, le Code civil aurait besoin d'être remanié à peu près complètement. La seule partie que s'en occupe, le contrat de louage, renferme en effet des règles qui apparaîtront comme bien insuffisantes quand on réfléchira qu'elles se sont formées à une époque où n'existaient ni le machinisme, ni la grande industrie, ni cet amour des humbles, qui est bien pour quelque chose aussi dans le progrès de la législation sociale, sans qu'il faille oublier le sentiment de la dignité et de la force des classes ouvrières, qui est sûrement l'agent le plus actif de leur émancipation et de l'amélioration nécessaire de leur sort' (at 914).

about the law as a technique for furthering pluralisation and politicisation – yielding a jurisprudence that co-constitutes legislative activities. Let me explain.

There has been increasing awareness that each piece of special private law legislation constitutes an autonomous legal realm that: introduces sets of rules applicable to specific fact situations and involving special legal consequences, breaking away from the 'formal unity' of law typical of the nineteenth-century codes; delivers the objective of protecting the interests of certain social groups by implementing the commands of the constitution, thus breaking away from the 'substantive unity' of the nineteenth-century codes by deconstructing the subject (the 'individual') as the only addressee of rules, and by designing rules and protectionist standards also for groups rather than just individuals; entails a disintegrative impact on the 'systematic coherence' and 'comprehensiveness' (or 'completeness') of private law as a whole, as purportedly provided for in the code, given that the work of the scholar becomes one of applying individual substantive regimes as incorporated into each piece of special legislation rather than 'the law' as 'descending' from an interpretation of the whole of the code understood as a 'system'.[54] From a comparative constitutional perspective, the de-codification consciousness has been a chapter in the story of welfare states managing to adopt the coordinative or interventionist stance, or variations thereof, depending on which specific country one considers.[55] It has been argued that, as a result of the enactment of special laws under the shadow of the code, private law has been 'de-codified' as a result of the subtraction of key regulatory areas from it, which involved a profound change in the formal organisation of sources of private law (from unity to fragmentation), the substantive orientation of it (from liberalist individualism to welfare provision) and the methodological practices surrounding the interpretative task (the losing of systematic coherence of private law as contained in the code-book according to then mainstream scholarship, given that all of the code-based legal constructs would no longer be capable of making sense of, or of directing, interpretation).[56]

De-codification is, however, a complex process that may happen through not just the enactment of pieces of special legislation isolated from the code but also through the rewriting of the code itself from within – and, rather than renumbering, legislatures may insert new articles in the structure of the code, but leave formally intact the pre-existing numerical sequence of articles by using Latin prefixes such as *-bis*, *-ter* etc, which has been the case, for example, in Articles 1469-*bis* et seq *Italian codice civile* based on the Unfair Terms Directive (now Article 33 et seq *Italian Codice del consumo*). Some may label this operation 're-codification', but

[54] Irti, *L'etá della decodificazione* (n 11) 97 et seq ('Esegesi e costruzione dei micro-sistemi si intrecciano e si implicano vicendevolmente'). See FC von Savigny, *Vom Beruf unserer Zeit für Gesetzgebung und Rechtswissenschaft* (Heidelberg, 1814) 21: 'Men longed for new codes, which, by their completeness, should ensure a mechanically precise administration of justice; insomuch that the judge, freed from the exercise of private opinion should be confined to the mere literal application'.

[55] Niglia (n 3) (for substantive aspects); Irti, *L'etá della decodificazione* (n 11) (concerned more with the structures of private law interventionism and less with substantive details).

[56] Irti, *L'etá della decodificazione* (n 11) (concurring with Kötz (n 51) 12–13).

only formally, for the placing of a special body of rules in the code is disruptive of the alleged coherence of it.[57] At a deeper level of analysis, and strictly speaking, adoption of the re-codification technique is about defending the coherence of the code vis-a-vis the practice of de-codification understood as a legislative-based process that creates a variety of specialised regimes in lieu of the 'unity' of the code-regime.[58] In a similar fashion to the typical ways in which systematisation was historically deployed in the context of the *code corpus* paradigm itself before the age of de-codification, re-codification patterns have been used as means to resist the de-codification phenomenon perceived, by those who support re-codification, as consigning the law to chaos, that is, as an attempt to reframe it around what they perceive to be the minimum conditions of legal certainty. In this understanding, the rights of tenants may well have been contained in the relevant Italian special legislation on *disciplina delle locazioni di immobili urbani* (Law of 27 July 1978, n 392), but they still need to be conceptualised having in mind the 'overarching' 'categorical logic' of the code. However, system thinking has not always been really articulated in the sense of re-enacting the reasoning of heavenly concepts ('strong re-codification' or 'strong systematisation'). Instead, a weaker form of system thinking may be in operation[59] that aims at balancing the need to protect special interests (eg, those of tenants) with the need to ensure that protection takes place in the light of the requirements of the public interest, with the code being used instrumentally as a channel for doing so – as a matter of fact, the national constitution is equally referred to as a further basis for reconstructing private law in this way.[60] Re-codification understood this way (or 'weak re-codification') is just another way in which to articulate the de-codification interpretative strategy. This is a perspective exemplified by statements such as the

[57] For discussion, see, eg, S Patti, *Diritto Privato e Codificazioni Europee* (Milan, Giuffrè, 2007) 171 et seq.

[58] For arguments in this sense see, eg, Kötz (n 51) 13 (in relation to debates during the proposal of the legislative bill for the German Standard Terms Act, recalling scholarly arguments making 'the case for incorporating the new rules into the Civil Code', rather than enacting a special legislative act, 'on the ground that this would keep the Code in tune with present notions of contractual fairness and thus help to prevent its contract rules from gradually decaying into obsolescence').

[59] If the task of the judge (and of scholarship) is 'il compito di integrare nel sistema del diritto privato, rivedendone le strutture dogmatiche, i nuovi punti di vista e i nuovi valori costituzionali, mediando il principio individualistico, che sta all'origine del sistema, con i principi dello Stato solidaristico contemporaneo' (at 23–24), then re-codification, whether by legislative insertion of new articles in the code or by rewriting of old articles or by interpretation, is about reconstituting the private law system weakly, that is, around a variety of principles overcoming the old prejudice according to which 'the explanation based on one principle only is the best' ('é tempo, anche nella scienza giuridica, che lo spirito sistematico abbandoni "l'antico pregiudizio che la spiegazione in base a un unico principio sia la migliore"': L Mengoni, *Diritto e Valori* (Bologna, Il Mulino, 1985) 145, quoting Hartmann's *Il problema dell'essere spirituale* (Florence, La Nuova Italia, 1971) 23. Note that in France, some argue that re-codification should be about ensuring an 'effet d'ordre et de systématisation' rather than 're-codification tranquille' understood as a form of de-codification, that is, as aiming just at a 'collection de lois ordinaires' (see L Vogel, 'Re-codification civile et renouvellement des sources internes' in *Livre Bicentenaire* 159, 164).

[60] See Irti, *L'etá della decodificazione* (n 11) 53 et seq (placing the Italian Constitution, rather than the code, at the centre of the universe of private law; ranking the code alongside special legislative acts in relation to the interpretative operations of private law actors).

following,[61] which are heavily influenced by the work of Irti, but emphasise aspects of 'manageability, order and accessibility' as being coterminus with the maintaining of the code as a reliable technique of organisation of private law material:

> [T]here are good reasons for keeping the code up-to-date by means of amendment or revision if one possibly can rather than enacting special legislation. These are not of course the reasons that used to be given in the early days of codification, when a code was said to be a symbol of national identity or of social or political reform, or to help the legal education of the citizenry. The case for reforming the law by revising the code is based strictly on operational and technical grounds. The argument is that special legislation tends to be prolix and verbose and to introduce byzantine distinctions and technical details which later turn out to be not only unnecessary but actually harmful in opening up new areas of dispute. A code, on the other hand, stands for the ideas of internal economy and discipline, so *codification tends to keep the law manageable, orderly, accessible and teachable without depriving it of the needed flexibility.* At the same time it acts as a check on the legislature's propensity to rush off into special enactments whenever desired, instead of first asking whether the new proposals might not be fitted into the existing structure or expressed in existing terms. For these reasons, the routine work of legal practice and adjudication may arguably be easier in a system with a code than in a system rife with ill-coordinated special statutes.

Here the code is clearly interpreted in the sense of no longer being self-standing or comprehensive and not even understood to be standing on a closed set of overarching principles, for it is just one instrument that is useful to the work of balancing interests and values at stake in disputes.[62] Within the interpretative horizon of the 'weak re-codification' position, whilst some argue that a conceptual system might still be considered worthwhile in the context of contemporary private law, and others insist that private law has instead largely overcome system thinking, no one denies the diminishing power of the code as the conceptual grid with pretence of supremacy over the private law realm including special legislation – in striking contrast to the 'strong re-codification' strands of thought, in particular those rehabilitated in the context of the current codification process, as I will discuss in chapter four.[63] Mengoni's words are worth recalling in that they portray the new 'equilibrium' found in the private law discourse within the horizon of 'weak re-codification':

> L'idea di codice può ridursi, e ormai si è ridotta, a un concetto puramente tecnico, ordinato alla funzione di apprestare un nucleo sistematico di principi e di categorie ordinatorie adeguato alla selezione strutturale dei conflitti di interesse e all'organizzazione delle relative decisioni nell'unità del sistema giuridico, garantendo il primato dell'argomentazione giuridica sulla contingenza delle valutazioni politiche.[64]

[61] Kötz (n 51) 14 (emphasis added).

[62] But on the proposal of a code of principles (code open) as not really suitable for doing the balancing job, see below, ch 4.

[63] In ch 4 I discuss this position in terms of 'strong systematisation'.

[64] L Mengoni, *L'Europa dei Codici o un Codice per l'Europa?* (Rome, Centro di Studi e Ricerche di Diritto Comparato e Straniero, 1993).

In brief, the interpretative patterns at work in de-codification contexts have become other than the old ways of *code corpus* thinking, for they are about re-arranging the law as a technique for governing a private law fragmented along the lines of the many, conflicting values making up welfarist constitutional politics[65] and by preserving law's autonomy in doing that job.[66]

iii. Contexts of Constitutional Politicisation

The techniques just discussed, involving a wide deployment of special pieces of legislation and related de-codified interpretative patterns, have been part and parcel of a broader context. 'Clashing normativities'[67] have been at stake that derived from pluralisation processes and the dynamics of conflicts among the many societal expectations implicated in those processes, expectations rooted in a variety of private institutional settings,[68] from associations to companies to contractual arrangements. Legislatures, in being committed to and in incorporating in legislation the relevant social interests also had in mind a certain worldview, that is, welfare strategies with distinctive features in each country ('varieties' of active politicisation).[69] The basic strategy, common to welfare states, was the commitment to incorporate the plurality of often conflicting values (market-orientated efficiency and solidarity-based interventions)[70] by way of balancing and compromising, in contexts in which: 'The welfare states of the late 20th century . . . achieved a peculiar balance between a state constitutionalism, which progressively extended its principles to social spheres, and a constitutional pluralism, in which the state in fact respected a certain autonomy of social sub-constitutions.'[71]

My own reconstruction of these developments is that, to take the case of the core private law area, that is, contract law applicable to standardised terms as regulated in the second half of the past century and up to today,[72] systems of private law interventionism have been calibrated to fit the type of welfarism as preferred by the respective governments.[73] Here we must recall that 'interventionism' and 'coordination' have been the representative patterns of 'active politicisation' of the welfare states in private law matters.[74] This is a story that has a common thread across countries (the commitment of balancing, and compromising among, the

[65] See Mengoni (n 59), as quoted above at n 59 and below at n 88.

[66] On law's autonomy and politicisation, see, eg, Mengoni (n 59), as quoted above at n 59 and below at n 88; Niglia (n 3) and *ibid*, 'Introduction to Part III' in *Foundations*; *Vesting* (n 31).

[67] See Niglia (n 18) (discussing the importance in contemporary pluralist literature of the theme of 'conflicting authorities' in pluralist perspective, in normative terms).

[68] *cf* Teubner (n 14).

[69] Niglia (n 3).

[70] *cf*, eg, Wilhelmsson (n 8) 715 ('the welfare state is characterised by a continuous balancing between market-oriented efficiency and solidarity-based interventions of the state').

[71] Teubner (n 14) 6.

[72] See Niglia (n 3).

[73] ibid.

[74] See above at section B.ii, also referring to parallel developments in constitutional law.

relevant values within the welfarist horizon),[75] but that otherwise varies in relation to each domestic legal regime that one looks at, depending on which organisation of values happened to have emerged out of the aggregated choices of decision makers. Thus, and looking at four jurisdictions (the English, the French, the German and the Italian), one must note a variety of capitalist styles which correspond to the contingent forms of legal structures implementing them. In some countries, the role of the legislature consisted of enacting pieces of special legislation (eg, special laws on unfair terms in standard form contracts) aimed at protecting weak contractors. In other countries, instead, the provision of protectionist private law rules on unfair terms were avoided altogether by both the legislature and the class of jurists and judges, which was in turn traceable to a context in which heavy state interventionism in the economy meant that calculations of welfare and redistribution interests were somehow incorporated into decisions regarding the overall organisation of an economy, for example, the governmental organisation (including arrangement of contracts) of the operations of state-owned companies in the utility, banking or insurance sectors. Here economic interventionism of the state meant that weak contractual parties were taken care of in the context of the overall policies of economic interventionism. By contrast, legal protectionism of weak parties was the central concern of those legislatures that chose to restrain state activities in the economy, but that felt the need to ensure a degree of justice in contexts in which a free market could flourish. One can label these opposing types of private law organisational schemes 'welfarist interventionism' and 'welfarist coordination'. In this way private law has been made instrumental to the complex and conflicting requirements of state interventionism (active politicisation). This is because state interventionism means that private law becomes a piece of social regulation, which in turn means that the concern of the legislature is to ensure that private law rules accommodate the workings of the market (whether practised as welfarist interventionism or as welfarist cooperation), whilst placing limits on it towards protecting individuals and groups considered to be 'weak'.[76] Legislative activities have been part and parcel of the broader engagement of social actors in the pursuit of a plurality of social objectives, for, in welfarist contexts, social objectives do not exist in a vacuum, but are the reference point of activities and goals of social groups that articulate them and struggle for their success. I will clarify this note in the following pages, which focus on the role of jurists and judges.

[75] For a synthetic analysis, see Kennedy (n 8) 213 (discussing a connection between the socialisation of private law and balancing with the example of the so-called constitutionalisation of private law in Germany). See Wilhelmsson (n 8) 715.

[76] For the relevant range of complex and often conflicting requirements underlying state interventionism in private law, see Wilhelmsson (n 8).

C. Into Politicisation II: Of Agency and Techniques (Jurisprudential Vocabularies)

All of the above indicates how the national legislature has played a key transformative role in the re-organisation of private law. However – and this is the point to which the remainder of this chapter is dedicated – legislative activities happen in jurisprudential contexts (both judicial and scholarly). The legislative governance of conflicts and related centralised resolutions around state structures has been grounded on a jurisprudential terrain. We should recall that the history of private law of the last century or so, and indeed of the modern age,[77] has been not just one of legislative choices and instruments, but of a continuing process of 'renewal' of European legal science.[78] Indeed, it has been and continues to be pre-eminently a story that revolves around the jurisprudential forces, a key point that must be emphasised towards understanding the politicisation processes as previously discussed. This is a story that complements the one told in the previous pages, that is, jurisprudential forces that have managed to synthesise the conflicts emerging out of the phenomenon of pluralisation alongside, and in assistance of, the legislature in doing a similar job. From this vantage point, politicisation, understood as an active exercise in the governing of and settlement of the relevant conflicts (the challenge of settlement),[79] took place via the jurisprudential forces. 'Totality' explains this story, that is, the consideration of the work of the legislature and of jurisprudence in tandem. The work of constitutional synthesis put in place by the

[77] For a retrospective account see, eg, Tarello (n 17).

[78] In approaching the codification phenomenon from the vantage point of the role of jurisprudence, this book must agree with the tenet that the distinction between codification and consolidation has been largely overdone. I am thinking of historically orientated writings whereby codification indicates not just the legislature's choice to place all private law in a code-book, but a historical process of 'renewal' of legal science (*cf* P Caroni, 'Kodifikation' in A Erler and E Kaufmann (eds), *Handwoerterbuch zur Deutchen Rechtsgeschichte* (Berlin, Erich Schmidt Verlag, 1978) 907 at 908 ('die Erneurung der Europaeischen Rechtswissenschaft in der Neuzeit'), consisting of the overcoming of the universalism of Roman law through the establishment of national laws and national science of law (908–09) – with the code-book becoming the 'most important' of all sources. In this view, the distinction between consolidation and codification has little reason to exist, for any legislation at any point in time is about conferring new functions to old material (910); one must contrast to this the more conventional view that understands codification as designating the modern character of codes, as opposed to consolidating laws as was the case for past 'codes' (see, eg, RC van Caenegem, *A Historical Introduction to Private Law* (Cambridge, Cambridge University Press, 1992) 12 (contrasting 'compilations' to code qua 'exhaustive regulation of a particular area . . . involves a coherent programme and a consistent logical structure'; T Ascarelli, *L'idea di codice nel diritto privato e la funzione dell'interpretazione* (1945) in T Ascarelli *Saggi Giuridici* (Milan, Giuffrè, 1949), at pp 48–49, as cited in M Bellomo, *L'Europa del Diritto Comune* (8th edn, Rome, Il Cigno Galileo Galilei Edizioni di Arte e Scienza, 1998) 12–13; commenting on the distinction as having been introduced by Mario Viora 'Consolidazioni e codificazioni' in the 1930s (Bologna) is M Bellomo, *L'Europa del diritto comune*, (8th edn, Rome, Il Cigno Galileo Galilei Edizioni di Arte e Scienza, 1998) at pp 11–13; for discussion in France, see J-P Dunand, 'Entre tradition et innovation. Analyse historique du concept de code' in J-P Dunand and B. Winiger (eds), *Le Code Civil Francais dans le droit europeen* (Brussels, Bruylant, 2005) 3 (code-compilation versus code-innovation). The contemporary private law *history* that I am recounting, however, involves 'breaks' such as those that I consider in this chapter, so it would be wrong to make of the 'argument-from-renewal' an absolute, as happens in some legal historical writings.

[79] On the category of 'settlement' in pluralist literature, see Niglia (n 18).

jurisprudential forces has been one of an eminently political tenor. The example of the AGBG, to which I return in the remainder of this chapter, is exemplary – here scholars and judges co-created a protectionist regime for addressees of standard form contracts with the legislature stepping in at a later stage and consolidating much of that jurisprudence in the form of special legislation.[80] *En bref*, de-codification has been a jurisprudential phenomenon and it would be appropriate to coin a new term for what really happened – that of *jurisprudential de-codification*.[81]

The state of politicisation in which private law as a whole finds itself, ever since the changes discussed in the previous section, has been the product of a shift from 'professional' to 'constitutional' private law. If one considers the 'quality' of the work of scholars and judges, 'professional' indicates the legal profession's work of elaboration of formal law (classical law) towards creating or reinforcing the centralisation of power around the state – the paradigmatic models in the nineteenth century being the exegetic school of thought in France and the Pandectistic school of thought as developed in Germany first and then abroad, both embodying what Tarello called the *tecnicizzazione* of juristic work.[82] 'Constitutional' private law in the de-codified age indicates instead the work of scholars and judges towards synthesising the conflicts emerging out of fragmentation, in the sense that a revolutionary methodological shift towards de-formalisation, consequentialism, proceduralisation and contextualisation has transformed the work of scholars and judges towards making it functional to achieving the overarching objectives of private law's materialisation. Whereas *tecnicizzazione* indicates a climate in which social conflicts have tended to be marginalised and ignored (in the nineteenth century), *materialisation* indicates the turn towards active engagement and management of them. A de-professionalisation or, better, re-professionalisation process,[83] as a result of the politicisation of the private law discourse, has taken place that has consisted of re-inventing classical categories (from the nineteenth century and earlier centuries) so as to make them adapt to the requirements of the welfare state. Private lawyers have engaged with reconstructing law according to those requirements. Passive and active forms of politicisation (legislative)[84] have been co-constructed via the law's discursive structures, with questions of private law caught in the categories of classical legal thought being 'translated' into questions of material justice. The critique of system thinking and of code-based formalism has been an inevitable part and parcel of this process. One can call this process 'constitutionalisation' (in the contemporary sense of the word, as opposed to the eighteenth- and nineteenth-century sense),[85] given that scholars and judges

[80] Niglia (n 3).
[81] Contrast the phenomenon of *jurisprudential codification* that I discuss below, ch 4.
[82] Tarello (n 17).
[83] For a historic perspective behind this vocabulary, *cf* Tarello (n 17).
[84] See above, Section II.
[85] On constitutionalisation entailed in 'bourgeois-enlightenment codification' see Tarello (n 17) 25 (at n 7) referring to the works of Gioele Solari (cf Gioele Solari *Individualismo e Diritto Privato* (Turin, 1959) and G Solari, *Filosofia del Diritto Privato. Volume II. Storicismo e Diritto Privato* (1st edn, Turin,

have re-deployed all of law's resources (those of private law and of constitutionalism) towards that work of 'translation'. Out of this translation a core set of material rights have been established, that is, the heritage of socialised contractual, tortious and property rules and institutions that constitutes the kernel of contemporary private law. For example, a powerful way in which material rights have been framed has been the act of reconfiguring codes' norms in relation to the values enshrined in the polity's constitutional charter, sometimes absorbing private law material found in the codes into the constitutional dimension ('direct effect'), as in a German line of interpretation alternative to dominant understandings (*unmittelbare versus mittelbare Drittwirkung*),[86] while at other times, maintaining distinct layers of legal orders (private law, constitutional law), although holding the argument that the constitution should be the 'unifying force' that keeps the whole of the law's edifice in one piece via demanding the compliance of special legislation with the substantive commands coming from the constitution, an interpretation put forward in Italy.[87] Here the task of ensuring legal certainty via conformity with the constitution has been delegated to the judge (chiefly, but not exclusively, the constitutional courts),[88] de-codification being at root a

Giappichelli, 1971, 1940)): 'la codificazione corrisponde nel campo del diritto privato a quello che furono le dichiarazioni dei diritti e le costituzioni nel campo del diritto pubblico . . . Come queste erano dirette a garantire le liberta' politiche dei cittadini nel loro rapporto con lo Stato, cosi' le codificazioni mirano ad assicurare la libertá civile dell'individuo nella sua vita privata contro le indebite ingerenze del potere politico'.

[86] For scholarship in support of the 'indirect effect' view, see, for example, the classical writings of Günter Dürig (eg, 'Der Grundgrechtssarz von der Menschenwuerde – Entwurf eines praktikablen Wertsystems der Grundrechte aus Art. 1 Abs. 1 in Verbindung mit Art. 19 Abs. II des Grundgesetzes' (1956) *AöR* 117). For a synthesis of the debate, see Matthias Ruffert, *Vorrang der Verfassung und Eigenständigkeit des Privatrechts* (Tübingen, Mohr Siebeck, 2001) 7 et seq. The landmark contribution of Günter Dürig has shaped the mainstream understanding of the relevant case law up to the present day in Germany. A classical work favouring instead a reading based on 'direct effect' is Hans C Nipperdey *Grundrechte und Privatrecht. Eine Universitätrede*, in Hans C Nipperdey (ed) *Festschrift für Eric Molitor* (*München, Beck,* 1962), 17. A vigorous debate between the 'direct horizontal effect' (*unmittelbare Drittwirkung*) and 'indirect effect' (*mittelbare Drittwirkung*) schools of thought has developed in Germany, for a recent synthesis of which, see, eg, Ruffert *Vorrang der Verfassung* 12 et seq and, in English, G Brüggemeier, 'Constitutionalisation of Private Law – The German Perspective' in T Barkhuysen and S Lindenbergh (eds), *Constitutionalisation of Private Law* (Leiden, Martinus Nijhoff, 2006) 59 (stressing the role of the writings of Günter Dürig); and M Kumm, 'Who is Afraid of the Total Constitution? Constitutional Rights as Principles and the Constitutionalization of Private Law' (2006) 7 *German Law Journal* 341.

[87] Irti, *L'etá della decodificazione* (n 11) 6 ('Il carattere rigido delle norme costituzionali ha introdotto nel sistema un elemento di certezza e di stabilità. Queste garanzie, già prestate dal codice civile, si sono trasferite dal piano delle norme ordinarie al piano delle norme costitutionali').

[88] Contrast ibid 44 ('Le leggi disperse e frammentarie non possono essere ricondotte ad unità dalla mediazione del giudice ma dai rapporti di forza tra lo Stato ed i gruppi e dalla capacità, dell'uno e degli altri, di impedire l'espansione di particolarismo e di arbitrarie prerogative. Il giudice, al quale fosse affidata quella funzione unificatrice, si troverebbe dinanzi a logiche diverse e contrastanti: né sarebbe in grado di affermare il primato delle clausole generali nei confronti della legge, che esprimono, anch'esse, princìpi generali, dotati di efficacia regolativa per intere materie o classi di rapporti'. 'Al di fuori del controllo di legittimità costituzionale, non c'è altro modo di ristabilite l'unità di trattamento giuridico, e cosí di tutelare la concreta eguaglianza dei cittadini, che un rigoroso sistema di rapporti di potere dello Stato e potere dei gruppi'). Caught in this legislation-centred understanding of things, Irti must remain hostage to reconstructing the work of scholarship as 'exegetic', paradoxically re-deploying a term that signified the work of the jurist when codification reached its highest point. However, in my

jurisprudential story of *constitutional* engagement. From this vantage point, 'de-codification' and the 'constitutionalisation of private law' must be seen as coterminus phenomena, and not as legislative (the former) and jurisprudential (the latter), with 'de-codification' being connotative of both.

One visible illustration of these developments has been the 'fragmentation' of private legal thought, that is, the formation of diverse schools of thought in relation to the ways in which the insiders have taken a position as to how to implement the welfarist strategy in its many versions (interventionism or coordination or variations thereof).[89] This is a story of parallel developments – as the 'social world' of private law gets fragmented along the lines of conflicting interests and goals (pluralisation), and as concerns for delivering material objectives of justice gain ground (politicisation), the doctrinal discourse also gets fragmented along divisive interpretative lines concerning the substance of materialisation. The pluralisation of currents of thought has been the intellectual support of the materialisation developments, both detecting and constituting them, with scholars proposing often competing views as to how to understand the societal demands for justice in the private law realm. At times, scholarship has presented us with deep divisions. This has been the case for the strands of German critical legal thought that have proposed a mode of protecting consumers caught in standardised contracts that would take into account the circumstances of the disputes, towards ensuring a greater degree of protection for weak contractual parties than just applying the protectionist standards – doctrinal proposals only episodically and controversially incorporated into the living law.[90] It has also been the case

view, the jurists are creative interpreters of the law of the 'microcosm' (each piece of special law), reinventing principles that suit the world of microcosms – the jurist is not just exegete. The issue of the role that the judge should play in decodied contexts has been contentious; see, eg, ibid (taking a position whereby it is the legislature to be entrusted with the task of mediating conflicts and criticising those who defend the view that the judge should play that role). See also L Mengoni, 'Problema e sistema nella controversia sul metodo giuridico' (1976) *Jus*, 3 and Mengoni (n 59) 11, who explicitly acknowledges the role of the judge (and of the jurist, at 24) in the task of mediating the relevant conflicts: 'le tensioni sociali generate dal dinamismo della struttura pluralistica, nella misura in cui non sono assorbite mediante strumenti politici produttivi di nuovo diritto – legislazione o contrattazione collettiva – si trasformano in domande di giustizia indirizzate agli organi di applicazione del diritto esistente. Il giudice viene chiamato a compiti quali ad esempio . . . di supplenza del potere legislativo o di concretizzazione di direttive generiche del legislatore in ordine al regolamento del conflitto collettivo e dei modi di esercizio dei poteri e dei contropoteri in esso coinvolti. Si pensi ai problemi che la giurisprudenza deve risolvere circa i limiti di esercizio del diritto di sciopero e i limiti correlativi di legittimità della serrata difensiva; compiti di differenziazione o di rielaborazione di istituti giuridici, quali il contratto e la responsabilità civile, in funzione delle esigenze di tutela della collettività connesse alla produzione di massa e al sistema di distribuzione dei prodotti . . . compiti di tutela della funzione di certi istituti contro possibili distorsioni da parte di imprese dominanti, che di fatto usano come strumenti di normazione nei confronti della collettività dei consumatori. Si pensi al problema delle condizioni generali di contratto . . . più in generale. il compito di integrare nel sistema del diritto privato, rivedendone le strutture dogmatiche, i nuovi punti di vista e i nuovi valori costituzionali, mediando il principio individualistico, che sta all'origine del sistema, con i principi dello Stato solidaristico contemporaneo' (at 23–24).

[89] See Niglia (n 3).

[90] On this position in Germany and on the category of 'rules-as-applied', see ibid.

for[91] Italian legal thought critical of the dominant non-protectionist mode of regulating standard form contracts (use of burdensome general conditions of contract terms made only conditional on the minimal requirement that the 'adherent' to the contract specifically subscribes to it as per Article 1341 Italian Civil Code) and struggling for changing the law to make it revolve around a protectionist kind of legislation and case law. Any resolution of the interpretative conflicts has taken place via operations of *synthesisation* as implemented by the jurisprudential actors – alongside scholars, judges equally engage in the work of mediating social conflicts,[92] in interaction with the legislature's synthesisation patterns. A paradigmatic example is the AGBG and its incorporation of previous judicial decisions, as inherited by the BGB (the AGBG having then been incorporated into the BGB) – which visibly demonstrates that a combination of synthesisation processes operating 'in parallel', legislative and scholarly/judicial, have characterised the decodified ways of welfarist-orientated private law, rather than just the workings of legislation. The application of the clusters of protectionist rules for consumers in France, such as the law of unfair terms (*Loi Scrivener*), is another good illustration of scholarship and adjudication managing to settle conflicts in tandem with the overarching welfarist plans set out in the context of governmental activities. Illustrations of the paramount role of judges and scholars in the materialisation of private law also include: the reconstruction of general private law so as to make it instrumental to protectionist objectives (for example, the doctrinal construction of the *contract for the protection of third parties* in Germany); the work of constitutional courts in relation to the balancing of rights, including private law rights. Here materialisation on the basis of the *Wertordnung* of the Constitutional Charter has meant that conflicting values have been balanced according to internal parameters of rationality built up by the courts. Whenever a constitutional court intervenes in the private law field through the balancing of fundamental rights and the demand on ordinary courts to read private law in the light of that balancing, it is effectively rewriting the private law script by using fundamental rights as a key vehicle for the regulation of contract, tort and property law. Remarkably, it does this with the imperium of, and indeed above the imperium of, a legislature.[93] For the many constitutional cases developed along these lines have constituted another path for the materialisation of law,[94] no less important that that undertaken by the legislature via issuing special laws, considering the higher ranking of constitutional material over legislative decisions. The resolution of the relevant conflicts here has taken place via a synthesisation that operates in the terrain of constitutional values (constitutional synthesisation). This has certainly been a process driven by the (constitutional) courts, but scholarship coparticipated through contentious debates over the extent to which the

[91] See Niglia (n 3).

[92] Mengoni, as discussed above at n 59 and at n 88.

[93] See C Moellers, *The Three Branches* (Oxford, Oxford University Press, 2013) 141 (constitutional courts may be understood as hybrid entities that are neither appropriately described as courts nor as purely political actors).

[94] See, eg, *BVerfGE* vol 7, 198, 201 (*Lüth*).

constitutionalisation of private law could be held to be acceptable or otherwise.[95] Nothing more than the 'constitutionalisation of private law' speaks for the 'jurisprudential de-codification' thesis that I am putting forward whereby judges (and scholars) co-participate in the phenomenon of the 'de-codification' of private law.[96]

III. PLURALISM BEYOND THE STATE: THE DEVELOPMENT OF A EUROPEAN PRIVATE LAW JURISPRUDENCE OUT OF DOMESTIC STRUCTURES

The many pluralist processes of adjustment within domestic private law for the accommodation of clashing normativities that emerged out of social conflicts, in the shadow of what has become known as law's materialisation,[97] have given birth to nationally based, entrenched 'identities'.[98] From the mid-1980s, such 'identities' then had to confront the wave of legislative interventions coming from the EU and to reconstitute themselves around the supranational challenge of private law re-regulation and its underlying instrumental *fiat* (market building).[99] Such national identities in turn have been instantiating a new, European-wide 'pluralist interpretative game', with legal traditions domestically re-created[100] by way of both supranational (whenever preliminary references are placed before the CJEU by national courts) and infra-national (effect of changes brought about by the private consumer law Directives on rules and institutions of national private law, such as the application of the Doorstep Directive to guarantees) engagements.[101] I understand this story to be one in which in the first instance judges and scholars have re-articulated domestic private law in relation to the new wave of private law

[95] In a vast literature, see, eg, Barkhuysen and Lindenbergh (n 86); G Brüggemeier, A Colombi Ciacchi and G Comandé (eds), *Fundamental Rights and Private Law in the European Union*, vol I, *A Comparative Overview* (Cambridge, Cambridge University Press, 2010).

[96] See Mengoni (n 88) (in my view exemplifying an interpretative attitude that I am reconstructing as, and labelling, jurisprudential de-codification; contrast Irti, *L'etá della decodificazione* (n 11) 44 (defending the conventional view of an allegedly exclusively legislative-led de-codification process).

[97] For a theoretical grounding of this perspective, *cf* L. Niglia 'Pluralism in a New Key' in Niglia (n 18).

[98] Niglia (n 3) (recounting processes that show how the 'unity of law', according to the classical vocabulary of comparative and historical studies, was a simplifying way to describe concrete constitutional practices; what really happened was, to put it in the vocabulary adopted in the previous pages, pluralisation processes, governance of conflicts and synthesising constitutional operations). See also below, ch 4.

[99] On Europeanisation as private law's instrumental functionalisation to the market-building objective see C Joerges, 'The Europeanization of Private Law as a Rationalization Process and as a Contest of Disciplines: An Analysis of the Directive on Unfair Terms in Consumer Contracts' (1995) 3 *European Review of Private Law* 175; Niglia (n 3); Christoph U Schmid, 'The Instrumentalist Conception of the Acquis Communautaire in Consumer Law and its Implications on a European Contract Law Code' (2005) 1 *European Review of Contract Law* 211; Christoph U Schmid, *Die Instrumentalisierung des Privatrechts durch die Europäische Union. Privatrecht und Privatrechtskonzeptionen in der Entwicklung der Europäischen Integrationsverfassung* (Baden-Baden, Nomos, 2010).

[100] See above, Section I.

[101] See, eg, C-45/96 *Bayerische Hypotheken und Wechselbank v Dietzinger* [1998] ECR I-1199.

politicisation as coming from the EU.[102] EU law could be successfully enforced[103] in circumstances of 'value compatibility' between the national and the supranational levels of regulation. One could generalise by arguing that, in this initial period (roughly until around the turn of the century), a similarity of values has underlined the harmonisation process centred on the Directives.[104] In other words, the new politicisation (the project of market integration) has corresponded to a new wave of jurisprudential constitutionalisation (from entirely domestic to European) characterised by an identical value horizon,[105] and by its mediating between the requirements of the national constitutional heritage as relevant to private law and those of European integration. Once more,[106] law's questions have been reframed as questions of material justice.[107] Institutions of private law as engineered by European legislation (the Directives) around a re-deployment of the individualist register have been measured against sociality as defined by national private law, that is, by the welfarist 'identity' based on the de-codified practices of active politicisation and constitutionalisation described above. Thus, cancelling a concluded contract for the sake of protecting the consumer-contractor and the related sacrifice of the *pacta sunt servanda* dogma have been held to be operations compatible with national private law (its social standards, constitutionally entrenched) via adopting systematic re-interpretations of the private law repertoire (weak systematisation) refocused around the notion of consumer protection. This has resulted in a widening of the reach of domestic notions of social (consumer) protection.[108] This was a period in which, at times, normativities as incorporated into the nation state could be held to be compatible with the requirements of market integration, such as in the example just mentioned, but, at other times, could be held to be clashing directly with the new instrumental requirements coming from the EU, with judges ultimately keeping national law in its place (the preservation of national law).[109] In either case, by mediating between individuals' interests and social objectives this way, judges and scholars

[102] On waves of politicisation and private law, see above at Section II.

[103] On the complexity of 'enforcement' in EU law, see Niglia (n 3); L Niglia, 'The Non-Europeanisation of Private Law' (2001) 4 *European Review of Private Law* 575.

[104] See Mengoni (n 64); Niglia (n 3) (arguing that England and Italy shifted towards implementing the new unfair terms regime contained in the Unfair Terms Directive in contexts in which similar private law values happened to prevail in the two countries).

[105] For the changing patterns of politicisation proper (legislation as changed in relation to the impact of the Directives) and of jurisprudence see Niglia (n 3).

[106] See above, at Section I.

[107] For a *synthèse*, see Wilhelmsson (n 8) (a reading of European private law measures in the light of a 'scheme describing six welfarist directions in modern contract law', that is, the plurality of contingent values and policies that surrounds the European harmonisation project). For a common law voice confirming the weight of pluralism of values in private law, see R Brownsword, 'The Theoretical Foundations of European Private Law: A Time to Stand and Stare' in Brownsword, Micklitz, Niglia and Weatherill (n 8) 171 (emphasising the role of 'how we understand the relationship between and the application of . . . values' and noting how 'In the field of consumer transactions, regulators have given up on full-blown freedom of contract (*qua* private ordering) in favor of a pluralism that prioritizes the interests of consumer security' (coupled with the efficiency of a marketplace with one set of rules).

[108] For details, see Niglia (n 103).

[109] ibid.

have been reframing private law issues related to integration as questions of material justice, in tune with, and in continuation of, their work at the domestic level and independently of Europeanisation.[110] Once more,[111] judges (and scholars whenever writing in support of them) have been working towards incorporating social values (national) in the individualistic private law structures (European).[112] The axiological horizon of the diverse living private law has remained unaltered and, where compliance with the Directive has taken place, has even expanded.[113]

At a certain point in time, then, courts (and scholars)[114] have been starting to play a more sophisticated kind of pluralist interpretative game in which individualist European values are measured against social private law (national) by way of an explicit deployment of the technique of balancing. As cases have been growing more complex over the last 15 years, as opposed to the previous 20 years or so, the judges have been pushed to review the heritage of private law's social values towards rationalising them (for example, avoiding protecting individual consumers claiming rights before the courtrooms whenever they feel that to do so would mean to unnecessarily and unfairly hurt other consumers).[115] The ever-present work of mediation between individuals' interests and social objectives as practised earlier – that is, incorporating social values (national) into the individualist structures of the Directives[116] – increasingly takes place via interpretative operations of

[110] See above at Section I.

[111] See above at Section I on constitutionally orientated mediation via incorporating social values in the individualistic structures of private law.

[112] On the consumer private law Directives as structures of individualism, see Niglia (n 3). See also L Niglia, 'Form and Substance in European Constitutional Law: The Social Character of Indirect Effect' (2010) 16(4) *European Law Journal* 439.

[113] I refer to the relevant case law under consideration as 'living law', considering that it is a law applied in the courtrooms as opposed to the orthodoxy of the common rules that continues marginalising these developments (on the mechanics of marginalisation, see L Niglia, 'Taking Comparative Law Seriously – Europe's Private Law and the Poverty of the Orthodoxy' (2006) 54(3) *American Journal of Comparative Law* 401).

[114] As to scholarship, see L Niglia 'Taking Private Law Rights Seriously–Of Balancing and the Court of Justice of the European Union' in L Niglia (ed) *Symposium–Balancing in European Law* in *16 Cambridge Yearbook of European Legal Studies* (Oxford, Hart Publishing, 2014) (indicating those scholars who pay attention to the judicial developments, in contrast to the orthodoxy that tends to ignore them altogether). As to the legislative side of the Europeanisation story, see Niglia (n 3).

[115] See Case C 215/08 *E Friz GmbH v Carsten von der Heyden* [2010] ECR I-2947.

[116] For a critical description of what private law scholars understand by 'individualism' and by 'social', see, eg, R. Michaels 'Of Islands and the Ocean: The Two Rationalities of European Private Law' in Brownsword, Micklitz, Niglia and Weatherill (n 8), 139; Duncan Kennedy, 'Three Globalizations of Law and Legal Thought: 1850–2000', in David M Trubek and Alvaro Santos (eds), *The New Law and Economic Development: A Critical Appraisal* (Cambridge, Cambridge University Press, 2006) 19; Niglia (n 3). One can derive the following sets of binary notions as distinctive of each vocabulary among the many: private autonomy; free will; freedom of contract; system; relations of individuals; commutative justice; intrinsic rationality; individual freedom; personal shortcomings such as lack of information or wealth fall in the individualist camp as opposed to notions such as solidarity; deduction; teleological reasoning; relations of society; distributive justice; extra-legal goals; appropriate allocation of goods; social justice; balancing that belongs instead to the 'social' camp. Such vocabularies have always played a constitutional role (in the sense of 'constitutionalisation' as discussed in this chapter) in tandem with arguments from positions (ideologies) – for example, the three individualistic principles typically held to have been at the core of the *Code civil* (see discussion below in ch 4) *or* the social principle of solidarity (see polemic over the principles to be inserted into the DCFR in ch 1) are good illustrations of

balancing values (individualist and social), in a horizon in which, importantly, the ensembles of social values associated with consumer protectionism are more improved by rationalisations and less sacrificed to individualist values.[117] Here one notes the employment of constitutional-like techniques (centred on the objective of accommodating the 'clashing normativities') that avoid sheer compliance or non-compliance, and that instead produce 'value balancing' towards a strategy of adjustment and accommodation.[118] This mimics, at the transnational level, transformation processes from 'conflicts' to 'accommodation' as they have been taking place in the nation state, as recounted in the previous pages (mediation or synthetisation). Once more, jurisprudence plays the role of 'synthesising' conflicts among interests and values entailed in the new wave of pluralisation (the fragmentation brought about by Europeanisation via the Directives) and of politicisation (engagement with European legislation) processes.[119]

The new European jurisprudence that has emerged out of this balancing scenario thus consists of a Europeanised version of the jurisprudential model of 'constitutional synthesisation' as developed nationally, and as described above in section II. It has been (and still is)[120] a categorical mistake of both the historical school of thought (*acquis commune*) and the positivistic school of thought (*acquis communautaire*) to conceive of the Europeanisation of private law as entirely revolving around texts (both 'formal' texts, such as the Directives, and 'informal' texts, such as the common rules)[121] rather than (also) the synthesising constitu-

positions/ideologies that intersect the vocabularies (discourses, reasoning) of individualism and sociality respectively (albeit not always overlapping). I analyse this intersection from the vantage point of the role of positions/ideologies in the contemporary codification project in ch 3 when discussing 'de-constitutionalisation' and 're-constitutionalisation', and from the vantage point of the role of vocabularies in that same context in ch 4 when considering the lasting power of the vocabularies of individualism and of sociality.

[117] See Case C-484/08 *Caja de Ahorros y Monte de Piedad de Madrid v Asocación de Usuarios de servicios bancarios (Ausbanc)* [2010] ECR I-4785 (Unfair Terms Directive); *Friz* (n 115) (Doorstep Directive).

[118] For an account of pluralism in terms of conflicts and accommodation, see Niglia (n 18) and (n 114).

[119] See above, at Section II and Niglia (n 3). The narrative intends to contribute to a line of constitutional law writings attempting to trace pluralist structures and processes within the nation state, as opposed to believing that pluralism only came to exist as a result of post-national globalisation processes: *cf* D Halberstam, 'Systems Pluralism and Institutional Pluralism in Constitutional Law: National, Supranational, and Global Governance' in M Avbelj and J Komarék (eds), *Constitutional Pluralism in the European Union and Beyond* (Oxford, Hart Publishing, 2012). For a focus on the problematic aspects entailed in the new European jurisprudence, see L Niglia, 'Constitutionalising European Private Law' (essay 2014, on file with author) (alerting to the risk of playing down the 'learning capacity', and the axiology of, domestic private law values, and critical considerations on how to counter that risk).

[120] For discussion, see ch 4.

[121] Even social thought as it emerged in the European group on social justice, in displaying scepticism vis-à-vis the role of the courts in Europeanisation, places itself in the same level as the historical and the positivist positions insofar as the authors of the 'Manifesto' defend 'social justice', but nevertheless agree on the technique of identifying 'common rules': see Manifesto of the 'Study Group on Social Justice in European Private Law' (2004) 6 *European Law Journal* 653: 'Agreement on common rules will symbolise more clearly than any Treaty or Constitution the emergence of a post-national form of governance.' On informal versus formal authorities, see H Micklitz, 'Monistic Ideology versus Pluralistic Reality – Towards a Normative Design for European Private Law' in Niglia (n 18) 29, 32; N Jansen,

tional operations discussed above – mistaking the structures of contemporary private law for (just) a nineteenth-century enterprise *à l'école de l'exégèse*[122] rather than (also) a continuation of twentieth-century developments (a constitutional jurisprudence of synthesis of conflicts).

Let me discuss each chapter of this story in turn.

A. Constitutional Private Law I: 'Low Intensity'

The impact of the private (consumer) law Directives on domestic private laws has been a story of re-creations of private law, by which I mean the re-organisation of domestic laws as a result of the encroachment on them by the private consumer law Directives.[123] It has been decided, for example, that contracts could be 're-opened', despite having been concluded in the context of the saga on the Doorstep Directive in which cancellation rights have been held to trump *pacta sunt servanda.*[124] One must register various types of reaction of the courts vis-à-vis the Directives, oscillating between compliance and non-compliance, the combination of which gives rise to 'fragmentation'.[125] Such fragmentation has been due partly to some hesitation, and even confusion, regarding how to effect an application of the domestic techniques of jurisprudential constitutionalisation to EU law-based litigation, as instigated by the new politicisation[126] entailed in the project of market integration and partly to sustained patterns of resistance towards some of the Directives (or of the rules contained in the Directives), which are perceived as endangering the integrity of national private laws (as constitutionally understood).[127] Judges (and scholars) have always avoided changing the deep structures of constitutional values implicated in private law[128] whenever it was felt that they would have to be unduly sacrificed for the purpose of enforcing the Directives. This indicates that these processes of 'law's re-creations' have been of a low-intensity constitutional character, as opposed to those of high-level calibre that have developed over the past 15 years or so and that I will consider in the remainder of this chapter. Let me now discuss, briefly, the low-intensity kind of 'law's re-creations' as they have developed over the last 20 years of the twentieth century.

'Legal Pluralism in Europe: National Laws, European Legislation, and Non-legislative Codifications' in Niglia (n 18) 112 (opening up to political settlements in relation to formal sources, but not to informal sources, whilst in the narrative I see both being involved in political and constitutional settlements).

[122] For a recent treatment of the role of texts in the context of the Europeanisation of private law, see Jansen (n 19).

[123] Niglia (n 3).

[124] See *Dori* as discussed in ch 1.

[125] See ch 1 (with relevant literature).

[126] On politicisation and pluralisation in the shadow of Europeanisation, see also Micklitz (n 121) (adopting a regulatory perspective).

[127] In terms of the welfarist material constitution, see Niglia (n 3).

[128] For a detailed analysis of this process in relation to welfarist interventionism or welfarist coordination, see Niglia (n 3).

Compliance has been about re-arranging domestic laws so as to make them conform to the requirements of European law as manifested in the relevant Directives. Cases of compliance include 'outright compliance' *and* what one can call 'creative compliance'. The right of cancellation understood as applicable to consumer contracts (as opposed to the problem of its applicability to so-called 'linked contracts' as discussed in the remainder of this chapter) is a good illustration of *outright compliance*. This is because it has been enforced slowly yet widely throughout domestic jurisdictions and it has certainly changed the face of at least one key traditional aspect of contract law. The traditional principle whereby contracts, once concluded, cannot be revoked other than via mutual agreement has been set aside whenever implementing the right of the consumer to revoke the contract after a prescribed period of time following its conclusion. Scholars have gone so far as to say that one should reconceptualise the entire doctrine of conclusion of contracts by considering 'conclusion' to take place at the moment that the consumer decides not to exercise the right of cancellation.[129] Europeanisation in this case has really succeeded in pushing contract law towards changing its classical reasoning and systematic structures in pursuit of accommodating the demands of market integration as encapsulated in the Doorstep Directive. Here the politicisation of market integration has given rise to a piece of EU legislation largely felt to be acceptable to domestic legal actors interested in crafting renovated forms of consumer protection in order to ensure reflected choice. Different and often conflicting rationales have been offered for the shared purpose of implementing and enforcing the right of cancellation in consumer contracts.[130] Legal actors that operate in countries with heavy consumer protectionist private law systems (welfare interventionism) have accepted the new principle as a form of improving the existing standards of consumer protection; legal actors operating in countries more keen to rely on the workings of market processes (welfare coordination) have seen in cancellation rights an instrument for fostering reflected choice towards taming market power.[131]

Creative compliance has taken place through reception processes that have enforced the commands of the Directives in ways that were not originally intended by the legislature. This is the case, again, for the right of cancellation as provided

[129] N Jansen and R Zimmermann, 'Restating the Acquis Communautaire?' (2008) 71(4) *Modern Law Review* 505. For a more ambitious suggestion towards a reconceptualisation of the system at the level of its operating principles, see L Mengoni, 'Note sul rapporto tra fonti di diritto comunitario e fonti di diritto interno degli Stati membri' in N Lipari (ed), *Diritto Privato Europeo e Categorie Civilistiche* (Napoli, ESI, 1988) 32 (in relation to the right of cancellation, arguing for a re-organisation of the system around a 'reticolo di principi e modelli di decisione differenziati').

[130] At times, this trend has led to complex turns in jurisprudence and sometimes conflicts between supreme courts and lower courts in Germany; for example, see N Reich, 'Balancing in Private Law and the Imperatives of Public Interest' in Brownsword, Micklitz, Niglia and Weatherill (n 8) 221. See also Mengoni (n 129) 23, 29 et seq (discussing the case law of the Italian Corte di Cassazione).

[131] Respectively, in countries adopting interventionist welfarism and in countries adopting coordination welfarism: see Niglia (n 3) (also detailing how the shift in some countries' governmental policies, and in jurisprudential thinking, towards marketisation facilitated the process of adaptation to European private law legislation).

for in the Doorstep Directive and as invoked by guarantors. Here the courts have been struggling with disputes in which guarantors have relied upon the Doorstep Directive. Their hope has been to use the Directive's provision that allows for the cancellation of the contract within a prescribed period (the so-called 'cooling-off period') with a view to back out of the obligations descending from their position as guarantors, despite the fact that the Directive was not intended to apply to guarantors. Legal actors, rather creatively, have been managing to re-interpret the Directive so as to hold that it applies to guarantees. For, not only domestic legal actors have been arguing for the application of the requirement of the right of cancellation to disputes in which guarantors of commercial loans were interested in backing out of their obligations, but, when reaching the CJEU, the Court itself decided that guarantors of consumer loans, albeit not guarantors of commercial loans, could rely on the right of cancellation on the basis of the Doorstep Directive. The details of this story show how private law's re-creations may happen in contexts in which legal actors re-invent the field in unexpected and unpredictable ways. As I argue in the remainder of this chapter, *Heininger* is another example of creative compliance in relation to the Doorstep Directive.[132]

Non-compliance instead has been about defending the 'integrity' of domestic laws against the encroachment of the Directives. Here a clash between the new politicisation of private law (based on market integration) and the old constitutional structures of private law has taken place, with some judges holding it neither possible nor feasible to accommodate the new law. I understand in this way the position of courts that have at times outrightly rejected pieces of European law incorporated into Directives. A *fin-de-siècle* decision of the *Bundesgerichtshof* exemplifies this,[133] that is, situations in which private law's materialisation as practised nationally manages to remain in place as opposed to situations in which compliance (outright or creative) with the Directives takes place.[134] However, it should be noted that even a piece of domestic law implementing a Directive, being defended as 'required' for compliance with EU law, may have been, on closer inspection, an opportunity for changing domestic law according to internal (domestic) requirements, albeit at odds with the requirements of the Unfair Terms Directive. This has been the case in France, where legal actors have taken the opportunity to 'implement' the Unfair Terms Directive for reforming national law towards pursuing a revised kind of materialisation strategy, disguising that reform of national protectionist legislation as a faithful adaptation to the Directive.[135] And even cases of 'outright rejection' of a Directive amount to 're-creating' law in a minimal yet important way, for they may bring about debates on available alternatives to domestic models and related plausible changes as well

[132] For discussion, see Niglia (n 114) (on literalism and balancing in the case law of the CJEU).

[133] BGH, 7 July 1998, 1998 *Der Betriebs-Berater* 1864 (as quoted in ch 1). Note also *Office of Fair Trading v Abbey National plc and others* (2009) UKSC 6 (no reference to the CJEU of the bank charges case; interpretation of the 1999 Regulations, implementing the Unfair Terms Directive, is a matter for domestic law only).

[134] For details in relation to countries shifting to marketisation policies instead, see Niglia (n 3).

[135] Niglia (n 3).

as a renovated awareness of the value of the relevant domestic laws being kept in place.[136] After all, keeping in place domestic law vis-à-vis an incoming Directive is never a complete act of mere defence of the existing law, but something that changes domestic law itself to some extent – Teubner has called these processes 'irritations'; I have called them 'transformations.[137]

Overall, it has been typical of this stage of Europeanisation (the last 20 years or so of the twentieth century) that the background structures and techniques of private law, whether or not changed at the national level as a result of the impact of the Directives, have remained in line with the horizon of established values as nationally constituted,[138] values that in any case have become open ('Europeanised') rather than exclusively centred on the national constitutional heritage. To the extent that this is true,[139] one must say, let me stress this point once more, that the axiology of private law (materialisation) has been expanded but not altered.[140]

B. Constitutional Private Law II: 'High Intensity'

In the last 15 years or so, the courts have been developing a new kind of approach that goes considerably beyond the parameters within which adjudication had been operating in the previous period of 'low-intensity constitutionalism'. It is of a maximal kind of 'constitutional' jurisprudential re-creations of private law that one must talk ('high intensity') as opposed to the 'minimal' constitutional activities ('low intensity') of the previous period. The minimal way has been about respecting the nationally established value choices embodied in the rules and institutions of private law affected by Europeanisation,[141] with judicial adjustments of national private law having been engineered within the axiological parameters of the pre-established national material constitutional settlement, and with values having been at most applied to even wider areas. Instead, the maximal way has been about actively engaging in explicitly making new value choices. Specifically, in the line of controversial cases that I consider below, the courts have been actively employing a constitutional technique of adjudication, 'balancing' as they do the relevant rights at stake. What is peculiar in terms of this new practice[142] is that the judges have shown themselves to be actively aware of the constitutional implications of their work, consciously taking a stance as a counter-force vis-à-vis the market-orientated drive of European interventions through the

[136] ibid.

[137] See respectively Teubner (n 14); and Niglia (n 3).

[138] *cf* Wilhelmsson (n 8).

[139] This is no doubt a complex process with national variations: see the cases of England and Italy (in Italy, the Corte di Cassazione ultimately managed to justify cancellation in the context of the existing constitutional private law arrangements: see Mengoni (n 129), in the context, I should add, of a deeper shift in governmental policies towards marketisation (see Niglia (n 3)).

[140] *cf* Mengoni (n 64).

[141] *cf* above at Section II (where relevant literature on material constitutional arrangements).

[142] See Niglia (n 114).

Directives[143] – they have tended to protect the weaker party (the consumer). There is a third reason, alongside the deployment of balancing and the conscious incorporation of the value of consumer protectionism towards taming market forces, for reading the case-law as embodying 'high-level' constitutionalism qua transformative constitutionalism that changes the value structures within which private law operates. In some of the relevant cases, one can find a convergence of judicial opinions that marks the rise of a true constitutional dialogue[144] in lieu of contestation and resistance as has been typical of private law adjudication under the paradigm of low-level constitutional re-creations.[145] Such dialogue presents us with the following characteristics.

First, the key judicial objective has been the pursuit of rationalising (bettering) consumer protection by avoiding excessive protectionism in the circumstances of the case and by re-inventing old social values to suit complex cases such as 'linked contracts'. Second, the decisions revolve around respect for national private law, as shown inter alia by *Hamilton* (absorption in European law, as interpreted by the CJEU, of the balancing act made by the national legislature, that is, of the legislation limiting the time period within which the right of cancellation can be exercised) and *Friz* (absorption in European law, as interpreted by the CJEU, of the domestic judge-made law on the sharing of contractual risks in partnership contracts). Third, the decisions resemble other lines of cases as one can find them in domestic legal systems where constitutional courts 'balance' and 'protect the weaker party' relative to the interests (reputed to be stronger) of the other party.[146] Specifically, in these decisions one can see the new way ('European') in which the incorporation of social values (national) in individualist private law structures takes place (materialisation) that continues the same kind of mediation as practised nationally in contexts of welfarist settlements. For the CJEU is showing a 'disposition towards protection of the weaker party'[147] through balancing the

[143] In this book I emphasise the positive aspect of the jurisprudence of constitutional synthesisation as countering the politicisation as built around legislative material by the European Commission. Elsewhere I discuss the problematic aspects that underlie this practice: see Niglia (n 119).

[144] For a discussion of this, see ibid (considering the complexity of this case law in relation to wider issues of social legitimacy in relation to which critical discernment of the relevant case law is required).

[145] Niglia (n 103).

[146] For example, in Germany see *BVerfG* 19 October 1993, *BVerfGE* 89, 214 (the Bürgschaft saga) and BGH 24 February 1994 NJW 1994, 1341 as inter alia discussed in H Collins, *The European Civil Code: The Way Forward* (Cambridge, Cambridge University Press, 2007) 106 et seq and Hesselink *The New European Private Law* (The Hague, Kluwer Law International) at 184 et seq. See also Niglia (n 119); Niglia (n 114). Alexy has famously called the work being undertaken by constitutional courts as consisting of a practice of 'rights' optimisation', that is, making the most of the rights' of the parties: 'The greater the degree of non-satisfaction of, or detriment to, one principle, the greater the importance of satisfying the other.' See R Alexy, 'Constitutional Rights, Balancing and Rationality' (2003) 16(2) *Ratio Juris* 131, 136. One must bear in mind this framework of analysis for understanding the European courts' decisions that I am about to consider: for discussion, see Niglia (n 119); Niglia (n 114).

[147] Here I am quoting H Collins, 'The Impact of Human Rights on Contract Law in Europe' (2001) *University of Cambridge Legal Studies Research Papers Series* 8, who, however, refers to the case law of the German Constitutional Court only, a case law which he explains in terms of the balancing of competing constitutional rights and principles (Collins openly criticises an explanation offered by strands of German constitutional scholarship, labelled *Schutzpflichtern*, whereby it is considered that the judges are less balancing and more applying indirectly the Basic Law, that is, implementing a positive

relevant rights at stake, which in my view[148] is similar to what constitutional courts do nationally when applying constitutional charters to the private law realm independently of the Europeanisation phenomenon. Fourth, and in structural terms, in the three cases that I consider below, it should be noted how the clashes take place 'horizontally', so to speak ('horizontal pluralism'),[149] that is, within the body of EU law and national law rules and principles as combined through interpretative practices – as opposed to 'vertically', that is, through the clashes of supranational rules and national rules and the hierarchical placing of one set of rules (national or European) over the other (European or national), depending on whether one respectively considers cases of non-compliance or compliance.[150] For the impact of Europeanisation on private law has certainly created an 'intermediate body' of rules and principles (in chapter one, I have labelled this practice 'persuasive reasoning') that encapsulate both European and national elements, and within which scholars and judges 'deliberate' over the relevant stakes. Fifth, and at a further level of analysis, the new jurisprudence is about participating in what can be called European 'composite constitutional law',[151] placing itself alongside private law cases which involve the European Convention on Human Rights, as occurred in the CJEU case *Mostaza Claro* – where the Advocate General reconstructed the position of the consumer as being entitled to the 'right to a fair trial' – or, another good illustration of such composite interrelations, the decision of the Italian Constitutional Court of April 2012[152] – where the Court relied on the European Convention on Human Rights rather than just the Italian Constitution with a view to support a finding of unconstitutionality of ordinary legislation that made it practically impossible for bank customers to act against the bank out of *repetitio indebiti* for breach of law in relation to the incorrect calculation of interest on bank contracts.

Let me now consider three cases that exemplify this new practice.

The first case consists of a turning point in the case law of the CJEU, having previously taken a more textual approach to the interpretation of the Doorstep

constitutional duty to intervene in private law towards 'guaranteeing a minimum level of enjoyment of rights in the private sphere'). For my own opinion on this aspect, see Niglia (n 119).

148 On this point, see Niglia (n 119); Niglia (n 114); Kennedy (n 8); Kumm (n 86).

149 On vertical, horizontal and diagonal pluralism, see Niglia (n 18).

150 Technically speaking, one may still categorise the balancing cases in terms of the classical vocabulary of compliance and non-compliance, depending on whether the output of judicial opinions lead to greater or lesser compliance with the Directives, but the point that I am making is a different one – that is, it is that the courts are employing balancing as their preferred mode of interpretation and that balancing is about combining, and compromising around, the relevant normative clashes as they occur as a result of the encroachment of the Directives on domestic private laws and as relied upon by the litigants before domestic courts.

151 On the notions of multi-level constitutionalism and of composite constitutionalism in general, see, eg, I Pernice and F Mayer, 'De la constitution composée de l'Europe' (2000) *Revue trimestrelle de droit européen* 623 et seq; I Pernice, 'Multilevel Constitutionalism in the European Union' (2002) 27 *European Law Review* 511, 514; Leonard FM Besselink, *A Composite European Constitution. Een Samengestelde Europese Constitutie* (Groningen, Europa Law Publishing, 2007). For the theoretical and comparative approach behind my argument, see Niglia (n 18).

152 See Italian Constitutional Court 78, 2–5 April 2012.

Directive, in line with the climate of interpretation in vogue before the embracing of balancing on the part of the CJEU.[153] In *Hamilton*, the Court dealt with a dispute that arose as a result of the fact that Ms Hamilton had not been allowed to cancel (on the basis of the Doorstep Directive) a loan contract for the acquisition of shares.[154] Considerations regarding certainty of transactions led the Court to hold that the right of withdrawal should not be considered applicable in the circumstances, despite the fact that she had not been informed of her right to exercise that right. Here the conflicting considerations regarding legal certainty and the duty to inform about the right of cancellation have been weighted to the advantage of the bank, the judges barring the exercise of the right of cancellation from the moment of completion of the performance on the part of both parties as provided for under the domestic legislation (as opposed to the moment of having given information about, or having made the consumer aware of, the right to cancellation), rather than allowing the consumer to cancel the contract indefinitely. Thus, to cancel a contract indefinitely is allowed in the noted circumstances, but not where all obligations have been performed, this being the solution adopted in a German piece of legislation providing for the expiring of the cancellation right one month after the performance of all obligations (see the fourth sentence of paragraph 2(1) of the Law on the cancellation of doorstep transactions and analogous transactions (*Gesetz über den Widerruf von Haustürgeschäften und ähnlichen Geschäften*)). This case is representative of a line of cases in which the adoption of balancing may or may not lead to the protection of the consumer, for it all depends on considerations regarding the actual balancing of the interests at stake.

In contrast to *Hamilton*, in *Heininger*,[155] at stake was the issue of the applicability of the right of cancellation provided for in the Doorstep Directive to credit agreements secured by a charge on the purchase of land in circumstances in which a piece of national legislation imposed a time limit on the exercise of that right. The Court held in favor of Mrs Heininger, rejecting the argument based on legal-certainty raised by the trader and holding that the trader could have avoided the legal uncertainty by informing the consumer of the right to withdrawal. This makes concerns about the security of transactions less of an issue, whereas in *Hamilton* the consideration that the obligations pertaining to the contract had all been performed played a heavy role in the Court's decision not to protect the consumer. Again, balancing may or may not lead to the protection of the consumer on the basis of considerations regarding the actual balancing of the interests at stake.

[153] For a classical understanding of the previous case law, see W van Gerven, 'The ECJ Case-law as a Means of Unification of Private Law?' in AS Hartkamp et al (eds), *Towards a European Civil Code* (The Hague, Kluwer Law International, 2nd edn, 1998) 91. For the thesis of the extent to which the CJEU adopts balancing, see Niglia (n 114) (with further cases in which balancing is equally employed).

[154] Case 412/06 *Annelore Hamilton v Volksbank Filder* [2008] ECR I-2383.

[155] Case C-481/99 *Heininger and Heininger v Bayerische Hypo-und Vereinsbank* [2001] ECR I-9945.

A third case worth mentioning is *Friz*, a decision regarding the interpretation of the Unfair Terms Directive.[156] The case shows how the balancing technique, understood as a tool of high-intensity constitutional adjudication, is actively deployed by domestic courts and not just by the CJEU. Thus, domestic courts do not just engage in dialogue with the CJEU by posing interpretative questions that then empower the CJEU to continue adopting its balancing technique, as it happened for example with the *Hamilton* and *Heininger* preliminary reference cases and the many more being increasingly brought before the CJEU. This is because in *Friz* the German court explicitly placed before the CJEU a question regarding whether a line of interpretation entirely based on balancing (the equitable apportioning of risks among contractors) could or not be held compatible with EU law. The line of interpretation consisted in holding that 'a satisfactory balance and a fair division of the risks among the various interested parties' is all that the domestic judge-made law aims at in the circumstances. What is remarkable is that the CJEU then transformed this reference into a 'constitutionalising' decision, in that it operationalised an explicit balancing of the values involved in the case. The value of consumer protection is implemented through the balancing of the collection of contractual rights at stake, that is, the rights of each participant to the share contract, rather than individually, as is usually the case in similar balancing decisions before domestic courts. A piece of judge-made law is thus transformed into a piece of constitutional law, that is, a contractual right gets 'materialised'. Specifically, the German judge-made balancing rule that protects the community of the shareholders to the partnership contract is implicitly a truly 'constitutional' requirement, for it is about protecting a social organisation from unjust redistributive effects,[157] which, in the circumstances, means protecting a closed-end real property fund from cancellations of membership whenever this might disadvantage those remaining in the fund or third-party creditors, as a way to contain the unequal redistribution of the risks involved in the partnership contract. The CJEU decision makes explicit that constitutionality by rephrasing it in the vocabulary of constitutional protection of consumers under EU law:[158]

> [W]hile there is no doubt that the aim of the Directive is to protect consumers, that does not imply that that protection is absolute.[159]

And, discussing the:

> [N]ational law according to which, in the event of cancellation of membership of a closed-end real property fund established in the form of a partnership, entered into following a doorstep transaction, the consumer has a claim against that partnership, to his severance balance, calculated on the basis of the value of his interest at the date of his

[156] For further cases in which balancing is equally employed in relation to the Unfair Terms Directive, see Niglia (n 119).

[157] For a synthesis of the workings of private law as protectionist of social spheres in Germany, see Teubner (n 14).

[158] See Arts 169 et seq Lisbon Treaty ('high level of consumer protection'), which is at the core of the case law of the CJEU on the Directives: see, eg, *Ausbanc* (n 117).

[159] *Friz* (n 115) [44].

> retirement from membership of that fund, and may therefore get back less than the value of his capital contribution or have to participate in the losses of that fund.

By way of faithful reference to the reasons offered by the German court:

> [F]irst, such a rule offers the consumer cancelling his membership of a closed-end real property fund established in the form of a partnership the opportunity to recover his holding, while taking on a proportion of the risks inherent to any capital investment of the type at issue in the main proceedings. Secondly, it also enables the other partners or third party creditors, in circumstances such as those of the main proceedings, not to have to bear the financial consequences of the cancellation of that membership, which moreover occurred following the signature of a contract to which they were not party.[160]

Note the explicit 'cooperative act' on the part of the CJEU in relation to the preliminary question as placed before it by the domestic courts:

> As the *Bundesgerichtshof* observed in its decision for reference, that rule is intended to ensure, in accordance with the general principles of civil law, a satisfactory balance and a fair division of the risks among the various interested parties.[161]

Friz shows a full commitment on the part of domestic courts in engaging with the CJEU in a dialogue on and about balancing, for the domestic courts are willing to expand the reach of materialisation of rights incorporated into the pattern of constitutional balancing applicable to shared contracts to the European case law concerning the Directives.[162] Exactly at the moment that judges are more than ever shifting away from nationalism (preservation of national values) to a European perspective (altering national value choices through balancing with a view to accommodate European legislation), the European Commission and its legal brethren are engineering the codification move by proposing a Common European Sales Law (the CESL Optional Code) – which, as I discuss below, is antithetical to, and works against, the remarkable judicial moves of the last decade and a half that have given rise to a Europeanised version of the materialisation of private law via the practices of constitutional synthesisation. I will explain why this is so in the next chapter.

[160] ibid [49].

[161] ibid [48].

[162] For contrasting cases in which the domestic courts act out of a position other than that of the CJEU, and on the extent to which that critical positioning can co-exist with the ongoing patterns of cooperation through balancing among courts, see Niglia (n 119) (inter alia discussing *Schulte*).

3

Code vs Jurisprudence

IN THIS CHAPTER I argue that the codification project as engineered by the European Commission, now taking shape through the *Proposal for a Common European Sales Law* (the CESL Optional Code) – the CESL code-text, presented as a 'comprehensive and self-standing' set of norms – entails an assault on the deep pluralistic structures of private law qua jurisprudence as I have described them in the previous chapter. In other words, on the structures that emerge through law's patterns of re-creations which I have labelled 'low-intensity' and 'high-intensity'. At stake is a confrontation between code (European) and jurisprudence (national and European) rather than between code (European) and codes (national) as per the conventionalist renderings of codification with their tendency to focus on the legislative side of legal developments only. For on the ground, there is no such thing as national codes as powerful as they were historically, as one might be led to believe in reading various conventional analyses,[1] but rather a sophisticated jurisprudence that operates both at the national and the European levels – a jurisprudence that the new codification movement threatens to undo, towards establishing a totalising realm of private law interpretation centred on overarching European law material (the individualist qua market libertarian vocabulary analysed in chapter one) and the related displacement of national law (the sociality vocabulary analysed in chapter two) altogether.

The move is problematic, and not just because it threatens to undermine the sustainability of jurisdictional diversity (the plurality of individual national jurisdictions),[2] as discussed in chapter one mostly on legal comparative and

[1] R Michaels, 'Code vs Code. Nationalist and Internationalist Images of the Code Civil in the French Resistance to a European Codification' (2012) *European Review of Contract Law* 277 is both a synthesis and a critique of conventional analyses.

[2] Jurisdictional diversity here pertains to the value (ascertainable on legal comparative grounds) of respecting the existence of the individuality of national legal traditions, while jurisdictional autonomy pertains to the value (equally ascertainable on legal comparative grounds) of the degree to which respect for the operations of the jurisprudential forces independently of territorial boundaries (that is, the jurisprudence of constitutional synthesisation as described in ch 2) can be defended, as I will argue below. For general legal comparative arguments in support of the idea that private law traditions may and should operate by trespassing territorial boundaries, see HP Glenn, *Legal Traditions in the World: Sustainable Diversity in Law* (4th edn, Oxford, Oxford University Press, 2010) 361 et seq. For further legal comparative and legal theoretical arguments towards a pluralist approach that engages with the trans-territorial operations of private law traditions and systems, see L Niglia (ed), *Pluralism and European Private Law* (Oxford, Hart Publishing, 2013); and L Niglia, 'Of Complexity and Tradition' (essay 2014, on file with author).

historical grounds, in the sense that any dissenting voices coming from the domestic realm would be bound to be placed at a disadvantage vis-à-vis code-based arguments. The deeper problem is the sustainability of the autonomy of the operations of the national jurisprudential structures, that is, what I described in the previous chapter as the many engagements of domestic jurisprudential forces with Europeanisation. For, in my view, as I argue in the following pages, at play is a sophisticated development which results in the impairment of 'constitutional synthesisation' as it characterises the workings of the European living private law jurisprudence. That is, the conflicts among interests and values (individual versus social; European versus national) as accommodated on the basis of national registers of constitutional authority,[3] in the two ways described in chapter two, depending on which strands of case law one looks at. Let me recall the two strands of cases.

In a first strand of cases, national registers are being *structurally* revised, whenever old private law institutions, such as *pacta sunt servanda*, are adapted so as to include the Directives' rights, such as the right of cancellation, thus expanding the reach of material rights for the purpose of taming conflicts between consumers and sellers ('low-intensity constitutional re-creations'). In a second strand of cases, national registers of constitutional authority are being both *structurally* and *substantively* revised, for here the revision affects the underlying *values* ('high-intensity constitutional re-creations'). This is the case of the courts' 'rationalisation' of private law material rights by avoiding to protect the consumer-litigant under the Directives in situations in which this may prove to be potentially harmful vis-à-vis other consumers affected by the case, as per the validation of the national legislative settlement in *Hamilton* and of the national judicial settlement in *Friz*.[4]

The EU Commission is concerned with 'fragmentation'[5] precisely because the implementation and enforcement of the Directives produce unwelcome results (from the point of view of the Commission), such as the preservation of material rights , as opposed to what the Commission has in mind when it attempts to instrumentalise law so as to make it accommodate market integration. But such fragmentary results are in turn needed, from the perspective of domestic legal systems, in order to safeguard the integrity of national constitutional private laws by keeping its underlying (materialisation) values in place.[6] As the jurisprudential

[3] On the interface between constitutional values and the actual organisation of private law in relation to the impact of Europeanisation, see L Niglia, *The Transformation of Contract in Europe* (The Hague, Kluwer Law International, 2003).

[4] On the challenge of bringing law-beyond-the-state into line with the imperative of ensuring conformity with a 'singular register of authority', see L Niglia, 'The Double Life of Pluralism in Europe'; and L Niglia, 'Pluralism in a New Key: Between Plurality and Normativity' in Niglia (n 2) 9 et seq and 249 et seq.

[5] See Memorandum of the 'Proposal for a Consumer Rights Directive' (discussing fragmentation in relation to subsidiarity).

[6] By 'safeguarding integrity', I mean that the private law values belonging to the national level are being safeguarded rather than altogether replaced (see Case 412/06 *Annelore Hamilton v Volksbank Filder* [2008] ECR I-2383 and Case-215/08 *E Friz GmbH v Carsten von der Heyden* [2010] ECR I-2947

forces move away from the Commission's harmonisation strategy, the Commission is now charging codification in order to bring jurisprudence in line with its strategy. The attempt is to replace the heritage of material rights by a neoclassical, formal set of rights channeling the strategy of market libertarianism.

The Optional Code targets the practice whereby judges base their decisions on a range of available domestic mandatory and default rules, that is, the heritage of material rights developed out of the national registers of constitutionalism. This is a practice currently guaranteed (under both EU law, in relation to the implementation and enforcement of the private law Directives, and private international law, in relation to the applicability of conflicts of law rules to transborder contractual disputes)[7] towards ensuring that, substantively, decisions are measured

as discussed above in ch 2). This is a practice that intersects and validates various arguments made in European constitutional law literature regarding the value of 'composite constitutionalism' as discussed in ch 2. It also intersects Braiberd Currie's work as adapted to the European law landscape, that is, his key argument whereby in conflicts of law situations, there should be a 'defence of the order most intimately concerned with the normative (public) consequences of the (private) material at issue' (see M Everson, 'The Limits of the 'Conflicts Approach': Law in Time of Political Turmoil' (2011) 2(2) *Transnational Legal Theory* 271, 273).

[7] At a minimum, enacting the CESL Optional Code would be bound to create a situation in which the range of legal material available for the judge to make decisions about applicable law would become dangerously limited to the CESL body of norms (this applying not only to business-to-business transactions, albeit only small and medium enterprises (SMEs), but also to business-to-consumer transactions) as can be seen from the legislative intentions in the *Memorandum* to the Proposal (emphasis added): 'The Common European Sales Law will be a second contract law regime within the national law of each Member State. Where the parties have agreed to use the Common European Sales Law, its rules will be the only national rules applicable for matters falling within its scope. Where a matter falls within the scope of the Common European Sales Law, there is thus no scope for the application of any other national rules. *This agreement to use the Common European Sales Law is a choice between two different sets of sales law within the same national law and does therefore not amount to, and must not be confused with, the previous choice of the applicable law within the meaning of private international law rules.* Under the normal operation of the Rome I Regulation there are however restrictions to the choice of law for business-to-consumer transactions. If the parties choose in business-to-consumer transactions the law of another Member State than the consumer's law, such a choice may under the conditions of Article 6(1) of the Rome I Regulation not deprive the consumer of the protection of the mandatory provisions of the law of his habitual residence (Article 6 (2) of the Rome I Regulation). *The latter provision however can have no practical importance if the parties have chosen within the applicable national law the Common European Sales Law. The reason is that the provisions of the Common European Sales Law of the country's law chosen are identical with the provisions of the Common European Sales Law of the consumer's country. Therefore the level of the mandatory consumer protection laws of the consumer's country is not higher and the consumer is not deprived of the protection of the law of his habitual residence.*' (Emphasis added.) On the impact of Europeanisation on private international law, see M Reimann, 'Comparative Law and Private International Law' in M Reimann and R Zimmermann (eds), *The Oxford Handbook of Comparative Law* (2nd edn, Oxford, Oxford University Press, 2008) 1375, 1390–91, pointing to the shift from 'occasional interference with national regimes' of EC conflicts law to adoption in the EU of 'comprehensive conflicts legislation, making law for whole, core, areas of the field' (eg, referring to the 'dramatic takeover' by Council Regulation 44/2001 of 22 December 2000 on Jurisdiction, Recognition and Enforcement of Judgments in Civil and Commercial Matters, OJ L 1-23, 16 January 2001 of the Brussels Convention of 1968) and arguing that 'private international law is decreasingly left to the individual member states as co-equal sovereigns, that is, less and less a matter of national legislation or voluntary international cooperation through convention making. Instead, conflicts law is increasingly turned over to central institutions wielding superior legislative authority, that is, made by command from above'.

relative to national standards of constitutionality.[8] Assuming that a rigorous implementation of the Optional Code takes place, the synthetisation of conflicts via reliance on domestic mandatory and default rules would no longer be practicable because all interpretation would be mandated to take place within the autonomous ('self-contained') regime of the Optional Code.[9] From this vantage point, the project of transferring the governing rules of major types of transborder contracts (sales; unfair terms) from Directives into Regulation, at the same time shifting from a horizon of minimum harmonisation to one of total harmonisation, and from one of conflict of law to one of substantive rules, is an ambitious move. This is because it aims at significantly altering the key material constitutional balance in which Europe finds itself, based as it is on the respect for the national private law dimension as constitutive of the synthesisation operations.[10] It is intended to make of the 'supranational dimension' the only regulatory level that matters, depriving jurisprudential decision making of the virtues of constitutional authority implicated in the national dimension and making of Europe's plural constitutional private law an empty shell.[11] In other words, the intention of the codifiers is to make it that constitutional synthesisation ('thick' private law constitutionalism) be outrightly displaced by the Optional Code-based 'totalising' disciplinary structures ('thin' private law constitutionalism).[12] The code-project effectively results in making of EU private law not only an 'applicable law' once the parties opt into the CESL, but the only 'applied law' in lieu of the existing constitutional private law.

In the remainder of the chapter, I will further discuss the ways in which the European community of interpreters has been reacting to the code-project in relation to three key aspects of the Optional Code proposal pertaining to 'mandatory rules', 'default rules' and 'choice' – although my analysis would obviously apply a fortiori to any future optional or non-optional European code to come, whether covering further sectors of private law or even the entire private law, depending on how the CFR agenda will be implemented in the near future.[13] From this perspective, it should be noted how the reactions of the European community of interpreters to the proposed Optional Code provide insight into what the codification strategy results in, that is, straitjacketing the key pillars of

[8] For discussion on this point, see the remainder of the chapter. This is another way in which enactment of the CESL Optional Code would, in my view, profoundly re-arrange the classical functions of private international law, as discussed above at n 7, to the detriment of the national constitutional dimension of law.

[9] In the sense that this will give rise to grammaticalist modes of interpretation that will make it harder for any of the potential opponents to code-based interpretations to see their views prevail: see ch 1 (the codification project as entailing a 'normalization' effect) and the remainder of this chapter.

[10] See also L Niglia, 'Form and Substance in European Constitutional Law: The Social Character of Indirect Effect' (2010) 16(4) *European Law Journal* 439 (with further literature).

[11] See n 6 above.

[12] See ch 1 on the mechanics of disciplinary interpretation via a *code corpus*.

[13] Let's recall that the Optional Code is a first step towards implementing a fully fledged strategy of codification, including via an optional code of greater scope (the whole of contract law) and not limited to transborder aspects. From this vantage point, my criticism in the remainder applies to any kind of optional code, regardless of its actual scope.

constitutional jurisprudence as they exist today in Europe. The narrative is about recounting a rising consciousness of a true assault on the structures of jurisprudential pluralism as they have been shaped over the past decades around the activities aimed at harmonising private law via the Directives. Seen from this perspective, the analysis of the 'code vs jurisprudence' contingency reveals a peculiar character, for it should be stressed that the scholarly debates around the proposed Optional Code that I recount below mark a shift in the character of the 'codifiers vs cultivators' dispute as articulated in scholarly writings.[14] That is, this dispute is no longer merely academic but historicised in that it involves contentious material – politically, it is about debating the merits of a concrete proposal being placed by the European Commission before the EU legislative institutions for approval, while constitutionally, it is about choosing what place to give to sociality in the European context.

* * *

Before addressing the main argument of this chapter, a few considerations need be outlined. The rest of the chapter consists of reflecting further on a series of polemical predicaments that characterise the current codification process with a view to advancing a new reading of them. Two such polemics are well known. The first is the one developed within the DCFR network of scholars over the role and number of the principles as initially inserted in the Interim Outline Edition (2008) of the DCFR[15] and as revised in the Outline Edition of the DCFR (2009).[16] The second polemic was raised by an independent group of German scholars vis-à-vis the Interim Outline Edition of the DCFR. The former began in relation to the argument put forward by some of those within the DCFR network of scholars that it would have been appropriate to make the code revolve around authorisation of the judge to balance a wide range of principles that would include, alongside the four that have remained in the last version of the DCFR, 11 'social principles'.[17] This has been about the proposition to place the balancing exercise at the core of European private law in a similar fashion to what judges are already doing.[18] The

[14] For the previous, academic formulation of this dispute, see the confrontation between 'codifiers' (eg, G Gandolfi 'Per un Codice Europeo dei Contratti' (1991) 45 *Rivista Trimestrale di Diritto e Procedura Civile* 781) and 'cultivators' (eg, 'European legal unity' to be achieved via academic development of synthetising principles: see B Markesinis, 'Why a Code is Not the Best Way to Advance the Cause of European Legal Unity' (1998) 5 *European Review of Public Law* 519).

[15] C von Bar, E Clive, H Schulte-Nölke et al (eds), *Principles, Definitions and Model Rules of European Private Law, Draft Common Frame of Reference (DCFR), Interim Outline Edition* (Munich, Sellier, 2008).

[16] C von Bar, E Clive, H Schulte-Nölke et al (eds), *Principles, Definitions and Model Rules of European Private Law, Draft Common Frame of Reference (DCFR), Outline Edition* (Munich, Sellier, 2009).

[17] M Hesselink, 'If You Don't Like Our Principles We Have Others' in R Brownsword, H-W Micklitz, L Niglia and S Weatherill (eds), *The Foundations of European Private Law* (Oxford, Hart Publishing, 2011) 59.

[18] Scholarship tends to ignore that balancing is taking place this way in the courtrooms, as I have argued above in ch 2. See also L Niglia 'Taking Private Law Rights Seriously–Of Balancing and the Jurisprudence of the Court of Justice of the European Union' in L Niglia (ed), *Symposium–Balancing in European Law: 16 Cambridge Yearbook of European Legal Studies* (2014); Niglia 'Constitutionalising European Private Law' (essay 2014, on file with author).

second polemic stems from considerations regarding the possibility of the jurisprudential discourse to articulate a more sophisticated and coherent body of private law rules than that embodied in the DCFR. The authors that put forward the critique are German; they take as the reference point for their criticism the Germanic legal system, and it is from this vantage point that they denounce the DCFR rules as inconsistent and badly drafted.[19] The constitutional critique that I put forward in the following pages is concerned with expanding on the material that underlies both sets of polemics with a view to making constitutional sense of them at once. I see the two strands of polemics as being representative of lines of argumentation that heavily draw on substantively rationalist (the polemic on private law principles internal to the DCFR) and formally rationalist qua doctrinal (the polemic external to the DCFR) positions; however, in my reconstruction of these writings, I emphasise what I consider to be implicit constitutional aspects. It is from this vantage point that, in my view, one can really grasp the extent to which the codification project results in unduly challenging the structures of the jurisprudential heritage as developed over the past few decades. Whilst I see much constitutional meaning in the reactions of some scholars to the CESL Optional Code proposal, I find it difficult to perceive a corresponding awareness about the constitutional meaning of that reaction. We urgently need a critical discourse characterised by such awareness. There is a tendency to articulate criticism in a piecemeal fashion rather than interpreting it all as part of the wider constitutional landscape, that is, related to the jurisprudential patterns described above in chapter two. In translating the debate in constitutional terms, I am deliberately attempting to move it all to a level at which one can gain the requisite awareness of what is at work, that is, not minor aspects but an ambitious codification project whose aim is to establish a law that lacks the kind of constitutional authority attached to the existing private law. In other words, let me stress this aspect again, the aim is to eliminate the core national private law dimension from the 'synthesisation processes' on which harmonisation rests today[20] and to create a new jurisprudential discourse based on an individualist horizon of values all contained within the code, thus making private law become instrumental in implementing a

[19] H Eidenmüller et al, 'The Common Frame of Reference for European Private Law – Policy Choices and Codification Problems' (2008) 28(4) *Oxford Journal of Legal Studies* 659 (criticising the DCFR, for example, for unduly expanding the grounds for contractual and tortious liability).

[20] I'd like to reiterate the importance of the position of JP Burgess, 'Culture and the Rationality of Law from Weimar to Maastricht in C Joerges and NS Ghaleigh (eds), *Darker Legacies of Law in Europe* (Oxford, Hart Publishing, 2003) 143, 165 on the value of 'resistance' to 'seamless conceptualisation' and 'homogenisation,' and specifically on 'adopting the rule of collectivisation *in order to preserve the right to dispute it*' (emphasis added) (for discussion see L Niglia, 'The Question Concerning the Common Frame of Reference' (2012) 18 *European Law Journal* 736) as the basis for constitutional authority, which, in relation to private law, means that there is a need to maintain the core dimension of *national* private law to the synthetisation operations. I have also defended this position in L Niglia, 'Beyond Enchantment: The Possibility of a New European Private Law' (2009) 28 *Yearbook of European Law* 60 (European private law must be about incorporating the legitimacy demands coming from the nation state) and in Niglia 'Pluralism in a New Key' (n 4) (arguing that normativity as inter alia articulated in the nation state must be a necessary component for the construction of a European private law legitimate).

set of aseptic, individualistic rules and principles. The disagreement between Whittaker and Basedow on the issue of subjection to the control of (un)fairness of standardised contractual terms such as those that provide for the 'opt-in' term (the term that allows the choice for the application of the would-be Optional Code) is a legitimate reaction to the proposed changes,[21] exactly because, as I argue in this chapter (if I may re-interpret the tenor of Whittaker's article in this way), it is about emphasising how the attempted break away from the established patterns of European private law interpretation, founded upon the constitutional virtues attached to the practice of 'synthesisation', is highly disruptive of established constitutional equilibria. On the basis of this analysis, I aim to show that all of the struggles currently emerging in the shadows of the proposed code – regarding the code's principles,[22] the content of the rules inserted in the code,[23] the mandatory rules contained in the code[24] and the 'opt-in' clause[25] – and many more that one can think of (for example, the culturalist struggle against a European civil code as it resurfaces in debates on the Optional Code) – [26] are discursive contexts out of which resistance patterns emerge vis-à-vis a European code as an instrument bound to sacrifice the integrity of the practices of constitutional synthesisation. They are the new juridical vocabularies in which the ever-present registers of individualism (today, market libertarianism) and of sociality (today, social welfarism) play out in juristic thought.[27] Shifting attention from (just) code to (also) jurisprudence makes it possible to capture these new variations on the old theme of the contested engagement of the juristic class in modern codification phenomena.[28]

* * *

The rest of this chapter consists of a two-step argument. First, I note how an optional code such as CESL would create significant and insurmountable obstacles to the operations of constitutional synthesisation that constitute the kernel of the living private law jurisprudence (section I), then I discuss a problematic de-constitutionalising and re-constitutionalising of private law as currently organised, implicated in the move to adopt an optional code such as CESL (section II).

[21] J Basedow, 'The Optional Instrument of European Contract Law: Opting-in through Standard Terms – A Reply to Simon Whittaker' (2012) 8 *European Review of Contract Law* 82; Simon Whittaker, 'The Optional Instrument of European Contract Law and Freedom of Contract' (2011) 7 *European Review of Contract Law* 371.

[22] See Hesselink (n 17); and ch 1.

[23] See Eidenmüller et al (n 19).

[24] See below at section I.A.

[25] See below at section I.C.

[26] P Legrand, 'Against a European Civil Code' (1997) 60 *Modern Law Review* 44.

[27] On the interface between vocabularies and positions/ideologies in the private law discourse, see ch 2.

[28] A theme that I explore below in ch 4.

I. REGIMENTING THE LIVING JURISPRUDENCE QUA EUROPE'S CONSTITUTIONAL PLURALISM

To aim at regimenting the European-wide structures of private law pluralism – the Directives and associated interpretative modes of engaging with them in the jurisprudential contexts considered in the previous chapter – through the proposed Optional Code entails a strategy of disregard for the 'clashing normativities' qua conflicting constitutional values that underlie the Directives' (non-) compliance processes and the European courts' re-creations of private law through balancing. For, from the vantage point of jurisprudential balancing as developed with regard to the Directives in cases such as *Fritz*, it would be much harder for judges to balance when the reference point is a code-book such as the proposed Optional Code, with its own set of crystallised principles and rules to be superimposed onto domestic legal systems. At the very least, it is counterintuitive to supplement code rules in an environment in which judges increasingly feel the need to act on the basis of arguments from policies and principles that they balance.[29] If Wilhelmsson is right when he holds that a code is too strict a structure to accommodate the variety of values that underlie modern welfarist private law, as I think he is,[30] then in an environment such as that of European private law, in which balancing takes hold of the imagination of judges, a code strikes at the heart of balancing by disrupting its operation – balancing and code-grammaticalism entail alternative ways of organising contemporary private law.[31] At another level of analysis, it must be acknowledged that the codification project is based on texts, from the DCFR to the proposed Optional Sales Law Code, that are ideologically biased towards accommodating free market processes (market libertarianism,[32] placing private autonomy above other values)[33] as opposed to a balancing jurisprudence that tends to be protectionist of consumers. Thus, consideration of both structure (*code corpus* as anti-plural *par excellence*) and substance (the value clashes at stake) leads one to argue that the codification move of the European legislature represents a blunt assault on the existing jurisprudential practices of constitutional synthesis and specifically on their output, that is, the heritage of material rights.

As a matter of fact, the stirrings of consciousness concerning the potentially adverse impact of the proposed optional code on the plural heritage of material

[29] On the balancing of policies and principles in European private law, see Niglia 'Taking Private Law Rights Seriously' (n 18).

[30] T Wilhelmsson, 'Varieties of Welfarism in European Contract Law' (2004) 10 *European Law Journal* 712.

[31] See, eg, D Kennedy, 'A Transnational Genealogy of Proportionality in Private Law' in Brownsword, Micklitz, Niglia and Weatherill (n 17) 214 (rise of balancing seen as disruptive of traditional code-based modes of thinking: 'The notion of interpreting a code through constitutional values leads eventually to the open acknowledgment of the potentially contradictory structure of private law'). For further discussion of this dichotomy see ch 4 and Epilogue.

[32] See ch 1.

[33] N Reich, 'Pluralism and Private Law in the Union' in Niglia (n 2) 73.

rights can be noted in various places. Examples that shed light on how the setting-up of a European code structure is tantamount to altering the deep constitutional structures of Europe's private law include: the debate about the role of mandatory rules were an optional code to be enacted and in particular the many implications of an optional code in terms of 'social dumping'; the debate about the role and function of default rules were an optional code to be enacted; and, always in relation to the eventuality of the enactment of an optional code, the debate about the role of 'choice' in 'opting in' the proposed CESL Optional Code. Let me now consider each of the three debates in turn. In each debate one can already sense a new interpretative climate that is being created by the proposed Optional Code. In the context of an expanding literature,[34] it is a climate in which scholars almost take for granted that this is a proposal that has serious chances for being approved, given that some kind of support exists at the level of the European Parliament. It is a climate in which scholars already discuss the possible impact of an enacted optional code on national laws, thus giving a sense of what would happen if an optional code were to be enacted. Interestingly, such issues are held to be so important that it has been noted how the association of German private law professors organised its *third* meeting in 55 years of existence to discuss the CESL Optional Code Proposal.[35] It is a climate in which scholars are slowly articulating critical narratives that, in my view, one can really make sense of more in terms of constitutionality and less in principled or doctrinal (such as the criticism regarding the ostracising of a set of private law principles, and the criticism coming from German scholars to the DCFR, both of which I have referred to earlier) or even culturalist (in polemical essays written before and independently of the Draft Common Frame of Reference and of CESL) terms.[36] It is to this complex debate that I refer to below, arguing that the proposed CESL Optional Code concretises a

[34] See, eg, n 35.

[35] See S Grundmann, 'CESL, Legal Nationalism or a Plea for Appropriate Governance' (2012) 8(3) *European Review of Contract Law* 241, 242: 'In April 2012, an extraordinary meeting of the German private law professors' association was organised – only the third in 55 years of existence! – dedicated to CESL (publication of the papers in the . . . *Archiv für die Civilistische Praxis*). This would seem to be a clear expression of the importance which German academia attributes to the question of an Optional EU Contract Law, and that all commentaries only addressed the flaws and the fundamental inadequacy of the proposal – without any focus on a comparison to the *Bürgerliches Gesetzbuch*. There was no opposition to an optional scheme as such, quite to the contrary.' The literature is large: see, eg, G Wagner and R Zimmermann, 'Vorwort: Sondertagung der Zivilrechtslehrervereinigung zum Vorschlag für ein *Common European Sales Law*' (2012) 212 *Archiv für die civilistische Praxis* 467 (with further contributions in the same issue); B Fauvarque-Cosson, 'Vers un droit commun européen de la vente' (2012) 188 *Recueil Dalloz* 34 et seq; R Zimmermann, 'Perspektiven des künftigen österreichischen und europäischen Zivilrechts: Zum Verordnungsvorschlag über ein Gemeinsames Europäisches Kaufrecht' (2012) *Juristische Blätter* 2 et seq; H Eidenmüller, N Jansen, E Kieninger, G Wagner and R Zimmermann, 'Der Vorschlag für eine Verordnung über ein Gemeinsames Europäisches Kaufrecht' (2012) *Juristenzeitung* 269 et seq; H Schulte-Nölke, F Zoll, N Jansen and R Schulze (eds), *Der Entwurf für ein optionales europäisches Kaufrecht* (Munich, Sellier, 2012); O Remien, S Herrler and P Limmer (eds), *Gemeinsames Europäisches Kaufrecht für die EU?* (Munich, CH Beck, 2012); 'Trenta giuristi europei sull'idea di codice europeo dei contratti' (2012) 1 *Contratto e Impresa/Europa* (special issue).

[36] For the culturalist approach see ch 4.

project whose ambitious objective is to change the living European private law from jurisprudence-centred to code-centred.[37]

A. Mandatory Rules

Mandatory rules are the backbone of domestic constitutional private laws. They are those rules-as-applied[38] that carry the weight of importance that entails obligatory compliance ('obligatory' in the sense of non-alterability via private law making) on the part of contractors. They are the chief, albeit not the only, instrument for regimenting institutionalised control on the exercise of private autonomy in order to prevent private parties from abusing it.[39] It is precisely such rules, which are so vital to the existing private law, that the CESL Optional Code Proposal targets in unprecedented ways. It is widely acknowledged that an optional code[40] would be bound to impact adversely on the range of mandatory rules as they exist in the nation state, in the sense that any of the national mandatory rules currently applicable to sale contracts would be bound to be displaced, and ultimately replaced, by the self-contained CESL Optional Code (in transborder sales transactions). Let me discuss this predicament in some detail. Below I note two major issues (replacement of domestic mandatory rules and the rise of the ideology of private governance) that are emerging in a debate to which the following pages aim to contribute. Let me discuss each issue in turn, while also noting their interconnectedness, given that both point to the problematic break away from the heritage of material rights as developed in the living jurisprudence of constitutional synthesisation,

First, a major critical position vis-à-vis the Optional Code stems from the substantive consideration that its impact would entail sacrificing the range of domestic mandatory rules otherwise typically applied to sales contracts when transborder in nature. These mandatory rules vary depending on each jurisdiction and may be, for example, pre-contractual information rules such as those that impose on the seller the duty to disclose a certain amount of information regarding the goods to be sold *or* liability rules. Critically, scholars object to the eventuality of a complete setting aside of domestic mandatory rules. In their view, this would lead to what they call 'social dumping'. By 'social dumping', they refer to the phenomenon whereby the elimination of the relevance of the range of domestic mandatory

[37] The problematic notion of 'European Union private law', as opposed to the more accurate notion of 'European private law' (see L Niglia, Review of *Cambridge Companion of European Union Law, ELR* 2011), fits well in with the strategy of the codifiers in that it completely disregards the role of the jurisprudential forces operating on the ground, only focusing on the upper echelon of Europeanisation rather than considering the developments affecting the terms of the interaction between the EU level and the national level.

[38] Niglia (n 3).

[39] ibid.

[40] Let me stress that my critique addresses the Optional Code on sales law (CESL), but it would equally apply to any other optional code incorporating further sectors of the DCFR, a path which is explicitly the intention of the codifiers to take (see Niglia, 'The Question' (n 20) 768–69).

rules applicable to sale contracts (when transborder in nature) providing for an opt-in clause would be bound to cause the lowering of key regulatory standards that protect the interests of weak contractors (and consumers) in each Member State, according to the domestic constitutional politics of social protection enshrined in private law systems.[41]

In contrast, there are strands of scholarship that defend the Optional Code as not raising any such social dumping concerns, since, they argue, sacrificing mandatory rules of domestic legal systems would be compensated and ultimately remedied by the code's institutionalisation of a new set of pan-European mandatory rules in lieu of domestic rules.[42] This is a scholarly position that reflects what the Memorandum to the Optional Code itself indicates. Specifically:

> In business-to-consumer transactions there would be no further need to identify the mandatory consumer protection provisions in the consumer's law, since the Common European Sales Law would contain fully harmonized consumer protection rules providing for a high standard of protection throughout the whole of the European Union.[43]

Both positions suggest a certain uneasiness with the code proposal, considering that both implicitly convey the idea that private law must revolve around a set of mandatory rules for it to be credible. I consider this debate to be entirely traceable to the 'ontological need' for private law to revolve around straightforward consideration of the relevance of collective values, since a private law that disposes of mandatory rules altogether would be self-defeating.[44] This consideration descends

[41] See, eg, M Hesselink, 'An Optional Instrument on EU Contract Law: Could it Increase Legal Certainty and Foster Cross-Border Trade?' *European Parliament, Policy Department, PE 425.642*, at 16–17; JW Kerber and S Grundmann, 'An Optional European Contract Law Code: Advantages and Disadvantages' (2006) 21 *European Journal of Law and Economics* 215; J Rutgers, 'An Optional Instrument and Social Dumping' (2006) *European Review of Contract Law* 199. For a summary of the view of an optional instrument as a tool for social dumping in the literature, see Fernando Gomez and Juan Jose Ganuza, 'The Economics of Harmonising Private Law through Optional Rules in Pluralism' in Niglia (n 2) 181–82 (arguing that the scholars who subscribe to the social dumping view believe that 'the optional instrument would be used – and imposed upon consumers – by firms involved in cross-border trade – or, if it is allowed, also in domestic transactions – only in order to escape higher levels of mandatory consumer protection, thus becoming an undesirable tool for lowering current levels of consumer rights').

[42] See, eg, in a theoretical study on optional codes in general, Gomez and Ganuza (n 41) 190 (addressing the question 'Is it possible for an optional instrument to be used willingly by firms if it contains rules conferring a higher level of protection than that existing in the consumer *acquis*, or even in countries with more exacting standards of consumer protection?' and arguing that it is possible for incorporating in an optional code a set of mandatory rules designed to ensure a higher level of protection than national mandatory standards, for example (at 194), arguing that, on certain conditions, 'it may be perfectly rational for a firm to use a European set of rules with a level of protection higher than all existing national standards, thus contradicting the iron law of social dumping'); O Bar-Gill and O Ben-Shahar, 'Regulatory Techniques in Consumer Protections: A Critique of European Consumer Contract Law' (2013) 50 *CMLR* 109 et seq (discussing mandatory rules contained in the CESL).

[43] See Memorandum of the CESL Proposal 2011, at 4: 'Consumers would benefit from better access to offers from across the European Union at lower prices and would face fewer refusals of sales. They would also enjoy more certainty about their rights when shopping cross-border on the basis of a single set of mandatory rules which offer a high level of consumer protection.'

[44] See B Lurger, 'A Radical View of Pluralism?' in Niglia (n 2) 176 ('States and citizens alike have a legitimate expectation to be subject to the mandatory rules in force in their political systems'). On collective values qua sociality see below, ch 4 and Epilogue.

from the recent history of the materialisation of private law as discussed in the previous chapter. Private law as a discipline has been constructed over the second half of the twentieth century and until today around the constitutional task of private law's materialisation. For it has been from the key operative practice of incorporating social values in the individualistic structures of private law that mandatory rules have originated, as shown by the absorption of protectionist judicial precedents into the AGBG (and, today, in the BGB), as discussed in chapter two. The preoccupation of scholarship with ensuring that mandatory rules as developed within national constitutional contexts remain in place is about defending this thrust of private law. As there is, contextually speaking, a social fabric in which conflicts unfold that need to be mediated, and as mandatory rules are justified in relation to that predicament, any attempt at abstracting from this context, that is, at decoupling so-called 'mandatory rules' from the social fabric, makes of any such 'mandatory rule' a sham.[45] Whilst much of the debate appears to be directed towards the interpretation of the CESL Optional Code's mandatory rules to be enforced in lieu of the existing range of mandatory rules, there is a more fundamental point that is of relevance to the issue of whether or not an optional code is acceptable in relation to the 'identity' of private law as a constitutional discipline. The point is that, viewed from the perspective of the Europeanness of private law, there is no credibility in an abstract rationality that determines the new mandatory rules independently of the national realm, unless one believes in the rationality of a European private law decoupled from the heritage of material rights engineered by the practices of the jurisprudence of constitutional synthesisation – a belief that betrays the deep constitutionality of private law in its European mode, whose historicity I have described and whose credibility I have defended above. Making sense of the debate over whether or not to dispose of national mandatory standards implies that one understands it for what it is, that is, a struggle regarding whether or not to maintain in place the existing constitutional private law, a struggle that manifests itself in the polemic over the Optional Code's potential 'social dumping' effects.

There is a second way in which the code proposal goes against the living law. At stake is not just the attempt to break away from the most visible product of the jurisprudence of constitutional synthesisation, the heritage of material rights contained in the mandatory rules (*pars destruens*), but a blunt attempt at replacing collective government (constitutional)[46] with private governance (*pars construens*). This should seriously worry those scholars who are voicing their critical

[45] This is not an argument against the possibility for developing legitimate European private law norms, but a warning that such norms should be crafted out of, and in relation to, the domestic realm in the ways discussed in ch 2 (that is, the practice of constitutional synthetisation – for example, in cases such as *Hamilton* and *Friz*, as recounted in ch 2). I am questioning the possibility of identifying, and the credibility of speculating about, mandatory rules in the abstract on the basis of acontextual economic and legal rationalities (*ex nihilo*) decoupled from social rationality (*ubi societas ibi ius*).

[46] See ch 2.

concerns vis-à-vis the CESL Optional Code Proposal as well as those who support the code move. Let me explain.

The strategic move towards disposing of domestic mandatory rules by freeing contractual transactions from them corresponds to a long-term goal of the European Commission, one that pre-dates the proposed Optional Code, for, in a previous proposal, the European Commission had already attempted to turn away from domestic mandatory rules. In 2005, a proposal was put forward for a Regulation of the European Parliament and the Council on the law applicable to contractual obligations, suggesting that the parties should be allowed to choose as the applicable law 'the principles and rules of the substantive law of contract recognised internationally or in the Community'.[47] By 'recognised internationally' is meant the product of private rule making,[48] that is, the 'body of rules relevant for business'.[49] This proposal was met with 'opposition by the Member States', which meant that it 'was dropped in the final compromise of the EU Institutions'.[50] The CELS Optional Code is a new chapter of an old story which sees the Commission continue to insist pursuing a goal that is central to its overall agenda in relation to private law matters. For the Optional Code's Proposal is about placing private rule making in the sovereign position to choose the whole range of contractual terms and conditions unrestricted by the operation of any of the body of domestic mandatory rules that would otherwise apply under the current international private law regime. The aim is to empower private parties to engineer a range of self-made private law rules for governing contractual relationships, subject to the scrutiny of the judge who, as discussed in chapter one, would only be bound by the rules and principles contained in the Optional Code, which are, in turn, in

[47] As noted by J Basedow, 'The State's Private Law and the Economy: Commercial Law as an Amalgam of Public and Private Rule-Making' (2008) 56(3) *American Journal of Comparative Law* 703, 720, commenting on the Proposal for a Regulation of the European Parliament and the Council on the law applicable to contractual obligations (Rome I), at 14, COM (2005) 650 final (15 December 2005).

[48] This is the context in relation to which Basedow (ibid) discusses that Commission's Proposal, holding that mandatory rules should be necessarily left with the state. Basedow interestingly discusses the role and nature of private rule-making (at 719). This deserves to be quoted in full: 'There is little hope that the dispute about the theoretical foundations of law in general and non-state law in particular will ever lead to a consensus. Private rule-making is a reality, yet there is also no doubt that the state may interfere with private rules by appropriate legislation or court decisions at any time. Given the risk of bias inherent in private rules, such state intervention may become necessary to restore the balance of rights and obligations. In this context, it is useful to identify the conditions that favor the emergence of private rules as well as those that make state law indispensable. The examples given above indicate that there are some matters which are left to state law by necessity but that in other areas private rule-making has a comparative advantage. Thus, mandatory provisions needed for the protection of markets or for the compensation of market failures can only be enacted by the state. In a similar vein, no private alternative is available in the field of rules on property rights. The adoption of dispositive contract law by the state is less urgent.'

[49] ibid 718.

[50] ibid 720. Whilst noting that 'a recital of the Rome I Regulation points out that it "does not preclude parties from incorporating by reference into their contract a non-State body of law"' (ibid 720, referring to the then Proposal for a Regulation of the European Parliament and the Council on the law applicable to contractual obligations (Rome I) – Outcome of the European Parliament's first reading, Doc 15832/07 (3 December 2007) 6), the current international private law regimes respects the value of mandatory rules and is therefore the target of the ongoing Commission's codification activities (see, eg, Memorandum to the Proposal for an Optional Sales Code, which summarises the current law).

themselves of a market-facilitating kind.[51] It all comes full circle. What is really interesting is to consider the kind of legal thought that stands behind this strategy as the discursive context out of which the Commission can confidently further it.

Behind the strategy of empowering private governance above 'collective government' in the form of the existing structures of constitutional private law is a rising literature that revolves around what has been called 'law market'.[52] This literature is by no means at the root the Commission strategy when this was initiated,[53] but, in recent years, it has undoubtedly become a significant factor in framing the cognitive conditions of the current codification phenomenon, reinforcing the long-term register of individualism rooted in the modern history of codification as re-enacted in present times. Belonging to this line of writings is the argument that the proposal for an Optional Code provides for a (new) set of mandatory rules that are no less protectionist than those that one can find at domestic level, as well as the casting of that argument in a highly abstract law-and-economic vocabulary that, in my view, overlooks contextual aspects that matter.[54] For law-and-economics scholarship adopts a free-market interpretation that reads the behaviour of market actors according to a particular view of efficiency thinking[55] rather than according to the plurality of often conflicting values that underlie consumer behaviour and that, as such, require explicit choices about constitutional values in the context of national social welfare constitutional settlements.[56] It all depends on which of the ever-present registers of private law interpretation, individualism or sociality, one adopts for 'reading' the relevant developments and for the acting out of them. Mandatory rules remind us of the centrality of a constitutional settlement for private law, that is, they are the product of true settlements that result out of 'dialogues' between scholarship and judges that happen to converge on rules that protect certain interests and classes of people in the logic of de-codification and of pluralisation, as discussed in chapter two. By contrast, professing the need for their disregard is the flipside of a 'philosophy' that contests the centrality of the collective in matters of private law and that proposes putting the 'individual' in the place of the collective instead.

I must now rephrase these notes in a more straightforward constitutional vocabulary, in order to emphasise the point concerning the constitutional dilemmas that the Optional Code's proposal must raise. Specifically, the Optional Code's encroachment upon mandatory rules that would follow enactment would not just consist in 'social dumping', as critical scholarship rightly maintains, but also in bringing about what can be referred to as 'constitutional dumping'. This is

[51] For details and examples, see ch 1.

[52] See the exchange between J Smits, 'A Radical View on Pluralism' in Niglia (n 2) 161 (upholding the law-market view) and Lurger (n 44) 173 (critical of such a view).

[53] Niglia (n 3).

[54] I am thinking of the 'argument from the social fabric' that I have put forward above.

[55] See, again, the exchange between Smits (n 52) 161 (upholding such a view) and Lurger (n 44) 173 (critical of such a view).

[56] *cf* J Wilhelmsson, 'Varieties of Welfarism' (2004) 10 *European Law Journal* 712 (considering the plurality of values that underlie consumer legislation) and note above the 'argument from the social fabric'.

because it would entail re-creating the domestic structures of constitutional private law[57] by placing some set of individualistic private law rules and principles, as chosen by the networks of European scholars and incorporated in the code-text, at a higher level of authority relative to the socially orientated rules in force in national jurisdictions. The enactment of the code would alter the hierarchy of values embodied in the existing webs of mandatory rules as organised within the plurality of national private law constitutional systems. In this way, social and constitutional dumping effects would be disruptive of the existing (European) jurisprudential pluralism in that they would alter it by dismantling the diverse basis of the domestic jurisprudence of constitutional synthesisation – by playing down the range of mandatory rules as one finds them in domestic jurisdictions.[58] It is a diversity that must be defended not just because it is grounded in the heritage of national constitutional private laws, but because it rests on the European-wide practices of constitutional synthesisation based on the ongoing adaptation and revision of values belonging to the (national) social fabric. This is all the more problematic, considering what one can call the foreseeable 'double impact' following the enactment of the Optional Code, for, as all domestic laws will be subject to adaptation to the code and not just sale contracts (transborder),[59] the code-based jurisprudence is bound to become applicable to the whole of the private law relations (non-sale contracts, tort and property, as well as any other areas that are indirectly impacted upon) within the nation state. There is even an article in the Optional Code's proposal that 'enables' Member States to apply the code to 'internal' (qua national) sales transactions as well, as opposed to applying it merely to cross-border transactions.[60] No doubt the codifiers must have in mind, and expect, an eventuality of that kind to occur spontaneously, so to speak, that is, independently of the national legislature's choice to extend the new code's regime to entirely national sales transactions.

On closer inspection, the effect of enacting the CESL Optional Code would not just be to alter value hierarchies (yielding a 'new' hierarchy), but to subvert them altogether. For the superimposition of European code-based 'mandatory' rules (and of the code's optional rules, as I argue below at Section B) in lieu of domestic mandatory rules would mean that one of the reference points of the twin processes of law's re-creations (which obviously operate on two levels – that of supra-

[57] For analysis and genealogy of these structures, see Niglia (n 3); and ch 1 above.

[58] Scholars have been raising criticism even against the mandatory rules contained in CESL (see H Eidenmüller, 'What Can Be Wrong with an Option? An optional Common European Sales Law as a Regulatory Tool (20130 50 *CMLR* 69, at 80: 'the proposed CESL is . . . clearly a defective product. This is principally because the proposed CESL contains many mandatory and inefficient rules'); Bar-Gill and Ben-Shahar (n 42) 115 (analytically considering mandatory rules contained in the CESL against the test whereby 'consumer protection comes at a price'). This is about repeating a classical criticism elevated against mandatory rules that, however, should take into account not just 'theory' (asymmetric information, imperfect rationality, at 115), but also the historical, constitutional conditions in which private law making develops, considering that decisions about mandatory rules develop out of such contexts.

[59] See English Law Society as cited below at n 79.

[60] Article 13 Optional Code for Sales Law Proposal.

national rules and that of national rules) would be bluntly eliminated. This would drive legal thought and practice away from the current plural practice of re-creating law and towards monistic modes of interpretation that are only reliant on the code. In setting aside the heritage of domestic mandatory rules, an Optional Code would entail dismantling law's re-creations based on the key role of mandatory rules, such as the mandatory system of protection contained in the AGBG as referred to in a remarkable BGH decision that rejected the application of the Unfair Terms Directive in Germany – [61] in the sense that, at a minimum, interpretative battles would be bound to unfold in which some legal actors will attempt to keep alive the heritage of mandatory rules, whilst others would embrace the aseptic logic of (mandatory) rules contained in the Optional Code. To give a flavour of the potential disintegrative effects[62] of the changes entailed by the enactment of an optional code, let me recall one major case of the CJEU. In *Ausbanc*, the Spanish courts referred questions to the CJEU regarding whether the choice of the national legislature not to implement Article 4(2) of the Unfair Terms Directive, as a means of ensuring a greater protection to the consumer in relation to the rounding-up of interests on loans, could be held to be compatible with EU law and specifically Article 8 of the Directive (minimum harmonisation). The Court held that 'greater protection' at the national level is allowed, implicitly assuming that domestic mandatory standards embody values that the Directive cannot do away with. In an interpretative environment in which an optional code would operate, the interpretative game would be completely changed, for the codifiers aim at centering interpretation only around the articles of the Optional Code and at playing down and ultimately excluding any domestic mandatory rules and ancillary domestic legal principles. This being their strategy, constitutional private law traditions are exposed to the risk of being silenced.

The gravity of the proposed code-based assault on the existing range of national mandatory rules is particularly evident in the position whereby limits on private autonomy should be placed through super-mandatory rules only and not through mandatory rules, the former being 'the fundamental values of the national legal order that cannot be made inapplicable by choice of a foreign law' (what is called public policy or *ordre public* in current private international law).[63] This suggestion for further reform is only a consequence of the overall premise of the proposed code-based optionality regime (in terms of magnifying private power) and is entirely dependent on a particular, and contested,[64] theoretical position, arguably traceable to neo-liberal assumptions.[65] It is neither historically founded nor

[61] See ch 1.

[62] See, eg, Christian Joerges, On the Legitimacy of Europeanising Private Law: Considerations on a Justice-Making Law for the EU Multi-level System' (2003) 7(3) *Electronic Journal of Comparative Law*, http://www.ejcl.org/ejcl/73/art73-3.html; Niglia (n 3).

[63] Smits (n 52) 169.

[64] See Lurger (n 44).

[65] See ibid for a critique of the position of Smits along these lines (arguing at 176: 'If ... "radical legal pluralism" is not efficient, does not expand the citizens' freedoms in a significant way, but seriously endangers the rights of all weaker parties to private law relationships, one last question might be allowed: in a Europe after a world financial and economic crisis, in the midst of State budgetary and

constitutionally justified. First, it is not grounded in history, and is indeed counter-historical, because the second half of the past century has seen states create a private international law system based on the respect for mandatory rules.[66] The position that defends the shift to a regime based only on super-mandatory rules (to use the vocabulary that I am adopting in this book, 'super-mandatory laws' are meant to be of a much lower 'protectionist quality' than mandatory rules) implies that setting aside the existing range of mandatory rules would after all be not so grave, given that there would remain a set of super-mandatory rules to take care of certain public interests. Second, the suggestion goes against the grain of the constitutional organisation of private law in nation states. This is true because mandatory rules channel key political choices that define the very existence of the nation state as democratic body politics,[67] and any attempt at having a set of super-mandatory rules replace mandatory rules in relation to private international law functionalities would amount to a de facto (let alone de jure) abolition of mandatory rules. The trouble is that an Optional Code would be about opening the gates for this kind of strategy, that is, the strategy of not only displacing domestic mandatory rules but also of replacing them with super-mandatory rules that limit private autonomy only in a few exceptional cases. According to this 'radically pluralist' view, one should see the world as rotating around the consideration that states are under increasing competition from other states; that states, if they wish to keep labour and capital within their territories, need to provide for legal frameworks that enable the accommodation of the contractual parties' 'overriding interest in the design of their legal relationship' – parties who, in this view, would otherwise move to other states 'or seek refuge in arbitration or in other alternative dispute mechanisms'.[68] There seems to be no room at all for the requirements of the public interest as contained in the mandatory rules in such a world in which all that matters is 'information' and 'choice'. Disposing of mandatory rules and placing private power at the centre of the legal universe is a strategy that turns arbitrariness into justified law making, repeating a historical pattern;[69] the Optional Code is no innocent tool of law making.[70]

debt crises, most of them having been brought about by the lack of necessary legal restrictions on financial markets and on State governments, should we really have so many positive expectations as regards the realisation of another neo-liberal idea, in the creation or radical liberalisation of an additional market – that of legal orders in the area of private law?').

[66] See, eg, ibid 175–76.

[67] ibid 176.

[68] J Smits, 'Party Choice and the Common European Sales Law, or: How to Prevent the CESL from Becoming a Lemon on the Law Market (2012) 50 *CMLR* 51, 52, inter alia referring to Eric A O'Hara and Larry E Ribstein, *The Law Market* (Oxford, Oxford University Press, 2009); H Eidenmueller 'Recht als Produkt' 64 *Juristenzeitung* (2009) 641.

[69] See below, 'Conclusion', in relation to the work of Gioele Solari; note Karsten Schmidt, *Lex mercatoria: Allheilmittel? Rätsel? Chimäre?* in Junichi Murakami et al (eds), *Globalisierung und Recht* (Berlin, de Gruyter, 2007) 153, 165 168 (on business law as having both 'authoritarian and anarchical roots', as quoted in Basedow (n 47) 718).

[70] For the position that state authorities should be exclusively entitled to issue 'mandatory provisions needed for the protection of markets or for the compensation of market failures', see Basedow (n 47) 719.

B. Default Rules

Once the parties have opted into the would-be Optional Code, according to the legislative plan, the only law applicable would be the one contained in the 'comprehensive and self-contained' Optional Code, that is, *all* code rules, whether mandatory or 'dispositive' (or, to put it another way, default). Also included in the code-based applicable law are default rules, that is, rules that the law provides for as a benchmark that the parties may adhere to or dispose of as they wish[71] and that 'liberate courts from having to decide which obligations are reasonable and which are not' as a whole rather than selectively.[72] In this context, 'default' rules are the major body of rules of the Optional Code other than those explicitly named, or implicitly taken to be, 'mandatory'.[73] This raises a dilemma.

Parties would be exposed to the application of any of the rules contained in the Optional Code taken to be 'dispositive', that is, all of the rules that are deemed not to be mandatory, for CESL default rules would become the reference point for judicial decisions regarding which reasonable standards to enforce.[74] All domestic default rules (that is, the whole body of domestic default rules and principles *ex hypothesis* applicable to sales contracts) should be disregarded by the judge minded to apply the Optional Code. For example, the argument referred to by the litigants in *Freiburger*, based on a German default rule such as the principle of contemporary performance of the parties' obligations, could no longer be relied upon before the courtrooms in disputes falling within the remit of CESL. In any case, any of the legal material coming out of domestic default rules that the judge might wish to deploy (if he were minded to enforce reasonable obligations as provided for in domestic default rules) would have to counter the interpretative constraints descending from code-based arguments as formalised in the 'prohibition' coming from the duty to apply the Optional Code on its own contained in Article

[71] In contrast to mandatory rules that cannot be deviated from. On default rules and on related theoretical discussion, see L Niglia, 'Standard Form Contracts in Europe and North America – One Hundred Years of Unfair Terms?' in C Rickett and T Telfer (eds), *International Perspectives on Consumers' Access to Justice* (Cambridge, Cambridge University Press, 2003) 101.

[72] For this interpretation, see T Ackermann, 'Public Supply of Optional Standardized Consumer Contracts: A Rationale for the Common European Sales Law?' (2013) 50 *CMLR* 11, 14 (contrasting the optional code as providing for default rules 'as a whole' with the classical concept of a contract code allowing for selective choice of the default rules). My critique of the adverse impact of the optional code on default rules is motivated by the difference between the current system of private international law, which allows for private parties to deviate from domestic default rules (see, eg, Lurger (n 44) 176: 'foreign legal orders may be chosen by domestic parties to remove any *default* rule of the domestic system'), and the system that would be inaugurated by enacting the optional sales law code, which would entail the setting aside of all domestic default rules.

[73] For an analysis of the content of the mandatory rules contained in the CESL, see Bar-Gill and Ben-Shahar (n 42).

[74] R Craswell, 'Property Rules and Liability Rules in Unconscionability and Related Doctrines' (1993) 60 *University of Chicago Law Review* 1, 12–14 and 32–34 (default rules are those that liberate courts from having to decide which obligations are reasonable and which are not). For example, see Article 89 CESL (in relation to 'change of circumstances', a court may 'adapt the contract in order to bring it into accordance with *what the parties would reasonably have agreed at the time of contracting if they had taken the change of circumstances into account*' (emphasis added)).

4(1) of the proposal, which in turn echoes the command of Article 5 of the French Civil Code.[75] This is because, as a (comprehensive and self-contained) *code corpus* is at stake, legal actors who are critical of code-based interpretations and are interested in furthering alternative interpretations to those allegedly based on the code would find themselves in a weak interpretative position.[76] Were the Optional Code to be enacted, in relation to any contracts falling within its remit, a code-led interpretative climate would develop in which interpreters would be empowered if they adopted code-based interpretations, but disempowered if they did not, which would be bound to produce the effect of marginalising the default rules of national law whilst implementing those contained in the code. Interestingly, there are courts in Sweden and Poland that have already spontaneously relied on the default rules of the DCFR and of the Principles of European Contract Law, such as rules on the termination of business contracts and on compensation for loss of holiday enjoyment.[77] *En bref*, organising private law around the judicial enforcement of the range of default rules contained in the proposed code on an exclusive basis would be bound to endanger, and radically stop, the practice of constitutional synthesisation whenever it entails the combined use of any national and European laws that the judge considers to be relevant, including reliance on the body of national default rules understood as benchmarks for reasonableness. Scholars have rightly pointed to the problem of the relative indeterminacy of the standard of reasonableness in applying the European code script as a result of the frequent use in the DCFR of the term 'reasonable'.[78] However, here I am pointing to the deeper problem of cutting the ties of private law from the implicit standards of reasonableness of domestic traditions, whilst replacing them with those contained in the Optional Code.

This 'default rules' issue is a specific problem that some of the insiders to the codification process have been pointing to in open statements levelled against the enactment of a European code. I am referring to the consideration of the English Law Society, whereby the regulation of cross-border contracts and their performance is connected to different areas of law, such as tort law and property law, areas which would still need to be governed by the laws of Member States.[79] Thus,

[75] Article 4 Code Civil reads: 'The judge who refuses to judge, under pretext of the silence, obscurity or insufficiency of the law, will be subject to prosecution for denial of justice.' Article 4(1) and (2) CESL (Annex I) reads: 'the Common European Sales Law is to be interpreted autonomously and in accordance with its objectives and the principles underlying it. Issues within the scope of the Common European Sales Law but not expressly settled by it are to be settled in accordance with the objectives and the principles underlying'.

[76] See ch 1 (discussing the 'disempowerment' entailed in the *code corpus*-based 'normalisation' effect).

[77] As to the DCFR see, eg, Case T 3-08 Swedish Supreme Court (Hoegsta domstolen) of 3 November 2009 in case note by M Grochowski 9/1 ERCL (2013), 95, applying Article IV.E. 2:302(3) DCFR as a gap-filling norm to a dispute on the termination of a business resale contract); as to the PECL, see Polish Supreme Court of 19 November 2010 III CZP 79/10 (OSNC 2011, vol 4, position 41 (Unidroit and PECL as grounds for allowing compensation for loss of holiday enjoyment (case referred to in M Grochowski 9/1 ERCL (2013), 95, at fn 10).

[78] Eidenmüller et al (n 19).

[79] See the Law Society (UK) at: http://international.lawsociety.org.uk/files/LSEW_FINAL_Contract-Law-Response_5_12_10_0.pdf.

commentators have noted that it would be inevitable that many of the tort, property and contract law notions (both mandatory and default) as applicable in general to private law will become relevant to the interpretative operations that engage with applying the proposed code. What they fear must be that the setting-up of a disciplinary interpretative structure such as the Optional Code would make it an impracticable exercise to refer to 'linked' domestic default rules in the context of those changing interpretative rules of the game that follow enactment of a *code corpus* – empowering those who uphold code-based arguments above those who do not. This is a criticism that comes from England, but that must a fortiori apply to the case of continental private law jurisdictions, accustomed as they are, because of the de-codification practices, to interpretative links between various groups of norms wherever they are located, from code to special legislation, as discussed in chapter two – links that remain in place even in our de-codified age, considering the existing weak systematisation practices discussed in chapter two. Hence, the polemic started by the English Law Commission vis-a-vis the European code proposal adds further criticism related to the legislative attempt to interrupt, via a code, the links between mandatory and default private law norm in the context of sociality as constituted in national realms. Once again, the registers of individualism and of sociality play out in juristic thought, defining its key features and seeing jurists defending the register of sociality (in this case, the web of domestic default rules constituting the social realm of private law) against the legislative attempt at implementing the register of individualism (market libertarianism) via blocking off the operation of the repertoire of reasonable standards of obligations contained in nationally provided default contract rules.

From this vantage point, the constitutional *problématique* entailed in the encroachment of the Optional Code upon national jurisdictions must be articulated so as to include default rules. I have argued above that the superimposition of European code 'mandatory rules' in lieu of domestic mandatory rules would mean that one of the reference points of the practice of constitutional synthesisation (the core dimension of national private law social, expressing itself via the heritage of material rights contained in the mandatory rules) would be bluntly eliminated, driving legal thought and practice away from the plural patterns of law's re-creations and towards monistic modes of interpretations that are only reliant on the code-text. The same argument must apply to default rules, for the enactment of the code would mean eliminating another reference point on which the jurisprudence of constitutional synthesisation is based, that is, the core dimension of national (social) private law, expressing itself via reasonable standards of obligations as contained in the default rules. This has constitutional implications, in that the Optional Code would be bound to dismantle the fertile terrain in which private law rules flourish in domestic and European constitutional contexts via the practices of constitutional synthesisation. As in the case for mandatory rules, here social dumping equally would lead to constitutional dumping, considering that many of the default rules in vogue in national laws incorporate sets of relevant social values, an example being the principle of contemporaneous performance based on the BGB as referred to in *Freiburger* insofar as it is relevant to defending the position of consumers.[80] From this vantage point, the attempt to close interpretation off from the existing non-code sources of law, such as domestic default rules, must rest on questionable grounds.

C. Choice

Up to this point, I have dealt with the deep meaning of the strategic entrenchment of private governance in transborder sales transactions and the constitutional dilemmas that are posed as a result. Let me now consider one more problem of constitutionality entailed in the project of enacting the Optional Code, that is, the possibility of subjecting the contractual term that elects the Optional Code as the applicable law[81] to the test of fairness *ex* the Unfair Terms Directive insofar as contained in a standard form contract as it is typically the case.[82] At issue here is another key dimension to the Optional Code, that is, 'choice' understood as a quintessential indication of how the making of the Optional Code is about attempting to shelter private power from public intervention. For the legislative attempt at instantiating the power to 'choose' for 'opting in' is, at root, about seeking to legitimise the authorisation to enable private parties' 'choice' to opt out of national mandatory and default rules that would otherwise apply to transborder sales law contracts – 'inclusion' as entailed in the opt-in regime is at root about 'exclusion'. The related question that I address in this section concerns the issue of whether such an authorising act should be left entirely to the discretion of private parties or should instead be subjected to the control of unfairness as critically argued in the literature. I am referring to a critical exchange between Basedow and Whittaker (that is, to a critical reply of Basedow to Whittaker's article),[83] which substantiates one more strand of academic 'polemic' that, alongside those above on 'social dumping' and on 'reasonableness', indicates rising concerns about the constitutionality of the Optional Code – concerns that, let me stress again, I am reframing using the vocabulary of a constitutional critique based on what I have analysed in chapter two as the pluralist practices of constitutional synthesisation.

Specifically, the question addressed in Whittaker's article is whether a choice-of-law standard term electing an optional instrument (such as the CESL) should be immune from judicial review under the test of fairness of the Unfair Terms Directives. Whittaker specifically argues that the relevant choice-of-law term

[80] Another example being *Friz* (n 6), as discussed in ch 2 (a judge-made rule regarding reasonable distribution of risks in contractual arrangements).

[81] Article 3 CESL reads: 'The parties may agree that the Common European Sales Law governs their cross-border contracts for the sale of goods, for the supply of digital content and for the provision of related services within the territorial, material and personal scope as set out in Articles 4 to 7.'

[82] Niglia (n 3).

[83] See above, n 21.

should be subject to the fairness test. [84] Basedow takes issue with this view, proposing what can be called the 'immunisation thesis', based on his own interpretation of Directive 93/13 and of the applicable rules on private international law. The opinions of the two scholars differ with respect to the characterisation of the choice-of-law standard term as a term arising out of a contractual practice (standard form contracts) marked by inequality of bargaining powers, as implicitly held by Whittaker – a characterisation that Basedow rejects as being an 'argument from policy' that, in his view, should be left outside the realm of the law (Basedow defends his thesis on the basis of articles of law such as Article 1(2) of the Unfair Terms Directive). One can, and should, re-read this dispute in the constitutional terms discussed in this chapter. It appears that authorising private parties to opt out of domestic law entirely, including immunising the 'opt in' from the control of fairness of the Unfair Terms Directive, corresponds to a radicalised position of denial of the application of key constitutional standards (that is, those standards enshrined in the practices of the jurisprudence of constitutional synthesisation)[85] to operations of private power such as standard form contracts. For private parties would be entitled to avoid the control of fairness of standardised terms that is central to the justice project of private law in the nation state and, now, as increasingly internalised in EU law via the case law of the CJEU and of the domestic courts acting in co-operation with the CJEU.[86] Immunisation would mean that the replacement of collective choice by private choice as entailed in the proposed Optional Code would be very profound in terms of its scope. This because it would be about denying the constitutionality enshrined in the dynamics of the production of mandatory rules out of the social fabric through 'collective decisions' that crystallise sets of mandatory protectionist standards in standard form contracts and place them beyond the reach of ordinary private law qua private autonomy – to use a constitutional analogy applicable to private law.[87] Judges defending established constitutional standards applied to private law under the paradigm of welfare-state materialisation would be disempowered. This is again a way in which the practice of the jurisprudence of constitutional synthesisation would be endangered, for it is about empowering the few (private parties) to make decisions for the many (the collective). At root, this is about assuming that individual market actors should exercise full control over the content of contracts and of property rules – the 'law market' rather than the 'republic of law' would become the province of transborder sales contracts.[88]

[84] Whittaker (n 21) interprets the test of (un-)fairness as being protectionist, a position in line with the case law of the CJEU (eg, Case C-484/08 *Caja de Ahorros y Monte de Piedad de Madrid v Asocación de Usuarios de servicios bancarios (Ausbanc)* [2010] ECR I) which should be contrasted with the overall Commission's private law agenda as discussed in ch 1.

[85] An example being *Ausbanc* (ibid; fairness applied towards ensuring protectionism of the consumer in standard contracts) as discussed above.

[86] See, eg, ibid; and above, ch 2, albeit that implementation happens in various, often conflicting ways depending on which country one considers. For details, see Niglia (n 3).

[87] On the parallelism between private law and constitutionalism in this sense, see ch 4.

[88] For a critique of the 'law market' theory as re-proposed in European private law literature, see, eg, ME Storme, 'The Foundations of Private *Law* in a Multi-level Structure: Balancing, Distribution of

Norbert Reich has stressed the point about the hierarchical structure implicated in the Optional Code when commenting on the consideration that optional codes are about placing 'autonomy' on a higher level and above other conflicting values.[89] 'Giving choice' to contractors in cross-border sale contracts means enabling private governance to prevail above public governance. By 'public governance', I mean the public structures devoted to the regulation of private law as developed in the context of the jurisprudence of constitutional synthesisation (national and European, as discussed in chapter two). By 'private governance', I mean instead the opinion made official in CESL, whereby the structures of private power should be enabled to rule 'without limitations'. This amounts to constitutionalise private power as a force of its own, that is, independently of the requirements of collective qua public governance. I say 'constitutionalising private power', having in mind the work of those rational choice writers who pursue the strategy of 'constitutional economics'[90] *or* those who pursue instead a renewed version of an ordo-liberal kind of constitutionalism,[91] for both strategies lend themselves to make intelligible what is happening here, that is, the strategy of enabling the constitution of private governance as a realm of unlimited private autonomy, over which the collective should exercise a minimum level of control, if any at all.[92] At this level of analysis, the proposed replacement of the jurisprudence of constitutional synthesisation is deeper in terms of scope than one would think, considering that it is about pursuing an alternative constitutional strategy to the one that characterises the living law (jurisprudential pluralism as enshrined in the practice of constitutional synthesisation) in its national and European modes of development. This becomes all the more evident if one looks at the character of the phenomenon under consideration. Whereas the jurisprudence of constitutional synthesisation stands on the shoulders of collective constitutional self-authorship,[93] the paradigm of market choice stands on the shoulders of private 'constitutional' self-authorship. Whereas the former is institutional (courts,

Law-making Power and other Constitutional Issues' in Brownsword, Micklitz, Niglia and Weatherill (n 17) 379, 391 (arguing that 'we need a "Market Law" rather than a "Law Market"').

[89] Reich (n 34) 76–77: 'The proponents of such optional regimes defend them with reference to "private autonomy", without realising that they contradict their pluralist argument, because they put autonomy in a hierarchical "first place", that is, beyond possible limitations imposed by public policy and the like.'

[90] See the work of James M Buchanan (see eg James M Buchanan, *Constitutional Economics* (Oxford and Cambridge, MA, Blackwell, 1991)) as discussed in G Teubner, *Constitutional Fragments* (Oxford, Oxford University Press, 2012) 33–34 (discussing the failures of constitutional economics thinking in relation to their 'exclusively' drawing 'upon rational principle choice').

[91] See E-J Mestmäcker, *Wirtschaft und Verfassung in der Europäischen Union* (Baden-Baden, Nomos, 2004) as discussed in Teubner (n 90) 30–33 (relating to the 'intolerably narrow economism' of ordo-liberal constitutionalism).

[92] I am also thinking of North American strands of legal economic thought that praise the virtue of the market as borrowed in current European debates on codification: see Smits (n 52) (drawing on writings that further the idea of a so-called 'law market'; proposing to limit intervention only for protecting super-mandatory rules, an aspect discussed earlier in this chapter).

[93] On the need for self-authorship in relation to transnational law, including private law, see M La Torre, 'The Poverty of Global Constitutionalism' in Niglia (n 2) 53 et seq.

legislators), the latter is just individualistic (private parties' choice). Whereas the former places trust in the tradition of law standing behind judicial interpretation, the latter places trust in the rationalism of choice as an abstract process organised around economic qua efficiency categories interpreted so as to justify whatever individual contractors wish to do. Whereas the former is sceptical of the terms included in standardised contracts as potentially leading to substantial inequality and injustice, the latter treats contractual terms as written by private parties as favourable, regardless of their being located in a standardised contract or in a 'fully negotiated' (no unequal bargaining powers) contract. The list could continue. This is the new vocabulary in which the registers of individualism and of sociality are re-engineered, the defining epistemic context in which the issue of how to re-organise private law is currently being addressed and in which socially orientated concerns are being voiced against the proposed individualist model of the Optional Code.

* * *

To synthesise our discussion up to this point – the superimposition of European code-based 'mandatory' rules in lieu of domestic mandatory rules would mean that one of the reference point of the practice of constitutional synthesisation would be bluntly disposed of, driving legal thought and practice away from the existing practice of law's plural re-creations and towards monistic modes of interpretations that are only reliant on the code-text. Equally, setting aside national default rules would mean eliminating another key reference point of the jurisprudence of constitutional synthesisation, this time no longer one that is necessary for the re-creational interpretative acts (the case of mandatory rules as currently incorporated in decisions such as *Ausbanc*),[94] but a reference point that the judge, under the current type of harmonisation regime, may make recourse to at any time that the judge is committed to enforce reasonable standards based on domestic default rules. To construct private choice as operating autonomously from a control of fairness (based on the Unfair Terms Directive and the corresponding national private law rules) would be bound to alter the practice of constitutional synthesisation in one more respect. For it would threaten to replace the work of the judge and of the jurist, understood as constitutional subjects in the private law arena articulating and synthetising the plurality of values of the national welfare-state paradigms, with that of the contractors (businesses or consumers) who, independently of any institutional constraints, 'autonomously' deliberate' out of the 'superior market-logic of 'informed choice'.[95] This is because judges would be asked to play the limited role of passive enforcers of the individualist rights

[94] In the sense that *Ausbanc* is a case in which national legislation more protectionist than the Directive (due to not having implemented Article 4(2) of the Unfair Terms Directive) is validated by the CJEU, which entails absorbing national mandatory standards into EU law.

[95] On 'consumers' as increasingly considered as if they were 'businesses' making informed choices see eg critically H Micklitz, 'The Explulsion of the Concept of Protection from the Consumer Law and the Return of Social Elements in the Civil Law', EUI Working Papers Law 2012/03, at 2.

contained in the code. *En bref*, implementing the Optional Code successfully would be the equivalent of eliminating the possibility of plural re-creations altogether, as all would take place at the level of monistic qua grammaticalist modes of interpretation that are only reliant on the European code-text. According to the proponents of the Optional Code, private law would have to be re-professionalised once more (*tecnicizzazione*), this time taking distance from the living jurisprudence towards a mechanical jurisprudence bounded by code-based rules and principles; the scholar would become the oracle of the code-text, the judge *bouche de la loi*. The gravity of the project of dismantling the existing jurisprudence of constitutional synthesisation is such that it deserves further consideration. To this end, in the remainder of this chapter, I expand my constitutional critique.

D. Further Criticism Towards the Proposed Optional Code – the Code vs Parliaments

Before continuing with the analysis of the constitutional tensions between the code-project and the living law, it is worth mentioning that the emerging struggles against the proposed code, as recounted above, are coupled with a further set of struggles between, on the one hand, the EU legislative institutions involved in the codification project[96] and, on the other hand, the national parliaments. These are clashes that are 'internal' to the legislative component as it operates in plural Europe and that only add to the many tensions between legislation and jurisprudence, as noted above. However, many of the scholarly voices critical of the Optional Code no doubt must have fed into domestic parliamentarian debates. This side of the story reinforces the tenor of the scholarly struggles against the code move. Interestingly, various parliaments have been raising a number of key constitutional objections vis-à-vis the proposed Regulation for an Optional Code on sales,[97] in particular, the critique whereby the Optional Code would be in breach of the proportionality principle must be made intelligible in relation to the many weaknesses of the project in constitutional terms, as discussed above. For it is about stressing the value of respecting the credentials of the national dimension, a value defended in the courtrooms through the jurisprudential practices of constitutional synthesising – insofar as proportionality is about warning against any EU legislative activities that arguably do what is not suitable *or* what may be deemed to be suitable, but that could nevertheless have been achieved by less intrusive means.[98] The same analogical argument applies to another set of objec-

[96] See ch 1.

[97] See H Micklitz, 'Monistic Ideology versus Pluralistic Reality – Towards a Normative Design for European Private Law' in Niglia (n 2) 29; L Niglia, 'Of Constitutionality and Private Consumer Law in Europe' (2012) 4 *Journal of European Consumer and Market Law* 223.

[98] See for further discussion L Niglia, 'Of Harmonisation and Fragmentation – The Problem of Legal Transplants and the Europeanisation of Private Law' (2010) 2 *Maastricht Journal of European and Comparative Law* 116 et seq; Niglia (n 97); L Niglia, 'Of Jurisdictional Balancing' in Brownsword, Micklitz, Niglia and Weatherill (n 17) 309 et seq.

tions coming from the parliaments and based on the defence of subsidiarity, which in turn echoes objections levied against those previous harmonisation initiatives considered to have been of dubious constitutional validity for failing subsidiarity, such as had been the case for the critical voices raised during the drafting of the Unfair Terms Directive.[99]

The voices of national parliaments equally count as a strictly speaking 'political' defence of the national layers of private law, conveying 'from the outside' to the juridical world the value of respecting the credentials of the national dimension. These national positions must be made intelligible in the classical vocabulary of the 'ontology' of political power, that is, as a defence of political 'voice' against 'technocratic engineering'. [100] They represent objections to the strategy that aims at abolishing the national layer of the existing 'dual level' (both national and EU) structure of private law.

The constitutional and political objections of parliaments that I am considering are arguably equivalent in importance to a line of decisions of the national constitutional courts, in particular the BVerfG,[101] insofar as they are about defending the deep pluralist character of integration against any attempt to make it into a unilateral process centered on the 'autonomy' of the CESL Optional Code regime. Moreover, insofar as the critical voices from scholarship raising constitutional concerns have only been 'half-made' or 'half-heard', that is, not fully elaborated in the constitutional terms that I have proposed in the preceding pages, national parliaments must have felt that they had to fill a gap, including deploying a constitutional vocabulary that explicitly draws on the standards of proportionality and subsidiarity. The 'half-made' critical reaction of scholarship vis-à-vis the Optional Code has translated into an open political battle (national parliaments versus the code legislative move) that is not really mediated by an active use of constitutional material. Awareness of the constitutional aspects implicated in the Optional Code's project should go towards re-enacting the role of scholarship so as to exercise its role of 'filtering' key political sensibilities. This would inter alia contribute towards avoiding further fragmentation as inevitably implicated in a predicament in which the Commission might insist on the enactment of the Optional Code despite the stance taken by national parliaments.[102] There is need for a renewed role of scholarship, the features of which I will discuss further in the remainder of the book.

[99] See Niglia (n 3).

[100] For a recent re-articulation of this dichotomy in the broader landscape of European integration, see C Offe, 'Europe Entrapped' (2013) 19(5) *European Law Journal* 95 et seq.

[101] For example, see BVerfG 129, 124 et seq (on state guarantees for Greece and the EFSF).

[102] On the value of constitutionality as contributing to remedy fragmentation, see Niglia, 'Of Harmonisation and Fragmentation' (n 98); Niglia, 'Of Constitutionality and Private Consumer Law' (n 99); Niglia, 'Of Jurisdictional Balancing' (n 97).

II. SYNTHESIS OF THE CONSTITUTIONAL CRITIQUE[103]

Reconstructing the patterns of critical reaction of scholarship to the move towards codification taken by the European Commission has indicated how the European codification project is orientated towards deviating from, obstructing and ultimately altering the living law as developed over the past decades via the processes of constitutional synthesisation.[104] Once one pierces the veil of conventional analyses, one must see how the polemics developed in relation to the Optional Code embody a constitutional meaning of 'resistance' vis-à-vis the code-based project attempt at disposing of the heritage of material rights contained in mandatory and default rules.[105] The critique of the codification project that I have put forward, including the proposed reconstructive analysis of the emerging scholarly debates, is, deep down, one that pertains to the dynamics of a private law community of interpreters that must face the reality of a revolutionary codification project whose aim is to erase the existing private law. In other words, setting a European *code corpus* against the living jurisprudence means attempting to play down and ultimately disposing of the living constitutional values on which the jurisprudential forces currently base their work (de-constitutionalisation), whilst at the same time replacing them with a new constitutional set of values (re-constitutionalisation). This is the real goal of the European Commission's attempt

[103] In the remainder of the chapter, I assume, *ex hypothesis*, a code-text enacted and fully implemented on the basis of a reasonable consensus among the jurisprudential forces, for the less consensus, the less de-constitutionalisation and re-constitutionalisation. I will reflect on the real-life dynamics of consensus or otherwise among the jurisprudential forces below in ch 4.

[104] For a 'visual mapping' of these processes, see L Niglia, 'An Age of European Re-Codification' (essay 2014, on file with author).

[105] I refer to the literature mentioned above (Hesselink (n 17); Eidenmüller et al (n 19); Basedow (n 21); Whittaker (n 21)). I interpret the article by Eidenmüller et al (n 19) in this way (as an article of defence of the existing constitutional private law arrangements) insofar as it makes the point whereby private law must reflect values and interests (at 669), be based on a shared understanding ('based upon a tradition of dispute resolution that may guide the application of the law': at 677), whilst linking the meaning of legal certainty to democratic legitimation premises (at 676). These are aspects which, at some deep level, are not incompatible with my own 'argument from the social fabric' and associated constitutional quality of private law. The article by Eidenmüller et al (n 19) is, however, complex (to an extent inevitably so, given that it is multi-authored) in that it embodies further meanings, not least some of which are patently contradictory with the interpretation that I am offering, including an interpretation of 'private autonomy' that lends itself to understandings that bring us back to nineteenth-century *code corpus* conceptions of individualism (*cf* Hesselink (n 17) 67, arguing, in relation to H Eidenmüller, F Faust, H Grigoleit, N Jansen, G Wagner and R Zimmermann, 'Der Gemeinsame Referenzrahmen für das Europäische Privatrecht – Wertungsfragen and Kodifikationsprobleme' (2008) 63 *Juristenzeitung* 529 et seq, that 'the Zimmermann group denounced the DCFR's value pluralism and, in particular, the reduction of private autonomy to merely one value among many others, including the 'political' notion of solidarity and social responsibility. It is striking that one article by a group of conservative German scholars (almost a pleonasm) can have such an impact on the editors of the DCFR'; and Kennedy (n 31) 186, arguing that the article by Eidenmüller et al is a 'conservative attack on the DCFR' in that inter alia 'it objects to the use of general clauses, reasonableness requirements and the augmentation of the role of business practice as an invitation to judicial law-making excoriated as undemocratic. At the same time, it objects to the generalisation of duties of good faith and cooperation, and the unstructured nature of the list of factors to be balanced, as inviting an unjustifiable erosion of private autonomy for the sake of an imprecise goal of social justice and solidarity').

at anchoring *nomos* (jurisprudence) to *thesis* (legislation qua code) in order to disempower *nomos* by placing it beyond the reach of the constitutional values that have shaped it over the second half of the past century and up until the present day; by making it 'powerful' only in the preposterous sense of delegating to the jurisprudential forces the job of applying the range of artificial, technocratic norms contained in the proposed code-text – towards the attempt at making them complicit in the legislative project of creating a 'new' private law world of artificial values.[106] For the code-text is made out of a set of model rules and principles mechanically transposed from document to document[107] and of which the more one investigates the genealogy and functions,[108] the more one understands their artificiality.[109] What the codification strategy ultimately denies (in epistemological terms) is the *carnalità* of law[110] typical of any really pluralist order, that is, the value of the 'particular' (sociality). Let me discuss this point further using a two-step argument.

A. De-constitutionalising Private Law

Let me preface the first argument by recalling a point that I have made in chapter one, that is, let's recall what the disciplinary impact of a code (having the features of a *code corpus*) is expected to be according to the plans of the codifiers. The enactment of a code is expected to repeat the normalisation effect attached to successful episodes of implementation of a *code corpus*, that is, 'grammaticalist interpretative utterances become key to the success and prestige of scholarly argumentation and judicial opinions' and 'such impacting processes in turn discipline law's application', for 'they exacerbate the work of those who, for whatever reason, wish to further decisions other than those dictated by the requirements of the impacted field'; 'dissenters have the extra burden of having to argue against code-based grammatical interpretative patterns (offering counter-grammaticalist arguments themselves based on grammatical reasoning)'; 'this represents an extra burden that does not exist in 'lowly impacted fields' with no such unified legal grammar – and in which legal actors base their arguments on policy or value considerations, or indeed on any chosen sort of authority and argumentative structure that they pick and choose from for being, in their view, conducive to sustain their own interpretative positioning on individual issues'.[111]

[106] See ch 1.

[107] See ch 1.

[108] In the sense that there is a need to investigate not just the origins and functions of general principles of civil law (as rightly indicated by M Hesselink, 'A Toolbox for Judges' (2011) 17 *European Law Journal* 441), but also the origins and functions of the model rules and the 'common legal principles'.

[109] See ch 1; and L Niglia, 'Taking Comparative Law Seriously – Europe's Private Law and the Poverty of the Orthodoxy' (2006) 54(3) *American Journal of Comparative Law* 401.

[110] P Grossi, *Universalismo e particolarismo nel diritto* (Editoriale Scientifica, 2011) 7 ('carnalità' defined as 'dimensione essenziale del diritto . . . per il suo essere scritto sulla pelle degli uomini').

[111] All passages taken from ch 1.

Seen in the light of the normalisation effect, implementing grammaticalism through the Optional Code means an attempt to replace the pluralism of jurisprudential interpretations (constitutional) as they currently exist, shifting the law from it being 'a lowly impacted field' to a 'highly impacted field'.[112] The 'high impacting' of the field would bring about the converse of the 'disorderly' predicament in which European private law finds itself today. In the words of Van Caenegem, law would once more 'merge with statute' or, in the words of the jurist-exegete Laurent: 'Statute, even if it were a thousand times absurd, would still have to be followed to the letter, because the text is clear and formal.' Enactment of the Optional Code would mean that constitutional balancing, the kernel of current jurisprudential activities, would be placed at a disadvantage vis-à-vis any of the grammaticalist interpretations based on the code. For constitutional balancing qua constitutional re-creations ('high-intensity') is a paradigmatic form of argumentation from policies and values[113] that codes aim at displacing. This because, if code (qua code corpus) is formalism (interpretation as an effortless and mechanical task based on recourse to, and transposition of meaning derived from, overarching and fixed norms), then the balancing incorporated into the jurisprudence of constitutional synthesisation in its de-codified shape is post-formalist, that is, about ad hoc compromising and reconciliation among values and policies.[114] For example, it must not be taken for granted that definitions (such as that of 'damages' in *Leitner*) can be automatically transposed from one case concerning the Product Liability Directive to another concerning the Package Travel Directive, as it all depends on the balancing reasoning context that the judges adopt – but this is exactly what the CFR is intended to do, that is, to regiment interpretation by conjuring up notions, such as that of 'damages', that can allegedly be easily transplanted across the range of relevant cases.[115] The same applies whenever the European code-in-the-making is held to incorporate principles emerging out of judicial balancing operations, such as imposing limitations on the exercise of rights towards ensuring legal certainty as per *Hamilton*, insofar as it is held to be amenable for incorporation into the CFR.[116] Here the idea is that a European code should crystallise the time limits once and for all rather than leaving them to the balancing decisions. Overall, a European *code corpus* is aimed at dramatically changing the patterns of interpretation to the detriment of 'free deliberation', as embodied in the practice of constitutional synthesisation. An optional code would de-constitutionalise private law in that it would make it

[112] See discussion above, at ch 1.

[113] See, eg, R Alexy, 'Constitutional Rights, Balancing and Rationality' (2003) 16 *Ratio Juris* 131, 133–34 (on balancing as involving values and policies; equivalence between values, interests and rights (and policies) in contexts of balancing).

[114] Respectively at ch 1 (code is formalism) and ch 12 (balancing is post-formalist).

[115] For a reconstruction, see Hesselink (n 108) 452; Case C-168/00 *Simone Leitner v TUI Deutschland GmbH Co KG* [2002] ECR I-02631.

[116] See Advocate-General Opinion in Case C-412/06 *Annelore Hamilton v Volksbank Filder eG* [2008] ECR I-02383 [24]: the placing of a time limit on the exercise of a right is 'a principle common to the laws of the Member States'. That principle 'might well ultimately appear at Community level in the context of the creation of a common frame of reference for European contract law'.

more difficult for actors clinging to constitutional balancing to operate, thus erasing much of the living substantive constitutional material from the theatre of private law interpretation. Erasing the national component of constitutional synthesisation as incorporated in mandatory and default rules means that the living constitution of European private law would be placed at a disadvantage, threatening to make it redundant. The blocking off, and the disposing, of the national dimension to constitutional synthesisation would bring about a kind of constitutional 'synthetic law', that is, a kind of truly artificial constitutional private law, given that all would be centered on experts' vocabularies devoid of any concrete relatedness to domestic constitutional private law realms.

B. Re-constitutionalising Private Law

One should not lose sight of the substantive aspects involved in the codification project, aspects that must be considered alongside the argument made above about de-constitutionalisation in the context of the critique that I am proposing. Having put forward the argument that the structures of jurisprudence would be unconstitutionally altered by an optional code, bracketing out constitutional values as they belong to the living law, I'd now like to consider the ways in which that alteration would be questionable in terms of its substantive aspects. Corresponding to the *pars destruens* qua de-constitutionalising would be a *pars construens*, consisting of 're-constitutionalising' private law along a partisan agenda. *Nomos*, once displaced, would be replaced by *thesis*, a code-text that incorporates an artificial world of partisan values in lieu of the plurality of values as they characterise contemporary private law.

Specifically, my constitutional critique is not only that any code would infringe upon private law pluralism by placing national constitutional material at a disadvantage, but also that this code-based infringement is undertaken with a view to actualising a partisan ideological project. Constitutionally, the superimposition of a European code amounts to entrenching a partisan ideological project above and beyond the usual patterns of contestation as they manifest themselves via the patterns of constitutional synthesisation emerging out of Europe's pluralist jurisprudence.

Constitutionalism includes furthering ideological projects, but political processes and settlements in general should not 'foreclose and exclude others' outrightly,[117] as that would diminish their quality and problem-solving effectiveness. Any such foreclosure would mean that the condition of 'mutual dependence' that 'requires parties to recognize the importance of the interests and claims of each other'[118] would not be ensured at all. The code-project is about re-constitutionalising private law by repositioning it away from 'procedural'

[117] D Chalmers, 'The European Redistributive State and a European Law of Struggle' (2012) 18 *European Law Journal* 667, 673.

[118] ibid 673.

conditions of mutual dependence and instead placing it on a terrain in which arbitrary determinations by the powerful contractual party over the weak would be legitimated. This is the case of the Optional Code's rationale in defence of a scheme of action in which powerful private contractual parties can draft sales contracts freely and opt into the Optional Code with no control aimed at taming any of the underlying bargaining power circumstances.[119] The template is self-evident – individuals are not taken to be part of a social fabric, but are seen as isolated market operators maximising their own interest; there is no room for social values and whoever relies on them must be prevented from doing so (via the code).

The above notes are all the more problematic considering that it is a constitutional 'mono-project' that we are discussing,[120] based as it is on a 'normativity of approximation' to 'a predetermined ideal state of individual interest-optimizing market convergence' as opposed to 'the evolved, sustainable and adaptable accomplishment of a self-determining, "multi-project" political community' (normativity of self-government). The code-project aims to reinforce the problematic character of integration insofar as its ideological framework fits into a libertarian type of normativity of approximation as presently practised in other fields of EU law.[121] The deep normativity is that of individualism, articulated through a register recovered from the historical repertoire of the private law discourse and re-arranged so as to become an absolute via the philosophy of private government, that is, the combined neglect of mandatory rules and of default rules and the immunisation of private choice from any substantive control of fairness. This is really about attempting to alter the material constitutional balance in which European private law finds itself.

As at work is the making of one more 'behaviour-regulating code', whenever 'the market's steering logic is given precedence within the more overt and reflexive regulatory code of law', one 'should not be surprised at the conformity-conducive consequences'.[122] The proposed European code cannot but reinforce this character of the integration project, insofar as it turns the reflexive code of law into a mechanical code (that is, the mechanics of interpretative grammaticalism) that rigidly implements the partisan ideological agenda that lies at its core (market libertarianism).[123] The proposed code reinforces all of those jurisprudential developments[124] that have gone in the direction of market holism, whilst disempowering exactly those judicial developments that have arguably gone in the opposite direction.[125] From this vantage point, the code-project acquires a

[119] See the discussion above in relation to 'choice'.

[120] *cf* Alexander Somek, *Individualism: An Essay on the Authority of the European Union* (Oxford, Oxford University Press, 2008, as commented upon by N Walker, 'The Anti-political Polity' (2010) 73(1) *Modern Law Review* 141, 148 (contrasting the constitutional mono-project of integration with the constitutional multi-project, centred on a political community, at the level of the nation state).

[121] *cf* Walker (n 120).

[122] ibid 149.

[123] See ch 1.

[124] For an account, see Somek (n 120).

[125] On such counter-developments that go against market holism and towards an acknowledgement of values of a different kind, see Walker (n 120) 150–51, criticising Somek (n 120) on this point.

problematic strategic relevance in relation to the direction that the whole process of European integration may take. Overall, the code-project is about attempting to replace the mechanics of Europe's composite constitutional order (through the patterns of 'constitutional re-creations') by the cold mechanics of a code-order based on the constitutional mono-project of market holism. But this is highly problematic, for the 'constitutional re-creations' that characterise the workings of the living private law via judicial decisions re-enact the logic of multi-project constitutionalism in beyond-the-state mode[126] as opposed to the constitutional mono-project that shapes the codification process.

If the way ahead should be about subjecting 'every invocation' over the meaning of the ideals of the EU to 'contestation by the member states',[127] then the proposed code is about attempting to do the reverse, that is, attempting to shelter every invocation of European private law based on the code from contestation from any dissenting actors, including those that operate at the domestic level, and to set aside the jurisprudence of constitutional synthesisation. Given that we are talking about would-be private law invocations based on a future code that rests on partisan ideological material, attempting to avoid contestation in such a way is all the more problematic. It epitomises the worst of what can happen whenever the opposite of a weak ethics of conversation and dialogue is practised in Europe. For if Europe should be about not subsuming the nation state or challenging it in some profound existential way, this is exactly what the proposed code purports to do.[128] From this vantage point, the voices of scholarly and parliamentarian resistance considered above are an obvious development. The proposed code is about glorifying universalistic claims in the name of Europe (rather than undermining them, as Chalmers argues should be the case),[129] whilst erasing what is otherwise needed. What is needed is 'contestation and debate about the central ethical issues through providing alternate meanings and horizons to those generated by the hegemonic national community'[130] – considering that a code proper (*code corpus*)[131] operates in the 'strong' logic of imposition of meanings and horizons of interpretation rather than 'weakly', that is, rather than providing alternatives to be discussed in conditions of arm's-length interpretation.[132] As the European codification project is about *thesis* (legislation) overriding *nomos* (understood as the

[126] Albeit 'not without' the state: see Michaels (n 1).

[127] D Chalmers, 'Constituent Power and the Pluralistic Ethic' in M Loughlin and N Walker (eds), *The Paradox of Constitutionalism* (Oxford, Oxford University Press, 2008) 313–14.

[128] On the need not to subsume the nation state or challenge the nation state 'in some profound existential way', see ibid.

[129] ibid.

[130] ibid.

[131] On *code corpus* versus weak conceptions of a code, see below, ch 4.

[132] Not even the proposal of a 'code of principles' (H Collins, *The European Civil Code: The Way Forward* (Cambridge, Cambidge University Press, 2007), on which see discussion below in ch 4) appears to fit this requirement, considering that it would be about the objective of identifying a set of principles detached from the real world understood as the practice of constitutional synthesisation out of which the private law values emerge: for a critical discussion of this view, see ch 4.

existing European-wide jurisprudence),[133] it is the opposite of the ideal of Europe as a place for dialogical intercourse among its many communities.[134]

If a contractual regime epitomises what private rule making can become whenever it is pushed to its extreme, that is, as 'a kind of constitution for the parties' ongoing relationships',[135] then the proposed CESL Optional Code represents an attempt at replacing 'the Constitution', that is,[136] the national constitutional charters as they exist independently of, and in relation to, the composite European constitutional order, with a 'private constitution'.[137] From this vantage point, the constitutional critique put forward here should concern both constitutionalists and private law scholars. The following chapter develops this aspect further, translating the confrontation code vs jurisprudence into the vocabulary of a deeper confrontation taking place among the jurisprudential forces. At this deeper level, I argue that the proposed Optional Code highlights the crucial point to which the playing out of the ever-present registers of individualism and of sociality has brought the private law discourse – creating a constitutional cluster of interpretations characterised by intense contestation over a radical version of individualism as embodied in the code proposal, due to its being deeply at odds with the existing structures of social welfare private law. It should then become evident that key sectors of the jurisprudential forces share responsibility with regard to the strategy of anchoring *nomos* to *thesis*, a development that, insofar as it can be equally read as being about restructuring *nomos* from within, reveals that strategy as traceable not only to legislative moves but, more importantly, to jurisprudential structures.

[133] I am adapting from RC Van Caenegem, *Judges, Legislators and Professors: Chapters in European Legal History* (Cambridge University Press 1987) 153, elaborating on FA Hayek's terminology ('nomos, the law made by the judges and thesis, the law edited by the legislator').

[134] See Chalmers (n 127) 314: 'the European ideal suggests that an emancipatory ethic of constituent power resides most happily in multinational democracies in which there is internal competition by different communities defining the ideals of the political imaginary'.

[135] A Riles, 'The Anti-Network' (2009) *American Journal of Comparative Law* 612.

[136] For critical discussion over the contentious issue of the status of private rule making in contemporary private law, see, eg, Basedow (n 47); Teubner (n 90); and the contributions in C Joerges and J Falke (eds), *Karl Polanyi, Globalisation and the Potential of Law in Transnational Markets* (Oxford, Hart Publishing, 2011).

[137] Considering the central place of national constitutional charters in the context of the phenomenon of de-codification as discussed above in ch 2.

4

Jurisprudence vs Jurisprudence

Au-delà du Code civil (R Saleilles, 1919)*

I. INTRODUCTION: THE VIEW FROM JURISPRUDENCE

IN CONTINENTAL EUROPE, codification (legislation) and jurisprudence (scholarship and adjudication)[1] are distinct yet profoundly interrelated phenomena. Legal writings have tended to emphasise the point of distinction between the two, making the widely established argument of a monopolising influence of the code over jurisprudence. But we need not underestimate the interrelationship between the two. There is an urgent need to change perspective in studies on codification if one is to make sense of the codification episode that we are confronting at present – there is a need to look at codification from the vantage point of jurisprudence.[2] Epistemic structures explain codification alongside legislative

* R Saleilles, 'Préface' in F Gény, *Méthode d'interprétation et sources en droit privé positif. Essai Critique* (Paris, LGD, 1919) xii, xxv (adding 'Il sera difficile désormais que cet "Au-delà" ne devienne pas le mot d'ordre de tous les juristes').

[1] Let me recall that, by jurisprudence (or *nomos*) in this chapter, I mean both scholarship and adjudication, unless otherwise indicated, in line with the jurisprudential perspective that this book takes, for, historically, not only scholars but also judges have participated in the making of codes (eg, see above, Prologue, n 7); the attitude of scholarship vis-à-vis a code-project has been shaped in contexts of exchanges with judges; it is the work of both scholars and judges to determine whether and to what extent a code is really implemented. I rely on the traditional understanding of the word jurisprudence as comprehensive of 'legal science' as held until the nineteenth century and, whenever specifically indicated in doctrinal writings, still today – see G Gorla Voce, 'Giurisprudenza' in C Mortati and S Pugliatti (eds), *Enciclopedia del Diritto*, vol XIX (Milan, Giuffrè, 1970) 490, 504 ('"giurisprudenza" significa quella dei tribunali (salvo che dal contesto risulti, eccezionalmente, che si tratti della scienza del diritto)'.

[2] Voices that indicate the need to point in this direction are those of P Caroni, A Gambaro and L Niglia, as discussed above in the Prologue at n 8, to which one may add N Jansen, *The Making of Legal Authority* (Oxford, Oxford University Press, 2010) 5–9 and 41 et seq (authority of legal texts, including codes, based on their 'acceptance' by the 'legal profession'); and Pia Letto-Vanamo, 'Fragmentation and Coherence of Law – A Historical Approach' in P Letto-Vanamo and J Smits (eds), *Coherence and Fragmentation in European Private Law* (Berlin, Walter de Gruyter, 2012) 152 ('the narrative of the emergence and development of modern (state) . . . underestimates the role of legal actors other than the legislator'; 'The European private law codifications of the 19th and 20th centuries were to a great extent based on legal concepts, classifications and ideas of previous centuries' and giving the example of continuity in the law based on the Roman law clause *clausola rebus sic stantibus*). Contrast, eg, RC Van Caenegem, *Judges, Legislators and Professors* (Cambridge, Cambridge University Press, 1987) 52 (depicting the 'background' to the Savigny–Thibaut codification debate as consisting of a 'struggle' 'between the professors and the legislators'; the code epitomising, in this view, the attempt of the

qua political will. There are major historical episodes that suggest that the role of jurisprudence is material to a real understanding of modern codification phenomena. They point to contested discursive landscapes surrounding the codification moves, with jurisprudential forces clashing over the code-idea – an idea sometimes proposed in its strongest version (*code corpus*) and sometimes in weaker versions,[3] sometimes opposed by arguments that are overwhelmingly critical of any codification move and sometimes based on the belief that a weaker version of the code would be the best course of action. The meaning of a code depends on the contingent character of the jurisprudential forces as they underlie each codification episode. Here are a few historical examples.

First, an 'unwillingness' of jurisprudence to support the codification move may entail that a code draft remains as such, with the codification project not materialising at all – a code may not be enacted if jurisprudence is not 'developed enough' (as contingently understood by the jurisprudential forces themselves) to make that happen. Nineteenth-century Germany is an illustration, considering that socio-political and intellectual circumstances appeared not to have been in place to further unification of law,[4] with key strands of jurisprudence (scholarship) voicing that condition and managing to bar the codification option[5] – tak-

legislators of the German states to replace the authority of the 'learned law' with that of legislation, and arguing that 'Savigny's ideas won the day because they voiced some deep seated anti-republican, anti-French and conservative tendencies of this time. As a consequence the learned law of the previous centuries remained predominant and Germany entered a phase where the professors of Roman law experienced their last and most glorious apotheosis, in the predominant school of the so called Pandectists'). For an application of the jurisprudential perspective that this book proposes to the case of *harmonisation* of private law (as opposed to legal unification, as discussed in this book) via EU secondary legislation (specifically the Unfair Terms Directive), see L Niglia, *The Transformation of Contract in Europe* (The Hague, Kluwer Law International, 2003) (analysing the implementation and enforcement processes of the Unfair Terms Directive in relation to the role of the relevant communities of interpreters). For a turn in EU law studies towards consideration of the wider community of interpreters, with a focus on the role of lawyers (rather than just that of judges), see A Vauchez and B de Witte (eds), *Lawyering Europe: European Law as a Transnational Social Field* (Oxford, Hart Publishing, 2013).

[3] For strong versions, see the recent re-statement of the code-corpus model in relation to the *CESL* in T Ackermann, 'Public Supply of Optional Standardized Consumer Contracts: A Rationale for the Common European Sales Law?' (2013) 50 *CMLR* 11: '[A] codification is a piece of legislation that claims to be the only source of law within its scope . . . The buzz about the CESL can only be explained against this background; the real point is that, for better or for worse, the CESL is treated as a significant step towards a European codification of private law pre-empting (codified and judge-made) private laws of EU Member States') and citing the 'classical' writings of F Wieacker, *Aufstieg, Bluete und Krisis der Kodifikationsidee in Festschrift fuer Gustav Boehmer* (Bonn, Roehrsheid, 1954) 34 (codes as exclusive sources of private law authority); Gilmore ('Legal Realism: Its Cause and Cure' (1961) 70 *Yale Law Journal* 1037, 1043: the code was 'assumed to carry within it all the answers to all possible questions') and with reference also to the work of J Bentham. For weaker versions of the code idea, see the 'European' lineage of writings from Nicolò to Rodotà and Collins, as discussed in the remainder of this chapter.

[4] *cf* G Solari, *Filosofia del Diritto Privato. Volume II. Storicismo e Diritto Privato* (Turin, Giappichelli, 1971, 1st edn 1940) 292: 'All'età del Savigny la codificazione in Germania era prematura o inopportuna e fu saggio l'averla impedita'; Van Caenegem (n 2) 52.

[5] Famously, FC von Savigny, *Vom Beruf unserer Zeit für Gesetzgebung und Rechtswissenschaft* (Heidelberg, Mohr und Zimmer, 1814) contra AFJ Thibaut, *Über die Notwendigkeit eines allgemeinen bürgerlichen Rechts für Deutschland* (Heidelberg, Mohr und Zimmer, 1814), reprinted in Hans Hattenbauer, *Thibaut und Savigny. Ihre Programmatisches Schriften* (Munich, Verlag Franz Vahlen, 1973).

ing as a parameter the position of Savigny in 1814 to have been representative of a lack of consensus towards the idea of a Germanic code.[6] It then took almost the whole of the century for the BGB to be enacted on the basis of the substantial support of scholarship that then came into being.[7] There have also been further modalities in which an 'unwillingness' of the jurisprudential forces could materialise, in opposition to the wish of the sovereign, for example, whenever codes were nevertheless made and yet significantly adapted to circumstances that required codes to be 'open' to other sources of law so as to ensure protection of local and feudal interests – avoiding a closure of the code that would just channel national and bourgeois interests,[8] this being the case for the Prussian *Allegemeines Landrecht* (which entered into force in 1794).[9] In cases such as this, the jurisprudential forces happened to be divided in relation to substantive issues and managed to achieve a compromise over a weaker (as opposed to a *code corpus*) form of codification. One more example is that of the code-projects that preceded the enactment of a code, but that did not manage entirely or partly to become the basis for the then approved code, such as a few that I refer to below – the three code-projects proposed by *Cambacérès* and the proposal for an Italian Code of Commerce – as they represent cases of 'failed codes' insofar as the clashes among the jurisprudential forces led to their partial or total dismissal.

Second, a code may not be implemented in the way that it had been intended to if the wider jurisprudentical forces turn out in reality to be not really supportive of it. This was the case of much of the first half of nineteenth-century France, a period during which arguably the deployment of pre-*Code civil* jurisprudential material remained solidly in place in the courtrooms up until the practices of exegesis established themselves,[10] with the modern and individualistic ideology of

[6] See Savigny (n 5).

[7] Jansen (n 2) 49 (referring to 'the decision of the German legal profession to make the *Reich*'s codification the exclusive textual authority of private law discourse', a decision taken 'at a conference in Eisenach in 1896, to replace the Corpus iuris with the BGB as the normative basis of academic teaching and doctrinal research' (at 47)).

[8] See Solari (n 4) 292 (in the early nineteenth century, the code form understood as channelling bourgeois interests; Germany was not ready to adopt the code in relation to that reason): 'La portata della dottrina storica doveva restringersi . . . nelle sue applicazioni al diritto privato, nel quale il programma della rivoluzione si era consolidato in ciò che presentava di più vero e di più solidamente acquisito alla coscienza giuridica universale. La critica del Savigny ai codici sotto questo punto di vista era assolutamente ingiusta e sproporzionata all'importanza e al significato storico della codificazione'.

[9] Pio Caroni, 'Il codice rinviato. Resistenze europee all'elaborazione e alla diffusione del modello codicistico' in P Cappellini and B Sordi (eds), *Codici. Una riflessione di fine* (Milan, Giuffrè, 2002) 263, 280 et seq.

[10] Contrast the official view of codification in the vocabulary of the myth of the omnipotent legislator in RC Van Caenegem, *A Historical Introduction to Private Law* (Cambridge, Cambridge University Press, 1992, translated by DEL Johnston) 7 et seq and 147 et seq (positivism at the core of the Code; the Napoleonic Codes inaugurated a 'century of sterility' as: 'The codes now existed; they suited the mentality and the interests of the citizens, and there was no reason to question them. Judges had only to respect them and apply them strictly; authors had merely to interpret the articles of the codes faithfully. It was out of the question now for case law or scholarship to attempt to innovate or play a creative role. Law had merged with statute. The statute was the work not of professors or magistrates, who had no mandate to act in the name of the nation, but of the legislator, the sole representative of the sovereign people') with views that see the first decades of the nineteenth century as not at all 'sterile': see, eg,

freedom of contract and property ('will theory') only gaining ground around the mid-nineteenth century with the works of Aubry, Demolombe, Duranton, Laurent and Rau among others.[11] Napoléon's reaction ('mon Code est perdu')[12] on reading the first commentaries on his code symbolises this phenomenon of the jurisprudential forces being in a condition of 'freedom'. Equally, the Louisiana Code of 1808 encountered sustained resistance as did the Prussian Civil Code (*Preußisches Allgemeines Landrecht* of 1794 –ALR) and the Spanish Civil Code of 1889 (insofar as the *derecho foral* gained in strength at the post-enactment stage).[13] In other words, the enactment of a code may entail the silencing of jurisprudence (the judge *qua* '*bouche de la loi*';[14] the scholar *qua* '*exeget*'),[15] but only if jurisprudence wishes to be silenced, so to speak. From this vantage point, and paradoxically, codes set the stage for a suspension of the normalcy of the interpretative workings of jurisprudence as developed in non-codified or in de-codified envi-

J Gordley, 'The Myths of the French Civil Code' (1992) 42 *American Journal of Comparative Law* 459 (the drafters of the Code did not innovate as the individualistic principles were 'taken from the Old Regime'; only a few decades following enactment of the Code, around the middle of the nineteenth century, did scholars develop modern individualistic principles (will theories); criticising contemporary scholarship that places the shift to modern individualism at the time of the making of the code, specifically: 'In his excellent recent history of the drafting of the Code, Halpérin termed the provisions governing family law reactionary and those concerning matrimonial property and inheritance a compromise. The truly revolutionary developments were the treatment of property, contract, and possibly tort law. He believes that these fields were reorganized around modern individualistic principles. The principles usually identified are the freedom of the owner to do as he likes with his property, the freedom of the parties to contract, and the liability of an individual for his own fault. These principles, René Savatier explained in an influential book, are the: 'three pillars [that] support the entire construction of the Napoleonic Code."' He refers to J-L Halpérin, *L'Impossible Code civil* (Paris, Presses Universitaires de France, 1992) 56–57, 276–78 and to René Savatier, *Les Métamorphoses économiques et sociales du droit privé d'aujourd'hui* (Paris, Dalloz, 2nd edn, 1959), § 2, at 5–6.

[11] Gordley (n 10) 467 (in relation to property law, citing the works of C Demolombe, *Cours de Code Napoléon* (1854–82), IX, § 544, 487, C Aubry and C Rau, *Cours de droit civil français* (1869–71), II, § 191, 175 and F Laurent, *Principes de droit civil français* (1869–78), VI § 101, 135 as giving rise to the idea of 'property in terms of the will of the proprietor', an idea not really contained in the Code, according to Gordley) and at 476 et seq (in relation to contract law, citing inter alia the works of Demolombe, *Cours*; and M. Duranton, *Cours de droit français suivant le Code civil* (3rd edn, 1834) IV, 202–03 and of Laurent, *Principes*, XV, §§ 424-–27, as the first to explain that 'the will of the parties formed a contract').

[12] Quoted in S Rodotà ,'Il Codice civile e il processo costituente europeo' in V Roppo (ed), *A European Civil Code? Perspectives and Problems* (Milan, Giuffrè, 2005) 183, 185.

[13] *cf* Caroni (n 9) 284–85 and Jansen (n 2) 46 (both on the Prussian code: *Preußisches Allgemeines Landrecht* of 1794/ALR); Jansen (n 2) 45–46 (on the Louisiana Code of 1808); Caroni (n 9) 284–85 (on the Spanish Civil Code). See also Caroni (n 9) 284–85 (the ALR gained terrain thanks to the 'inconcludenza dei legislatori provinciali', whilst in Spain 'fu il *derecho foral* ad acquistare vieppiù vigore', entailing a change of the intensity of the impact of the original codes as a result of contingent 'social and political changes' in both states). One must recall, however, that 'judges and academic scholars . . . never treated' the ALR as 'the comprehensive and exclusive basis of the law' (Jansen (n 2) 46) also because the ALR was meant to be of subsidiary application, a relationship between legislative technique and juristic craft to which I return in the remainder of this chapter.

[14] See, eg, Gordley (n 10) 485 (referring to Tribunat, Opinion du Tribun Mallia-Garat, séance du 19 frimaire, an X (10 December 1801), in Fenet VI, 151, 162, as having argued that: 'One who judges without a statute is not truly a judge. He is a Despot').

[15] In the words of the jurist exeget Laurent: 'Statute, even if it were a thousand times absurd, would still have to be followed to the letter, because the text is clear and formal' (quoted in van Caenegem (n 10) 147 et seq).

ronments[16] as long as that suspension is willed by the jurisprudential forces themselves.

Third, one more illustration is the fragmentation of private law around politicisation and pluralisation as it has taken place since at least the second half of the past century, and which has led to problematising the position of the code itself in the private law system, with the code becoming no longer a central tool as it had previously been (*de-codification*),[17] and with the constitutional charter becoming central to private law determinations, gaining authority alongside, and above, the authority of the code.[18] National civil codes remain in place, but the jurisprudential forces no longer place them at the centre of the legal universe, in dynamics that I have summarised in chapter two under the label 'jurisprudential de-codification'.

En bref, a jurisprudence that is supportive of a code warrants codification (if the legislature decides for the enactment of a code),[19] but a decisionist move of the legislature to enact a code in an unfavourable jurisprudential climate does not

[16] For the argument that codification entails a 'suspension' of the normal workings of jurisprudence (that is, a suspension of what I have called arm's-length interpretation) see the remainder of this chapter.

[17] See above, ch 2.

[18] On authority and codification, see the conclusion to this chapter. On the so-called *constitutionalisation of private law*, see, eg, T Barkhuysen and S Lindenbergh (eds), *Constitutionalisation of Private Law* (Leiden, Martinus Nijhoff, 2006); and Jansen (n 2) 48–49 (rightly emphasising the role of scholarship alongside that of judges in the making of the constitutionalisation of private law in Germany).

[19] Jurisprudence might be 'ready' in terms of having achieved a high level of formalisation (see below in this chapter for the concept of 'strong systematisation'; on code as mirror image of a fully systematised science of law, see, for example, critically recounting the influence of Germanic Pandectistic thinking on Italian codification, N Irti, *L'etá della decodificazione* (4th edn, Milan, Giuffrè, 1999); R Sacco, 'Rapport de Synthése' in *La circulation du modèle juridique français* (Paris, Journées franco-italiennes 1994), as discussed in F Ranieri, 'L'influence du Code Civil sue les codifications du 19e siècle: Essor et déclin d'un modèle européen' in *Das Europäische Privatrecht des 19. und 29. Jarhunderts. Studien zur Rechtsgeschichte und Rechtsvergleichung* (Berlin, Duncker & Humblot, 2007)), but no real codification may ensue as a result of a lack of action by the legislature. For example, in terms of the content of the contract and property law rules (as opposed to the modern individualistic ideological body of rules that developed during the nineteenth century), French eighteenth-century jurisprudence allegedly contained all of the elements for a code (see Gordley (n 10) referring to the works of Domat and of Pothiers as constitutive elements of the *Code civil*; previously for this opinion, see Savigny (n 5) 77 and the note of the translator of the 1831 English edition, A Hayward, at 77, mentioning Dupin's *Dissertation sur la vie et les ouvrages de Pothiers* as holding that 'three fourths of the *Code Civil* were literally extracted from his treaties'), but no sovereign's decision to codify (in the form of a *code corpus*) was made until the late eighteenth century. Also, to give another example, one should recall, first, that the idea of a European code has been around in scholarly circles for quite a while and that European scholarship has been ready for it (in terms of epistemic structures – see the remainder of the chapter), but that the EU legislature has only shifted from harmonisation via Directives to the code-project recently, with the turn-of-the-century CFR project. It should also be noted that the idea of modern codification itself precedes the actual making of modern codes, in that jurisprudence conceptualised it at an earlier stage, the Austrian General Civil Code (*Allgemeines Bürgerliches Gesetzbuch*/ABGB) of 1811 being an example: see L Mengoni, *L'Europa dei Codici o un Codice per l'Europa?* (Rome, Centro di Studi e Ricerche di Diritto Comparato e Straniero, 1993): 'il legame storico col concetto di Stato-nazione non è coessenziale all'idea di codice, nata nel secolo XVIII in concomitanza con lo sviluppo dell'autocomprensione della giurisprudenza come scienza. Il codice austriaco del 1811 è indubbiamente un codice moderno, fondato come il codice Napoleone sui principi di eguaglianza e di autonomia privata, ma non fu il codice di uno Stato nazionale, e tanto meno di uno Stato liberale con un ordinamento sociale borghese'.

warrant codification. The sovereign's decisionism[20] about making a code requires a crystallisation of supportive strands of jurisprudence.[21] A look at the actors involved in past codification episodes confirms this, for the drafters of a code are seen as, and perceive themselves as, transmitters of the existing jurisprudential material, both contemporary and past.[22] From this vantage point, it is fallacious not only to hold that the enactment of a code means that the legislature would somehow automatically take over jurisprudence, but also the conventionalist emphasis on a rivalry between legislation and jurisprudence in codification episodes has been overdone.[23] It all comes down to the contingency of the interactions between the legislative and the jurisprudential forces, a point that I will develop in the remainder of this chapter.

These lessons from history need to be taken seriously. One needs to map the ways in which the jurisprudential forces have participated in the legislative enterprise if one wishes to gain a realistic account of modern codification phenomena. As *nomos* and *thesis* co-constitute codification, one needs to explore the links between the two. The same argument applies to whoever ventures to understand the current predicament of a European codification, analysing the conditions in which European institutions have resorted to the idea of a European code and the ways in which that idea has been pursued in concrete terms via the legislative initiative of the CESL Optional Code, for, I argue in this chapter that behind the proposed codification project is a peculiar kind of jurisprudence that has led to the *Draft Common Frame of Reference (DCFR)* first and then to the CESL Optional Code legislative proposal now pending before the EU legislative institutions. A genealogical analysis of jurisprudence is needed to really decode the current codification phenomenon. It is from this perspective that this chapter discusses the contingent kind of jurisprudence that has made the code-idea take shape and reach the current stage of formal legislative proposal. I argue that it has been a convergence of various jurisprudential currents of thought towards the code enterprise that has led to the proposed Optional Code, constituting a crystallisation of jurisprudential material that in turn has been key to the decisionist move

[20] See, eg, L Muratori, 'Dei Difetti della Giurisprudenza. Trattato', *Venetiis* 1742 (calling for the necessity of a decision of the sovereign aimed at overcoming the clashes among jurists – that is, 'una decisione del sovrano che tagli i nodi divenuti inestricabili per la rissosa e verbosa attitudine alla contesa tra i giuristi'; arguing for 'a legge certa di fronte alla quale i giuristi, per l'obbedienza che debbono agli ordini del sovrano, saranno costretti a tacere') to put it in terms of the interpretation of M Bellomo, *L'Europa del diritto comune* (8th edn, Rome, Il Cigno Galileo Galilei Edizioni di Arte e Scienza, 1998) 15.

[21] One need not necessarily take an organicist approach, such as that adopted in conventional readings that draw on Savigny's *Vom Beruf* (n 5) to argue this – my own perspective in this book focuses on jurisprudential vocabularies and related legal consciousness.

[22] *cf*, eg, R Michaels, 'Code vs Code. Nationalist and Internationalist Images of the Code Civil in the French Resistance to a European Codification' (2012) *European Review of Contract Law* 277, 286 ('Lequette recounts how generations of French professors synthesised the principles of French law, until the code civil could be written in less than four months, based widely on the writings of Pothier', referring to Y Lequette, 'Quelques remarques à propos du projet de code civil européen de M von Bar' (2002) *Dalloz Chron* 2202).

[23] See Savigny (n 5) as re-read by Van Caenegem (n 2) 52: 'In this case the struggle [for the control of the law] was between the professors and the legislature (the enlightened princes and the deputies of the people).'

of the legislature – I propose calling this process 'osmosis'. As in previous modern codification episodes, no determinism but encounters of practices, both legislative and jurisprudential, have been leading to the structuring of the current codification phenomenon. In this sense, the EU codification episode is no novelty in the history of modern codifications – it is another chapter of the enduring age of codification that started more than two centuries ago.

To pursue this analysis, I propose starting with a description (analytic) of the structures of thought that have created the conditions for the EU codification move (section I.A), before considering the interface between them and the decisionist act of the EU legislature to promote a European code (section I.B). The new code proposal emerges as a Janus-faced object – the product of the work of the jurists, with section I.A exploring the legal material on which this work draws, and an economic constitution, with section I.B exploring the relatedness between the work of the jurists and the legislative economic constitutional agenda, explaining the two as contiguous material. It emerges that the code is 'nomothetic' (nomos-and-thesis) in that it merges certain strands of doctrinal and economic (state-building economic policies) material; it is thus force that constitutes (state-like) authority by selectively excluding whilst including legal and economic material.[24] Section I.C goes further in the investigation of the jurisprudential dimension to codification. It explains that the code-text is a contested piece of juristic work, both in terms of the legal material involved *and* of the ideological material that underlies it. For there is contestation over both the legal material chosen and the constitutional orientation of the enterprise, a contestation that comes from strands of thought that draw on the living private law as described in chapter two. On the basis of this analysis, I will conclude by arguing that at stake in the new codification episode is less a *code vs jurisprudence* clash[25] and more a clash that is internal to jurisprudence itself. The 'codification struggle' is not one 'between the

[24] To adapt the vocabulary of Niklas Luhmann, *Theory of Society*, vol 1 (Stanford, Stanford University Press, 2012, translated by Rhodes Barrett) 281 et seq. The unavoidable question of the legitimacy of the resulting authority structures, an aspect developed, for example, in J Habermas, *Between Facts and Norms: Contribution to a Discourse Theory of Law and Democracy* (Cambridge, MA, MIT Press, 1996, translated by W Rehg) 89 (criticising the ways in which private law theory qua doctrine of subjective rights developed, with its claim to 'normative independence from, and higher legitimacy than, the political process of legislation', in that it has led to 'the intersubjective meaning of liberty' being overlooked 'and with it the 'relation between private and civic autonomy in which both moments receive their due') remains open. For a critical analysis of functionalist theories *à la* Luhmann for their erasing the 'deontological dimension of normative validity', see Habermas *Between Facts and Norms*, 49 et seq. On exclusion and inclusion discussed in relation to the theme of normativity rather than the functionalist logic of evolution, see L Niglia, 'Pluralism in a New Key – Between Plurality and Normativity' in L Niglia (ed), *Pluralism and European Private Law* (Oxford, Hart Publishing, 2013) 249; and Habermas, *Between Facts and Norms*, 89 ('a statist understanding of objective law is misleading, for the latter first issues from the rights that subjects mutually acknowledge').

[25] This is the second step of my criticism of the *communis opinion* whereby the European codification process would consist of a confrontation 'code versus code' (see the critical synthesis of this opinion in Michaels (n 22)). Interestingly, note the unorthodox reference to the potential impact of the CESL on judge-made law in Ackermann (n 3) 12: 'The real point is that, for better or for worse, the CESL is treated as a significant step towards a European codification of private law pre-empting (codified *and judge-made*) private laws of EU Member States' (emphasis added).

legislature and the professors', as per conventional renderings,[26] but among scholars themselves, the outcome of which, I argue, is bound to largely determine the future of European private law.

A. Code as *Nomos*: The Jurisprudential Movement behind Codification

Looking at the characteristic modes of thought deployed by scholars from the various schools of thought that have been participating in the European codification enterprise, one must note a tendency on the part of scholars to selectively adopt those that are particularly suitable to implementing the code (*code corpus*) project. This is what I have described in chapter one as the practice of assembling private law material through the techniques of systematisation, coherence and neutralism.[27] The scholars of the CFR networks, emulating their predecessors who had engaged in the writing of the modern national codes,[28] have drafted a code-text using those techniques typically ordained to the task of compiling a supposedly 'complete' and 'self-standing' set of rules and principles (*code corpus*). Incorporation of much of the works of *Domat* and *Pothier* in the 1804 *Code civil de français* or, to give an example that is the closest to what is happening today,[29] incorporation of *Pandectistic* thinking in the 1900 BGB illustrate how, historically, the same kind of technical re-arrangements of private law geared towards the drafting of a modern code-text is at work – a pattern repeated now by the legal elites directly engaging with the Europeanisation project in the drafting of the

[26] Van Caenegem (n 2) 52.

[27] Neutralism has mutated conceptually but the basic pretense of depoliticisation has remained in the approach of scholarship – see ch 1. In this chapter, neutralism stands for depoliticisation. One must no doubt note a return to previous forms of jurisprudence that praised pyramids of concepts and deduction as central to the work of the jurist: see F Wieacker, *A History of Private Law in Europe* (Oxford, Clarendon Press, 1995) 239 et seq and 300 et seq (discussing the systematisers of the law of reason and Pandectism, including GF Puchta, *Das Gewohnheitsrecht* (Erlangen, Palm, vol I, 1828; vol II 1837)). This also explains why in ch 1 I have chosen to make sense of the DCFR in the vocabulary of a pyramid of concepts. But, as I discuss in the remainder of this chapter, it is a variety of sectors of jurisprudence (scholarship) that are behind the DCFR and not just one strand, including law and economics and 'law market' scholarship, constitutional economics and ordo-liberalism. Such scholarly strands are instrumental rather than conceptual, but they share with conceptual jurisprudential currents an attempt to mask utilitarian objectives under the cover of a pyramid-like code, as a way of securing the implementation of the preferred set of policies being defended.

[28] The committees of the jurists were composed of fewer members than those involved in the DCFR enterprise, but it remains true of both past and contemporary codification episodes that the jurists, willingly or unwillingly, have been representative of (sectors of the) jurisprudential forces. For example, as discussed below, the *Code civil* was not the product of cohesive scholarship (J-E-M Portalis, 'Discours préliminaire sur le Code Civil' in *Discours, rapports et travaux inédits sur le Code Civil* (Paris, Joubert, 1844) contains contradictory statements regarding how to understand law; the method of exegesis developed only about four decades after enactment); the newly proposed European code enjoys the consensus of various jurisprudential sectors but not all of them; the 1865 Italian Civil Code and the BGB were based on a vast jurisprudential consensus (Pandectist scholarship in Germany and scholarship as developed in the shadow of Germanic Pandectism in Italy: see Irti (n 19); Ranieri (n 19) 219 et seq; Wieacker (n 27) 363 et seq.

[29] Considering the key role played by systematisation and coherence in the construction of the BGB, similarly to the currently proposed European code (see above, ch 1): see also n 27.

European code-text. Scholars who have stressed, in relation to past codification episodes, the point of continuity between the structures of pre-code scholarship and the resulting code-text must be right in this sense.[30] The work of the strands of European private law scholarship that belong to the CFR networks have followed techniques crafted before the renewal of the codification project as explicitly taken up since the turn of the century with the launching of the CFR project. The move from adopting this platform of techniques to justifying the making of a code has been straightforward. It has been about re-enacting past practices.[31] More specifically, scholars are re-enacting ways of seeing the world which were in turn built through the history of codification (as made nationally). As always, these operations do not mean that a code necessarily follows, but that the intellectual conditions for it are re-created.

Let me now focus on a critical analysis of the employment of the technique of systematisation as an illustration of how the epistemic conditions for codification have been re-created via scholarly work, as a way of making sense of the role of scholarship, including the deployment of the complementary techniques of coherence and neutralism, and of completeness and autonomy.[32]

Systematisation can be taken to be a weak conceptual tool (weak systematisation) that allows the ordering of private law material according to value choices made in relation to social conflicts – the case of the 'weak re-codification' practices as discussed in chapter two in the context of contemporary private law. But it can also be taken as a heavy conceptual tool (strong systematisation) that acquires a value of its own,[33] 'inverting' standard interpretative arrangements as

[30] See, eg, P Caroni, 'Kodifikation' in A Erler and E Kaufmann (eds), *Handwörterbuch zur Deutchen Rechtsgeschichte* (Berlin, Erich Schmidt Verlag, 1978) 907, 908.

[31] On the intellectual background of techniques such as those of systematisation, coherence and neutralism, and on their influence on the making of a code, *cf* Wieacker (n 27) 257 et seq (on law of reason and natural law codes), 371 (on Pandectist thinking and the BGB and further codes) and 276 (natural law codes and Pandectist codes produced the same kind of 'complete' and 'exhaustive' law).

[32] On coherence, see D Kennedy, 'Thoughts on Coherence, Social Values and National Tradition in Private Law' in M Hesselink (ed), *The Politics of a European Civil Code* (The Hague, Kluwer, 2006); on neutralism qua depoliticisation, see L Niglia, 'The Political Foundations of European Private Law: Editorial' in R Brownsword, H-W Micklitz, L Niglia and S Weatherill (eds), *The Foundations of European Private Law* (Oxford, Hart Publishing, 2011) 177; on completeness (comprehensiveness) and autonomy (code as self–standing), see chs 1 and 3 and the remainder of this chapter. Note how depoliticisation remains in place despite its 'lower intensity' as a result of the more explicit endorsement of ideological material (market libertarianism) as discussed above in ch 1.

[33] See ch 2 (on de-codification). On the relations between constitutional private law (national) and jurisprudential professional work, see Niglia (n 2). A few quotations capture the many tensions in the field between weak and strong conceptions of systematisation. To start with, note the stress on the notion of systematisation in J Basedow, K Hopt and R Zimmermann, 'Preface' in J Basedow, K Hopt and R Zimmermann (eds), *Max Plank Encyclopedia of European Private Law* (Oxford, Oxford University Press, 2012) v:

'The various strands of development have led to European private law assuming greater significance as a theme in legal scholarship and, to some extent, even in legal practice. Yet they have not based on any grand systematic design but have followed a haphazard and uneven course . . . Today, the erratic character of the development still presents an obstacle towards systematizing the existing materials. But it is obvious that any meaningful scholarly advance has to be preceded by a thorough exercise of stock-taking . . . We are convinced that it is the task of legal scholarship today to comprehend and gather European private law in its entirety to lay a solid foundation for a later systematisation' and setting the

consolidated within contemporary national constitutional traditions.[34] This 'inversion' is problematic because it is about deploying an interpretative technique pre-occupied with ordering private law material along self-contained structured notions and categories presented as if they were independent of, and autonomous from, the underlying choices that must be made nevertheless, but that remain undisclosed. In private law vocabulary, a fictional world of individual(istic) rights (formal, neutral to sociality concerns) replaces the world of social conflicts, 'masking' them and, in so doing, freeing the arbitrary forces of private power, to put it in Solari's words, to which I will return in the following

'task of systematizing selected areas, and eventually European private law in its entirety' as a defining challenge to follow the overcoming of 'uncoordinated rules . . . formulated as answers to specific social and economic problems' (first phase) by way of 'discussion' ('second phase' – journals) and collection of materials and structured examination (third phase – the 'Encyclopedia').

See also C von Bar, 'Preface' in *The Common European Law of Torts* (Oxford, Oxford University Press, 1998) xxiii, his being explicitly an 'attempt to draw up a system of a common European law of torts': to put it in von Bar's words:

'It seemed possible to understand and portray each tort law as merely a manifestation of a single discipline'; 'although different legal practices which have each been grown naturally in their own environment do occasionally lead to different results, they can be dealt with in the same way as a single legal system in which a lawyer has to find his was through a variety of opinions. The person who looks, not only at his own, but also at surrounding laws, broadens the range of possible debate. In writing about different laws he undertakes work which is fundamentally no different from that on his own legal system, so long as the systems are equal in their basic values in the quality of their legal method, and have continuously learned from each other. This is the case in the countries of the European Union, and it is therefore possible to condense their difference national laws to a *common* European law of torts, or delict. To try to understand its structures does not mean leaving distinctive features of individual national laws out of consideration. Without an understanding of their effectiveness and their elegance, the treasure of judicial knowledge, which distinguishes European private law, will not be appreciated. However, to think in a European fashion means first to stress the common characteristics, secondly, to understand national laws as reactions to developments in neighboring countries, and thirdly, to tackle historical coincidences and rough edges, which, in view of the process of European codification, can be ground down without substantial loss'.

These aspirations, in particular those of von Bar, contrast remarkably with what German scholarship holds in relation to German private law independently of Europeanisation, a representative writing being that by HP Haferkamp 'Bürgerliches Gesetzbuch (BGB)' in J Basedow, K Hopt and R Zimmermann (eds), *Max Plank Encyclopedia* (Oxford, Oxford University Press, 2012), 120, 124 (commenting on the character of modern private law in Germany and arguing that a 'jurisprudence based on values . . . provided the backdrop for the re-orientation of the BGB towards the new constitution' such as discrimination and other leading principles including the protection of legitimate expectations; holding that: 'Since then, the older deductive reasoning firmly rooted within doctrinal principles has increasingly given way to a method of balancing the relevant interests in the case at hand, thereby evading the stabilising boundaries of a hierarchically structured system of rules which German law is usually known for. In fact, German private law today increasingly consists of judge-made law') and that by H Eidenmüller, F Faust, H Grigoleit, N Jansen, G Wagner and R Zimmermann, 'The Common Frame of Reference for European Private Law – Policy Choices and Codification Problems' (2008) 28(4) *Oxford Journal of Legal Studies* 659, 669: 'A legal code will invariably be more than simply a collection of technically integrated rules; it will reflect particular values and interests. Consequently, it is important that the normative goals and their relations to one another are plainly apparent. Only then is it possible to assess the body of law in terms of doctrinal clarity and consistency as well as of the realisation of policy interests.' The note by Wieacker (n 27) 487, to which I return later on, on the conflict between deductive and pragmatic strands in German legal thought remains as relevant and powerful as ever, that is, 'is the primary task of private law to provide a technique for solving problems or to construct an intellectually and logically coherent doctrinal structures?'.

[34] I refer to the standard interpretative arrangements described above in ch 2.

pages. Combined with deduction and coherence, we obtain what has been called a 'deductive-axiomatic system of thought'[35] which exists when 'the relationship between the individual pieces of knowledge is without gaps and can be presented in the form of deductions from certain axioms, in other words, the individual statements are able to be deductively derived as logical results from certain basic assumptions'.[36] This is a mode of thought that lies at the heart of European private law as conceptualised in orthodox writings. The reader will recall my analysis of the DCFR in chapter one and, specifically, how the schools of thought on the basis of which academic work has been carried out in the context of the Commission-appointed CFR networks have ended up with supporting this approach via the writing of a 'pyramid' of principles and model rules, the reduction of the relevant principles to four homogeneous principles, and the merging of the *acquis communautaire* and the principles, which indicates the attitude of scholarship to orchestrate (strong) systematisation. In furthering the systematising credo this way, scholarship is effectively promoting an interpretative climate geared towards protecting a set of abstract, individualist rights rather than considering 'rights' in relation to the social fabric (rights abstracted, that is, alienated, from the social fabric) – the juristic construction of 'individual choice'; the obliteration of mandatory rules in the *CESL*; the placing of individualistic principles ('efficiency') at the core of the DCFR; the exclusion from the DCFR of a set of social principles; all are fragments that belong to this credo. At this level of analysis, history repeats itself, for in the words of Gioele Solari:

> Quando si rimprovera ai codici l'abuso dell'astrazione e del formalismo non bisogna dimenticare il substrato economico da cui traggono vita e significato. La giustizia privata era il riflesso delle leggi economiche quali erano apparse alla mente dei fisiocrati, cioè esprimenti un ordine eterno di natura. L'individualismo economico aveva preparato l'individualismo giuridico, entrambi celebravano nei codici la loro salda, indissolubile alleanza, e nei principi dell'economia politica, oramai dopo Smith costituita su solide basi, era il miglior commento delle istituzioni del diritto privato. Le quali se parvero alla critica superficiale l'opera riflessa e arbitraria di filosofi e di legislatori, in realtà riassumevano le idealità, le aspirazioni di molte generazioni che per il loro trionfo avevano lottato, ed erano riuscite ad imporle nella teoria e nei fatti come condizione di ogni ulteriore progresso.[37]

For jurisprudence to pursue the organisation of private law material according to the parameters of strong systematisation is far from an exceptional development in modern times. Let me explain this aspect by considering the organisation of legal material by the insiders to the constitutional field as representative of what happens whenever scholars resort to sustained forms of systematisation. I suggest

[35] I borrow this definition from H Coing, *Zur Geschichte der Privatrechtsystems* (Frankfurt am Main, Suhrkamp, 1962) as quoted and translated in T Vesting, 'Constitutionalism or Legal Theory' in C Joerges et al (eds), *Transnational Governance and Constitutionalism* (Oxford, Hart Publishing, 2004) 33.

[36] Coing (n 35) as quoted in Vesting (n 35). See also Wieacker (n 27) 316 et seq, commenting on Puchta.

[37] Solari (n 4) 291–92.

looking at the parallelism between private law and constitutional law[38] as a way of understanding what system thinking is about in relation to its social consequences, which also means anticipating the argument that I will put forward in the remainder of this chapter that conflates the idea of a code with that of an (economic) constitution, which is as follows.

In the perceptions of constitutional lawyers, it has been held that forms of strong systematisation lead to adverse consequences for the arrangements of the body politic, that is, to the betrayal of the project of modernity understood as emancipation. Let me recall this story by considering a synthesis proposed by an author. Thomas Vesting has noted how a mathematical blueprint approach embraced in modernity has led in social philosophy (and then, arguably, in constitutionalism) to the assumption of 'the unity of politics and law' around a sovereign beyond the real and despite the multiplicity of the real (a reality of representation rather than a representation of reality). The myth of political unity was made.[39] There then arose an awareness of the problems arising out of this vision of political unity as conjured up more than two centuries ago. This awareness resurfaced in relation to the renewed 'divergence between unity and diversity in constitutionalism' that 'became even greater with the emergence of parties, associations and social organisations since the industrialisation of the 19th century'[40] and the related need for reconstructing it all as a spontaneous coordination of individual interests, that is, as administration and management of conflicting interests through forms of compromise and coordination rather than through implementation of an abstract system of individual rights and duties.[41] 'Weak constitutionalism'[42] has developed ever since as a way to promote constitutionalism understood as a 'coordination of individual interests'.[43] The two processes have gone hand in hand – as weak constitutionalism replaces its strong versions, 'sociality' replaces 'individualism'.

[38] See above, ch 3 (on constitutional private law).

[39] Vesting (n 35) 35 (discussing the myths of unity surrounding the nation state and 'system' in terms of a 'mathematical blueprint', which Vesting borrows from Heiddeger's *Die Frage nach dem Ding* (3rd edn, Tübingen, Mohr Siebeck, 1987) 42–92 at 69) in relation to constitutionalism and with references to private law (citing Wieacker (n 27) and Coing (n 35)).

[40] Vesting (n 35) 34–35 (discussing the 'discrepancy between the logic of identity, which the constitutional concept assumes for its idea of political unity, and the differences to the real world, which the constitutional recognises in its section on civil rights and liberties' as leading to 'the failure of the French revolution', arguing that '[t]he tension between the advantages of trade and human rights, on the one hand, and a single political will, on the other, resolved in the radical constitutional movement in favour of an alleged homogeneous civic virtue, ended in a reign of terror legitimized by messianism').

[41] Ladeur, KH (2008), 'We, the European People . . .' – Relâche? *European Law Journal* 14, 147–67, at p 148 (on 'the necessity of having a closer look at the social, political, economic and cultural conflicts which structure the constitutional discourse'); at p. 155 ('Constitutional courts, more or less successfully, adapt the individualistic principles of modern constitutions to groups, companies, political parties, patterns of public–private bargaining, and the rights of individuals within public insurance systems, etc. Nobody has claimed that this highly complex heterogeneous ensemble of patterns of inter-relationships which does not follow the established tracks of constitutional ordering, can ever be codified in a satisfactory mode which could be regarded as a functional equivalent to classical liberal constitutions').

[42] See Vesting (n 35) 36 (discussing the need for a 'weak conception of societal constitutionalism).

[43] Vesting (n 35) 35.

The same must apply to private law, at least if one directs one's attention to bodies of scholarship that have supported the adoption of what can be called 'weak forms of systematisation' as opposed to 'strong systematisation' as a way to accommodate private law's pluralisation and politicisation, as I have recounted it in relation to the past few decades (see chapter two). To link the private law predicament to the constitutional one, let me recall that the idea of 'a system' as essential to the private law discourse comes from a rich intellectual history (pre-nineteenth century) associated with the birth and development of the powerful individualistic model that runs in parallel to, and that has produced, the ideas that lie behind the making of civil codes (understood as *code corpus*).[44] We are talking of its re-deployment and transformation in the context of the project of modernity. From this vantage point, 'weak constitutionalism' corresponds to, and correlates to, the transformations of the private law sphere that I have described in chapter two – de-codification and constitutionalisation all being about organising private law around the management of conflict of interests in the context of the project of self-determination as implemented via national constitutionalism.[45] Systematic thinking has become part and parcel of this broader range of developments, no longer a value of its own but a 'weak' technique,[46] in the sense that it has become an instrument for dealing with concrete societal interests and their conflicts and synthesis. Not only de-codification but also 'weak re-codification' is a good illustration of this paradigm insofar as it is about maintaining system thinking, but 'weakly' so, for it is a compromise amongst interests and values that is concretised via forms of (weak) systematic reasoning.[47]

One can make a key point on the basis of this brief summary of intellectual material. Insofar as the present codification strategy re-proposes systematic thinking in its rigid and insulated version (the 'pyramid', the abstract 'merging' of legal material and the reduction of principles as described above as forms of strong constitutionalism), with the underlying faith in individualism (as operationalised in the various doctrinal notions orientated to absolute conceptions of private autonomy deployed in the DCFR and the *CESL*, as discussed at chapters one and three), it is a return to past, pre-constitutional forms of reasoning as held in high regard by the proponents of the move towards codification. Looked at in terms of the system idea, the present codification movement belongs to the strands of 'strong constitutionalism' as developed since early modernity, in the sense that it goes against the grain of 'weak constitutionalism' as developed in late modernity

[44] It is notable that the works of Domat and of Pothier (insofar as they are based on ideas of abstract systematisation) have been central to the drafting of the articles of the *Code civil*: see Gordley (n 10); G Tarello, *Storia della Cultura Giuridica Moderna. Assolutismo e Codificazione del Diritto* (Bologna, Il Mulino, 1976).

[45] See above, ch 2. Constitutionalisation indicates the judicial practices of constitutional courts whereby 'political principles are partially neutralized in favour of legal principles and consistency; the legal system is forced to take over the language of politics in its results-orientated weighing of interests' (Vesting (n 35) 36); the code itself having become an instrument understood in weak terms, that is, as technique instrumental for the resolution of interest conflicts (see Mengoni, as quoted at ch 2).

[46] See Eidenmüller et al (n 33) 669.

[47] On codes as technique for the resolution of conflicts see ch 2.

(particularly in the last 70 years or so) in consideration of the negative consequences of forms of excessive state unity, that is, the betrayal of the promise of the project of modernity of emancipating the masses by placing social values at the core of the legal universe. It is an attempt at reversing the trend from 'strong' to 'weak' constitutionalism in private law, taking it from weak to strong constitutionalism, from sociality to individualism (principles that are not 'social' are being excluded, whilst individualistic principles gain centre stage; obliteration of domestic mandatory rules; contractual choice held to be an absolute value).

* * *

From this vantage point, the revival of strong systematisation (and of associated *code corpus* techniques, such as neutralism, coherence, completeness and autonomy) that we are witnessing is a complex discursive phenomenon rooted not only in supranational movements of thought, whether neo-positivistic or neo-pandectistic,[48] but also in national movements of thought developed independently of the Europeanisation phenomenon. I refer to those movements that tend to think that a *code corpus* should be re-instated within national jurisdictions in lieu of the de-codified ways of private law,[49] rather than being satisfied with the current practices of 'weak re-codification', aimed as these practices are at balancing the protection of the diverse rights and interests, as considered relevant in the welfarist paradigm (as 'Europeanised'; see chapter two), with elements of legal certainty.[50] Willingly or unwillingly, such movements of thought act in defence of the classical, nineteenth-century private law world built on the individualistic model, vis-à-vis what they sceptically see as the 'intrusion' of new special laws, such as the Directives, and of constitutional values national and European,[51] that is, two pillars of the de-codification movement. Representative statements of this

[48] See ch 1 (pyramid of concepts, neo-exegesis).

[49] See above, at ch 1 (consciousness of re-codification of national private law developed nationally and linked to the position that favours a 'European' re-codification).

[50] See above, at ch 2 ('weak re-codification' positions consistent with the formal and substantive logic of de-codification).

[51] A consciousness has been built in scholarship around the criticism that the Directives disrupt the internal 'harmony' of private law; that private law should be defended from the intrusion of constitutional values incorporated in national constitutional charters (see the opposing views of Hans Nieuwendhuis, 'Fundamental Rights Talk. An Enrichment of Legal Discourse in Private Law' in T Barkhuysen and S Lindenbergh (eds), *Constitutionalisation of Private Law* (Leiden, Martinus Nijhoff, 2006) 1, arguing in favour of applying fundamental rights to private law disputes; and J Smits, 'Private Law and Fundamental Rights: A Sceptical View' in T Barkhuysen and S Lindenbergh (eds), *Constitutionalisation of Private Law* (Leiden, Martinus Nijhoff, 2006)); and that private law should be defended from the intrusion of constitutional values coming from the European constitutional level (P Rémy, 'Regards sur le code' in *Le Code Civil 1804–2004 Livre du Bicentenaire* (Paris, Dalloz, 2004) 99, 114–17, which critically discusses the 'contrôle conventionnalité' implicated in the obligations of civil law actors vis-à-vis the European Convention on Human Rights). This powerful vocabulary (its power comes from the fortune of the code-based individualist model) is in turn relied upon by scholars who favour the European codification project whenever they wish to articulate their criticism of the de-codified state of the art of contemporary private law as being unduly disruptive of the values embodied in private law via the code (for a representative writing see Rémy, 'Regards sur le code').

'neo-classical' position in national scholarship are those that defend the private law baseline from any encroachment of 'fundamental rights' as unduly disrupting the autonomy and functioning of the private law order as against those who argue in favour of applying fundamental rights in private law,[52] extreme points of a continuum along which scholars place themselves in debates over the idea of re-codifying private law, an idea discussed in relation to both national private law and private law in its European dimension. The two horizons have become indistinguishable. Two representative statements are:

> [L]e Code de 1804 n'était pas seulement notre vraie Constitution, c'était aussi la véritable charte positive de nos droits fondamentaux dans les rapports privés.[53]

> [F]aire intervener les droits fondamentaux dans les litiges entre particuliers, c'est bouleverser les base même du droit privé.[54]

The denial of any constitutional function for private law subscribed to by certain modes of thought, 'regulatory' and 'law-and-economics',[55] plays an increasingly significant role in the design of European private law, insofar as it creates the impression that private law is inherently a-constitutional (let alone allegedly a-political), this being another key factor that can only reinforce the claim that private law must be systematic (in the sense of 'strong systematisation') in order to be meaningful. What we are witnessing is a growing movement of thought, at both the national and the transnational level, that relies on the individualist model typical of the *code corpus* imagery for the purpose of reversing the living law based instead on the structures of welfarist de-codification. Below at section I.C I will focus on the jurisprudential forces opposing the European re-codification move (or, alternatively, proposing weaker forms of re-codification) as representing a distinct attitude of European legal thought that attempts to preserve the integrity of the living law. Before doing so, I must deal with the position of the legislature in relation to this jurisprudential predicament, but only after having dealt with another characteristic of the pro-code jurisprudential movement.

The substantial weight of the code-orientated jurisprudential forces (scholarship) is evident not only in its doings (the deployment of systematisation, coherence and neutralism) but also in their attempts at 'undoing', that is, in their ignoring and negating any patterns of law that develop on the ground and that are at odds with the dominant modes of thought. For a code-orientated jurisprudence has been developing that, even when not outspokenly in favour of the

[52] For arguments in favour, see, eg, Rodotà (n 12) 183.

[53] Rémy (n 51) 116.

[54] M Fromont, 'Les droit fondamentauz dans l'ordre juridique de la République Fédérale d'Allemagne' in *Recueil d'e'tudes en l'honneur de Ch. Eisenmann* (Paris, Cujas, 1975) 55, as quoted in G Comandé, 'Comparative Remarks, in G Brüggemeier, A Colombi Ciacchi and G Comandé (eds), *Fundamental Rights and Private Law in the European Union*, vol I, *A Comparative Overview* (Cambridge, Cambridge University Press, 2010) at 754.

[55] For a description of these schools of thought, see G Teubner, *Constitutional Fragments* (Oxford, Oxford University Press, 2012) 33–34.

DCFR-based codification,[56] sees positively European code proposals that tend to ignore and even to suppress and marginalise the living, constitutional jurisprudence, as noted in chapter two.[57] I have discussed these episodes of denial elsewhere.[58] They include scholarly tendencies to ignore and marginalise, first, the plural ways in which EU secondary legislation is applied on the ground and re-created in relation to local politico-constitutional sensitivities, for example, the case of the law of contract on unfair terms as provided for in the Unfair Terms Directive,[59] including episodes of boycotting of the EU Directives;[60] second, the jurisprudence of constitutional synthesisation as analysed at chapter two;[61] third, the many differences in the ways in which contract and tort laws are engineered throughout Europe independently of the Europeanisation phenomenon, differences played down and even negated for the sake of facilitating agreement on a common set of contract and tort rules.[62] In so doing, orthodox scholars ignore the 'Europeaness' of private law understood as the living law, for even resistance patterns vis-à-vis the Directives are a true 'European act' in claiming the value of one's own legal tradition as deserving a place in the wider European space of and for private law.[63] The end result of this predicament is to have created an ideal terrain for the codification move of the European legislature, considering that the harmonisation and unification legislative initiatives are about 'de-ranking'[64] much of the private law material that is being produced by the jurisprudential forces on the ground, as discussed in chapters two and three, in line with the denial of them by orthodox strands of European law scholarship. Displacing legal material has been a precondition for grounding the codification move. As *Normwissenschaft* replaces *Realwissenschaft*, the ground for codification is ready-made.

[56] Notably, Eidenmüller et al (n 33) 660, noting that 'the establishment of an authoritative European reference text promises to constitute a significant step forward', but criticising the attempted 'integration' on the part of the authors of the DCFR of 'the acquis commun, that has gradually evolved over many centuries of European legal history, and the acquis communautaire, relating primarily to consumer contract law' and adding (at 668): 'Yet, any more than superficial integration would have required a re-conceptualization of consumer protection law, which has neither been considered nor accomplished by the Acquis Group. Nor could the 'Compilation and Redaction Team', established at the beginning of 2006 and chaired by Christian von Bar and Eric Clive, deal with the matter because there was much too little time.' (at 668). For the complexity of the essay by Eidenmüller et al as embodying many meanings, see above, ch 3.

[57] In the sense of marginalising and suppressing political qua constitutional material rather than (just) cultural material (for a focus on the latter view, see P Legrand, 'Against a European Civil Code' (1997) 60 *Modern Law Review* 44).

[58] L Niglia, 'Taking Comparative Law Seriously – Europe's Private Law and the Poverty of the Orthodoxy' (2006) 54(3) *American Journal of Comparative Law* 401.

[59] Niglia (n 2).

[60] See ibid ('boycott' is a word that I borrow from E Hondius' review of Niglia (n 2) in (2004) 6 *European Review of Private Law* 855).

[61] See also Niglia (n 58); L Niglia, 'Constitutionalising European Private Law' (essay 2014, on file with author).

[62] See Niglia (n 58).

[63] If considered in relation to the context of the jurisprudence of constitutional synthesisation as I have discussed above in ch 2. For a theoretical elaboration on the value of the integrity of legal traditions, see ch 3, n 6.

[64] See Niglia (n 58).

B. Code as *Thesis*: The View from the Legislature

The convergence of key sectors of jurisprudence towards modes of thought that are all congenial to the codification strategy could not have managed on its own to produce the European code-text that we are dealing with these days. This is a lesson that one learns from history and that I am drawing upon towards making the new codification episode intelligible. For past codification phenomena in modern times, including those that I have enumerated in the historical summary to this chapter,[65] stem from both a decisionist act of the sovereign and jurisprudential material. Therefore, jurisprudential material, whilst necessary, is insufficient in itself for the making of a code. Examples abound as to how legislative decisionism (in the form of decisions coming from the legislative and administrative structure of the state such as emperors, ministers or ministerial committees) could determine much of the path of codification, examples that one must place alongside those that show the no less fundamental role played by the jurisprudential forces as discussed in the introduction to this chapter – acknowledging one truth does not mean that one should ignore the other, for that would be about repeating the positivistic 'mistake' of believing in the ominipotence of legislation, by changing its object, as one would by looking only at jurisprudence rather than at legislation. Examples include the refusal of Tsar Alexander I to introduce the French Civil Code in nineteenth-century Russia as traceable to his unwillingness to see the law of 'the enemy' become law of his country, despite the work of his principal minister MM Speransky towards codifying private law.[66] Further, in nineteenth-century Germany, the Imperial Ministry of Justice took a 'decisive position in re-shaping the First Draft of the BGB' by exercising 'decisive influence on the appointment process for the Second Commission as well as on the form and substance of the Second Draft'[67] through the insertion of a number of 'protective provisions'.[68] In

[65] See above, 'Introduction' to this chapter. Contrast Jansen (n 2) 45, who argues that 'in more recent times, it was often the legal profession, rather than the political legislator, which ultimately determined the sources of the law and their authority in legal discourse', including what he calls 'non-legislative codification'. As to contemporary modern times, I tend to think that decisionism (a variation on the theme of what studies of the codification phenomenon typically call 'political domination': see, eg, Jansen (n 2)) is behind all codes insofar as they are about the decision of the sovereign to entrench a market system ('market law'), but only if and to the extent that jurisprudence allows a code to come to existence. In this relational sense jurisprudence exercises legal authority independently of political domination (*cf* Jansen (n 2), who argues that legal authority, independently of political domination, is a feature of a certain set of non-legislative codifications). In turn, in my view, jurisprudential material (scholarly) that is not yet formally codified is 'authoritative' insofar as it creates the conditions for codification, an aspect on which I expand in the remainder of this chapter.

[66] Van Caenegem (n 2) 52–53.

[67] Haferkamp (n 33) 122.

[68] ibid 122 (arguing that a 'plethora of protective provisions' were inserted as a result; contrast Wieacker (n 27) below). Quoting the work of Werner Schubert (according to whom the BGB was 'the first modern codification influenced by social policy'), Haferkamp emphasises the role of the Second Commission in channelling interventionism alongside the more market-orientated character of the BGB understood as a liberal codification (at 124). I tend to think that Wieacker's account is more historically orientated and less influenced by the changes to the BGB that happened at a later stage (decodification) and that must have influenced the thoughts of Haferkamp and Schubert.

twentieth-century Italy, governmental support for the *code unique* project led to the unification of civil and commercial law, a move supported in scholarship, albeit controversially.[69] From this vantage point, today's quest for approval through a formal legislative act by the EU institutions such as the CESL Optional Code is no different, for it is, once more, about attempting to entrench a code formally via the sovereign's decisionism.

In order to grasp the renewed convergence between jurisprudence and the decisionist act of codification as it is taking place today at the European level, to which I dedicate section I.C below, let me first clarify in this section what I mean by decisionism of the sovereign[70] in relation to the modern codification phenomena, including the current European experiment in codification. Mine is a three-step argument.

i. *Decisionism qua administrativisation*

By decisionism, I do not mean conventional explanations on the interface between codification and nationalism, making codification intelligible as a technique directly related to the setting in motion of nation-state synergies, the code being understood simultaneously as a symbol of nationhood and as a carrier of 'cultural identity'.[71] These readings tend to play down the broader context in which nationalism and culturalism could develop, that is, that: 'The unification of private law on a national level had been one of the main demands of the liberal segment of the

[69] Alberto Asquini, 'Codice di commercio' in Francesco Calasso (ed), *Enciclopedia del Diritto*, vol VII (Milan, Giuffrè, 1960) 250.

[70] By 'sovereign' here, I refer to the combined participation of the EU Commission and Member States in the EU decision-making process leading to the deliberations over the proposed code; substantively, 'sovereign' refers to the weak sovereignty of the EU vis-a-vis the strong sovereignty of the nation state, although it is a matter of debate whether the EU is turning into a state (see recently D Chalmers, 'The European Redistributive State and a European Law of Struggle' (2012) 18 *European Law Journal* 667). On the complex relations between sovereignty and codification, see Mengoni (n 19) (noting the link between the two, but arguing that 'il legame storico col concetto di Stato-nazione non è coessenziale all'idea di codice' and illustrating this point by reference to the Austrian General Civil Code (Allgemeines Bürgerliches Gesetzbuch/ABGB) of 1811; then discussing a post-war turn towards codification understood as just technique, in the shadow of the phenomenon of 'constitutions without sovereignty' and arguing that 'L'idea di codice può ridursi, e ormai si è ridotta, a un concetto puramente tecnico, ordinato alla funzione di apprestare un nucleo sistematico di principi e di categorie ordinatorie adeguato alla selezione strutturale dei conflitti di interesse e all'organizzazione delle relative decisioni nell'unità del sistema giuridico, garantendo il primato dell'argomentazione giuridica sulla contingenza delle valutazioni politiche. La forza che l'idea di codice continua a esercitare in tutti i paesi del continente deriva precisamente dal senso profondo della sistematicità del diritto, che assegna ai concetti sistematici una funzione irrinunciabile di guida e di controllo dell'argomentazione giuridica, e quindi di razionalizzazione unificante dell'esperienza giuridica'; having noted the decoupling of codification and sovereignty, Mengoni then acknowledges that 'il codice civile conserva una forte valenza politico-culturale come deposito della tradizione giuridica nazionale e perciò elemento primario del complesso meccanismo che determina l'identità nazionale dello Stato'.

[71] For a critical synthesis of these understandings, see recently Michaels (n 22) (with a focus on France); and R Zimmermann, 'Codification. The Civilian Experience Reconsidered on the Eve of a Common European Sales Law' (2012) 8(4) *European Review of Contract Law* 367 (with a focus on Germany). *Cf*, Guido Comparato *Nationalism and Private Law in Europe* (Oxford, Hart Publishing, 2014).

bourgeoisie since the Napoleonic Wars.'[72] Closer to the truth of the matter is an understanding of the role of the legislature in codification phenomena as it relates to its position in shaping economic material by bureaucratic means, rather than just in terms of nationhood and of 'cultural identity'.[73] Let's recall the contingency of it all, considering that powerful notions such as 'nation' and 'culture' belong to a more complex history. To start with, let me recall the German context of codification according to the words of Wieacker:

> As the history of codification in the first Reichstag showed, the unity of private law was backed by the desire of the liberal bourgeoisie for the unification of the nation which they believed themselves to represent, but labor law at the beginning of the century, emergency law in the First World War, and the political and economic pluralism of the democratic Weimar Republic put paid to this pretension. The disappearance of the liberal economy involved the collapse of its greatest juristic creation, a unified private law.[74]

By decisionism, I refer to another explanation that brings back into the debate a dimension that has been played down.[75] I refer to the sovereign's decisionist move to make a code[76] as traceable to the contingent choice of placing economic relations under state-based, centralised administrative structures ('administrativisation'),[77] that is, the plan to make the behaviour of individuals and groups

[72] Haferkamp (n 33) 120.

[73] For criticism of conceptions of nationalism, see, eg, Glenn, *The Cosmopolitan State* (Oxford, Oxford University Press, 2013) at viii: 'All states are cosmopolitan. This may come as a surprise to all those who regularly use the expression 'nation-state' (and it has become a commonplace), but the coincidence or overlapping of a nation or homogeneous group of people with the legal and political structure of a state has never occurred, anywhere.'

[74] Wieacker (n 27) 431.

[75] I adopt the perspective of 'administrativisation' as a way of making really intelligible a range of materials that can be found in previous writings on codification, such as C Varga, *Codification as a Socio-historical Phenomenon* (Budapest, 1991)281 et seq and 289 (on rationalisation of the economy as central to the making of modern codes); Zimmermann (n 71) 376 (codification suited 'authorities eager to rationalize the administration of justice'). On the possibility of identifying features of the 'code' out of the contingent experiences of codification in modern times without having necessarily to incur in the danger of being ahistorical, see Varga, *Codification* 247 et seq.

[76] Whilst in episodes of national codification, the government took full control of the codification agenda by appointing a committee of jurists for its writing and by obtaining approval with little or no involvement from the Parliament, the case of the EU codification is starkly different: here the European Commission operates as the dominant legislative actor, but there is a high level of involvement of the Council of the European Union and the European Parliament in relation to the CESL. Obviously, in all modern codification episodes, a code has been technique that allows for little or no room for parliamentary deliberation insofar as it is a form of 'packaged legislation'. In reading my analysis of 'decisionism', one must take into consideration these factors.

[77] This point about the relevance of administrative structures in the organisation of market processes has emerged in the literature on codification. On *codification* in relation to *administration*, see M Weber, *Rechtssoziologie*, J Winckelmann (ed) (Neuwied, Luchthand, 1960) 249–50, as re-read by Varga (n 75) 289 (drawing on the Weberian explanation whereby bourgeois interests demanded a law that operated in a calculable manner, free from irrational administrative arbitrariness and the irrationality of real privileges, with modern codification being intelligible as accommodating the requirements for 'calculability', central to economic development, and mentioning 'a concerted functioning of the army of civil servants' and 'the technical needs of administration' as instrumental to the pursuit of 'calculatory forms of economic organisazion' (Varga (n 75) 289). See also Varga (n 75) 281 et seq (on the interface between advance of capitalism, state bureaucracy and codification, and drawing on

conform to a contingent set of overarching systematic objectives, a plan that is instrumental to the construction of a market economy.[78] Whilst the key market economic objectives pursued via codification may have been either lassez-faire (such as liberal-competitive capitalism in the nineteenth century, which was the case for the *Code civil* at least until the 1880s)[79] or liberist (which was the case for the *BGB*)[80, 81] *or* even sectorially interventionist (the case of key parts of the Italian

Weber). The link between codification and administrative rationality otherwise appears in standard writings on codification in relation to the broader objective of rationalising the administration of justice, that is, in a neutral vocabulary that tends to neglect the regulatory dimension of the market economy as I discuss it in the text: *cf* Zimmermann (n 71) 376 ('jurisprudence constructed *more geometrico* . . . appealed to the authorities eager to rationalize administration of justice'). Re-elaborating on Weber's approach, I am suggesting that 'the impersonal system of norms of the bureaucratic *Herrschaft*' (Varga (n 75) 289) has been a central characteristic of private law via codes qua regulatory structures (grammatical machineries) towards ensuring 'calculability'. In my view, bureaucratic organisation and the formalisation of law in codified form went hand in hand. It is in this way that 'the category of formal rationality' (Varga (n 75) 289) developed historically in relation to ensuring the liberal-competitive economy (nineteenth century) became less central with the rise of the 'free law' movement in relation to the need for adaptation coming from the changing economy starting from the late nineteenth century (the time of monopoly capitalism: see Varga (n 75) 282–83) and towards the twentieth century and beyond, which then led to the re-constitution of the 'rule of law' (rather than 'anarchism nihilism': see Varga (n 75) 273 et seq and at 283, drawing on Weberian writings).

[78] On *codification* and *market economy*, see n 77 above and the synthetic rendition of Mengoni (n 19) (discussing the 'codification of the bourgeois freedoms and of the relations of free market in the form of private rights'); F Ewald, 'Rapport philosophique: une politique du droit' in *Le Code Civil 1804–2004 Livre du Bicentenaire* (Paris, Dalloz, 2004) 76. For an account of the interface between codification and market economy, based on a critical re-reading of the works of Weber (n 77) and of G Lukács, *History and Class Consciousness* (Cambridge, MA, MIT Press, translated by R Livingstone) on the interface between rationalisation and economy, see Varga (n 75) 281 et seq (on the interface between rationalisation, economy and codification).

[79] See, eg, J-L Halpérin, 'Le Regard de l'historien' in *Livre du Bicentenaire* (n 51) 43, 54 et seq (metamorphoses of the *Code civil* reconstructed as 'three codes', that is, as two (types of) liberal codes in the period 1804–1880 and then, in the period 1880–1914, 'un troisième Code civil, authentiquement républicain').

[80] On the BGB as liberalist, see Wieacker (n 27) 382 (illustrating at 179 et seq the centrality of freedom of contract and arguing that only a few social elements can be found in it). Haferkamp (n 33) 123 quotes Wieacker in his *Das Sozialmodell der klassischen Privatrechtsgesetzbuecher und die Entwicklung der modernen Gesellschaft* (Karlsruhe, CF Mueller, 1953) as the author who 'successfully perpetuated the image of an 'unsocial' and formalistic' BGB and labelled the code a 'late born child of pandectism and the liberalist movement since 1848' that had been devised to fortify a social order unfairly favouring 'the affluent bourgeoisie', as well as noting how the BGB remained 'unloved', with centennial celebrations being 'rather low key'; see also Pio Caroni 'Codificare su due versanti: quello civile e quello penale. Riflessioni sul mito del codice-guida' in E Tavilla (ed), *Giuseppe Luosi, giurista italiano ed europeo. Traduzioni, tradizioni e tradimenti della codificazione. A 200 anni dalla traduzione in italiano del Code Napoléon (1806–2006)* Atti del Convegno Internazionale di Studi, Mirandola-Modena, 19–20 October 2006 (2009) 347–49.

[81] Considering the processes of 're-codification' ('weakly' understood: see ch 2), one should also note that a code may become an object embodying ordo-liberal qua welfarist objectives, as happened with the re-invention of the BGB as a result of what Wieacker called the breaking down of the 'unified private law'. See also Niglia (n 2) (on welfarism and private law in England, France, Germany and Italy); Haferkamp (n 33) 124 (discussing the changes that the BGB has undertaken in the twentieth century; 'Throughout the 20th century freedom of contract was confronted with far-reaching state interventionism [with] labour law . . . taken out of the code', whilst special statutes on tenancy were re-integrated into the code after 1945 and 'the Standard Contract Terms Act and most of the special consumer protection legislation . . . integrated into the BGB itself as part of a major reform of the law of obligations in 2001', pointing to processes that in this book I have termed 'de-codification' and 'weak re-

Civil Code 1942),[82] depending on which code one looks at and, obviously, on which interpretation of the code one adopts, a modern code typically consists of a set of administrative-regulatory structures for the enforcement of its rules and principles in disciplinary fashion[83] towards entrenching any of the preferred market economic objectives.. I am suggesting that 'the impersonal system of norms of the bureaucratic *Herrschaft*'[84] typical of modern capitalism has been a characteristic of private law via codes qua regulatory structures (what I have described in chapter one as the code-machinery that channels grammaticalism) aimed at ensuring 'calculability'. The engineering of the bureaucratic organisation and the formalisation of law in codified form went hand in hand. The ideology of the *code corpus*, that is, of the code as a 'complete' ('comprehensive') set of rules,[85] exemplifies at best this organisational character of the codification phenomenon – a project, I should recall, then more or less successfully implemented depending on the contingent state of the jurisprudential discourses, never really *fait accompli* as depicted by certain socio-legal and legal comparative reconstructions.[86]

codification'). Again, as noted above, I tend to think that ex post readings of the BGB that have emphasised a description of it as incorporating 'social oil' may have 'misunderstood' its substance as originally designed: see Wieacker (n 27) 381: 'All in all it seems clear that the draftsmen of [of the BGB] did not believe that private law had any special social function'; 'For all the good will of the draftsmen, concern for the economic interests of bourgeois society remains predominant'. However, on the extent to which the BGB remains implemented in ways that can be held to be substantively 'conservative' and 'formalist' even today, see N Reich, 'Pluralism and Private Law in the Union' in Niglia (ed) (n 24) 73.

[82] See Rosario Nicolò, 'Codice Civile' in Francesco Calasso (ed), *Enciclopedia del Diritto*, vol VII (Milan, Giuffrè, 1960), 240, 248–49 (property no longer absolute as per the *Code civil*, but limited by obligations; norms on *impresa* (enterprise) and on *lavoro* (labor law) held to be at the core of the 1942 Italian Civil Code as opposed to property being at the core of the *Code civil*; crisis of the category of *diritto soggettivo* as centred on the right to property; shift towards a plurality of property rights as opposed to a monistic conception of the right to property); Asquini (n 69) 254 (1942 Italian Civil Code, apart from family law and law of succession, based on protection of *impresa* (enterprise) and on *lavoro* (labour law) as opposed to being based on property as per the 1865 Italian Civil Code).

[83] Degrees of 'discipline', depending on whether one considers a *code corpus* or weaker codification forms.

[84] Varga (n 75) 289, drawing on Weber (n 77) 249–50.

[85] See eg Loi du 30 Ventôse an XII and P Remy, 'Regards sur le code', *Livre du Bicentenaire* (n 51),100: 'c'était un corps, un tout coherent, un systéme de droit civil prétendant à la completude'; Halpérin (n 79) 43, 46 ('C'est le mythe codificateur, insistant sur la complétude du Code, qui a créé dans nos esprits la conviction que le texte de 1804 était un "système" en soi'); notably, see the criticism of F Gény, *Méthode d'interprétation et sources en droit privé positif. Essai Critique* (Paris, LGD, 1919).

[86] The power of what I call the *code corpus* conception of codification in legal comparative writings cannot be underestimated: for a recent reading of the relevant legal comparative and doctrinal literature see, critically, Zimmermann (n 71) 371; note, critically, Varga (n 75) 247–48, from a socio-legal viewpoint, arguing that 'the phenomenon of codification has usually been taken as given, as a consequence of the normatively conceived requirements of defining the concept. It has been linked with definite ideas or models. The French Code Civil served as the model . . . it became the originator of a type . . . a pattern of the model concept of the code itself, indeed, the lowest common denominator . . . a pattern for the concept of codes, past and future. It established a form of higher organisation of the codification phenomenon, and by doing so, it became the originator of a tradition inspiring further development' and, but only partly, in socio-legal analyses (see Varga (n 75), as discussed above, but admitting of 'diversity' (at 247) and arguing that codification is a 'function . . . of a concrete socio-legal situation'; but adding that 'it did not obliterate old and/or different forms. In spite of its historical significance, it remained a particular manifestation' and criticising the theories that identified codification 'with this developed, but still particular historical manifestation, represented by the Code Civil' at

Specifically, the legislative plan to make a *code corpus* is about entrenching a true suspension of what one can call 'free interpretation' or 'arm's-length interpretation', relative to what otherwise applies whenever a code is not enacted – that is, interpretation that takes place unconstrained by code-based interpretative boundaries and that can refer to sources of law outside the code, such as policy arguments and normative considerations.[87] Such discipline is sought after instrumentally in order for the project(s) of a market economy to be effectively implemented. The parallelism between administrative power and the development of the industrial society has been noted,[88] which entailed the interest of the sovereign in organising structures of administrative power exempted from judicial control.[89] The same happened in relation to codification phenomena – the sovereign was interested in exempting power (via private law) from judicial control understood to be an obstruction to the operations of markets so as to pursue freedom of contract rights and absolute forms of protection of property rights based on the free will theory (*Code civil*), requiring from jurisprudence that exemption as a way towards ensuring the implementation of its preferred regulatory objectives. For example, Article 5 of the *Code civil* is emblematic of the practice of codification qua administrativisation – with the legislature interested in prohibiting 'full interpretation' as an end in itself (instrumental rationality)[90] towards implementing the value of 'calculability' in economic processes. In early nineteenth-century France, in terms of substantive rationality, the codification initiative was a move towards implementing a liberal-competitive market economy – the 'alliance of interests between the ruler and the bourgeois strata was the most potent driving force behind the formal rationalization of law',[91] that is, codification. Today, something similar is taking place, for, as discussed in chapter one, behind the code proposal is a market libertarian agenda. Embracing the code-form on the part of the legislature is about implementing an integrated system of interpretative patterns, that is, about 'impacting the field' so as to obtain mechanical pat-

248). Contrast the more nuanced position of Jansen (n 2) 86–87: '[M]odern codifications provide for comprehensive and therefore systematic legislation over a substantive part of the law. Seen from a formal, constitutional perspective, such codifications may be regarded as an expression of political domination in the same sense as statutory legislation . . . of course based on the sovereign's will . . . Yet . . . the normative substance of a codification is normally not determined by parliaments and governments. Codifications are typically drafted in the spirit of a largely declaratory restatement of the law. Usually, therefore, the legislator relies on professional advice and often even adds non-legislative, professional authority to a new code . . . with regard to law's substance, codification cannot be regarded as a full expression of political domination'), drawing on Max Weber's concept of 'legislative authority, or domination, as the sovereign's power legitimately to determine the law according to its free political choice': see M Weber, 'Die Drei Typen der legitimen Herrschaft' in M Weber, *Gesalmmelte Aufsäetze zur Wissenschaftslehre* (Tübingen, JC B Mohr, 7th edn, edited by Johannes Wincklemann 1988) 475–88 (translated by G Roth and C Wittich, M Weber *Economy and Society* 1968, I, at 53 et seq).

[87] See ch 1.

[88] See Weber, *Wirtschaft* as discussed above at n 77.

[89] *cf*, in the US, Pound's notion of 'administrative absolutism', epitomising the possibility of unlimited power of administrative structures.

[90] On calculability, see Varga (n 75), as discussed above.

[91] See ibid 289.

terns of law's application towards entrenching the preferred kind of market economy.[92]

In order for a codified private law to work in the way that the administrative state intends it to,[93] judges and scholars are meant to act as passive administrative agencies, that is, re-enacting as far as possible the model of the jurist-*exeget* and of the judge-*bouche de la loi* towards the delivery of that agenda.[94] Instrumentalisation to market systemic needs is supposed then to follow via the imposition of a certain behaviour on market actors; 'regulation' becomes the catchword; code as legislation cannot pretend to be a full-encompassing definition, for the phenomenon is above all about administrativisation and technique. Tarello's stress on the role of 'tecnicizzazione'[95] as a general trend of the work of the jurist in the age of modern codification episodes is a remarkable formulation that supports this understanding, as it is the argument of another Italian legal historian, who stressed how the primary concern of the legislator (for example, in France from the sixteenth-century onwards) was about forming 'un corpo di leggi unico unitario ed uniforme per tutti i territori dello Stato' in relation to the formation of 'uno stato burocratico e centralizzato a economia nazionale'.[96] From this vantage point, one must conclude that a code is not just 'legislation',[97] but a 'regulatory tool' aimed at organising market behaviour via administrative means – not the only one, obviously, but a major tool that could ensure the making of the project of modernity

[92] On the concept of 'impacting the field', see above, ch 1.

[93] This fallacy (the statist ideology that the *code corpus* 'must work') must be looked at critically. One cannot say in the abstract whether or not, and to what extent, a code 'works', considering the argument that this book is proposing that the conditions of the jurisprudential discourse determine the success or failure of the implementation of a code. I am thinking of the long periods during which formalistic strands of jurisprudence allowed the code to be implemented until then jurisprudence managed to set itself free from the code: examples are the 'time lag' that it took for a protectionist regime of product liability and of standardised terms to establish itself in France and Italy respectively. From this vantage point, one must consider critically the following statement by C Varga, 'The Contemporaneity of Lukács' Ideas with Modern Social Theoretical Thought' (2013) 99 *Archiv fuer Rechts- und Sozialphilosophie* 42, 49, recounting 'the development of created, written and formally enacted norm structures, intended to embody the law exclusively' as 'the scheme' whereby the idea of jus has been reduced to the mere factuality of the lex exacted: 'such a scheme presumes law-making to have been lifted to almost limitless all-mightness, to a freely fillable space of regulatory character. As a consequence, the lex will remain the exclusive genuine actor on the legal field, the sole creator of which can be considered at all relevant – and in which sense – in law. Thereby, law-making is sharply contrasted to law-application, which latter is downgraded to a merely executive role. As a consequence, the justice to be administered will necessarily degenerate into mere formal rule-conformism'.

[94] For a description of what this means in relation to the contemporary project of codification, see above chs 1 and 3.

[95] Tarello (n 44).

[96] V Piano Mortari, 'Codice (Storia)' in *Enciclopedia del Diritto* (Milan, Giuffrè, 1970) 227, 230.

[97] Zimmermann (n 71) 371 ('codification is an act of legislation, ie its validity is based on the intervention of the state'; explaining that this means the 'recording of the rules pertaining to a certain field of law' – quoting Jeremy Bentham, who argued that codification is 'Quite different [from] ordinary legislation' in view of the fact that here 'of the entire field of law . . . some very large portion . . . is to receive an entire new covering all at once': J Bentham, 'Papers Relative to Codification and Public Instruction' in J Bowring (ed), *The Works of Jeremy Bentham, Volume IV* (Edinburgh, Tait, 1843) 518 – along with ensuring internal coherence, with having a systematic nature and with being 'not intended to be a contribution to an academic discourse but . . . to be observed and applied in practice').

in terms of entrenching market economic systems of production and distribution of wealth.

Thus, a code cannot just be about nation-building, or about 'rationalism' in the sense of the objective of eliminating legal uncertainties, or about constituting 'cultural identity',[98] depending on one's preferred viewpoint on codification phenomena as read in conventional literature, for it is about the overarching administrative objective of implementing the chosen market-economic plan. Nation-building, the objective of eliminating legal uncertainties and, arguments based on 'cultural identity', have all in turn been epiphenomena instrumental to achieving that objective – but contingently and not by necessity, considering for example that the Allgemeines Bürgerliches Gesetzbuch/ABGB) of 1811 was neither about state-building[99] nor about nation-building,[100] nor was the 1992 Dutch Code about nationalism and cultural identity.[101] It has been a categorical mistake[102] of scholarship to look at factors other than economic regulation via administrativisation and to direct our attention to matters that are important in themselves but not instrumental for a full understanding of the codification phenomenon.[103] I agree with Zimmermann that there is a need for writing a critical history of modern codifications.[104] I take that to mean (this is my proposal) to pay attention to administrativisation as a decisive factor in the matter, alongside other aspects as considered above, whose role must also be investigated in relation to the practices of administrativisation. Conventional understandings of the codification phenomenon must be re-interpreted more realistically, that is, in relation to the administrative practice of economic regulation. Specifically, and firstly, codes can be held to have played a 'revolutionary' role because abolishing old laws

[98] This critique remains valid even if one by 'cultural' means, as in my view one should, complex traditions and cultural identities (Glenn (n 73); Niglia 'Of Complexity and Tradition' (2014 essay, on file with author)), for example, in the sense of the definition of codification according to Mengoni (see above, at ch 2) rather than in the more holistic sense in which scholars tend to understand the work of Legrand (*cf* Legrand (n 57)).

[99] See L Mengoni, *L'Europa dei Codici o un Codice per l'Europa?* (Rome, Centro di Studi e Ricerche di Diritto Comparato e Straniero, 1993) as discussed above, at ch 2.

[100] ibid (the *Allgemeines Bürgerliches Gesetzbuch*/ABGB of 1811 not about nation-building). See above, ch 2 (synthesis of conflicts representing the new constitutional 'identity' in a climate of constitutionalism without sovereignty).

[101] On the Dutch Code *Burgerlijk Wetboek* (BW) of 1992 interpreted in this way, see W Van Gerven, 'Codifying European Private Law: Top Down and Bottom Up' in S Grundmann and J Stuyck (eds), *An Academic Green Paper on European Contract Law* (The Hague, London, Kluwer Law International, 2002), 405, 409 (arguing, with regard to the *Code civil* and the *BGB*, that 'Where the two codes do resemble each other is that they had the same political goal which was to put an end to legal differentiation and thus to contribute to the shaping of a centralized Nation-State' and that 'Obviously the Dutch BW had a completely different function: it was no longer intended to achieve unity or to strengthen the concept of the Nation-State but constituted an undertaking carried out by lawyers in view of modernizing private law by turning judicial and doctrinal innovations into codified law'. For a critique of cultural identity as embodied in the *Code civil*, see Michaels (n 22).

[102] On an intellectual genealogy of this 'mistake' (in relation to natural law), see, eg, Wieacker (n 27) 215 (interface between 'the modern nation's claim to total control' and the 'Law of Reason').

[103] See the discussion in Michaels (n 22) (enumerating them and noting their deployment in contradictory terms).

[104] Zimmermann (n 71).

(feudal, pre-modern etc) meant furthering a market system that could not otherwise sustain itself; secondly, codes can be held to be about nation-building and 'cultural identity' insofar as one bears in mind that, the monopolisation of force via the nationalism that they embody is instrumental to market-building, an instrumentality that is indistinguishable from the nation-building exercise in the modern history of continental Europe.[105] These are accidental relations that cannot be turned into necessary relations, as conventionalism (that is, the schools of thought that draw on nationalism and culturalism) would have us believe. In the organisation of economic material via codification, everything is interrelated. From this vantage point, the repertoire of 'historical conditions' allegedly behind the codification phenomena of the past two centuries cannot be re-deployed so as to make intelligible[106] the proposed European code, for explaining the latter only on those terms in turn makes of it an object that is, historically speaking, existent but unexplainable. Taking administrativisation into account is a must in order to really explain codification past and present.

ii. Decisionism qua economic constitution

One must overcome those conventional explanations firmly based on nationalism and culturalism, whether strictly spelled out on historical or on theoretical-conceptual grounds.[107] Such explanations obscure our understanding of the phenomenon and, on this basis, one must explain codification not only in terms of administrativisation but also, let me argue now, in terms of constitutionality, for this is the other key decisionist dimension to the codification enterprise. Administrativisation is, deep down, about constitutionality[108] because it is about

[105] See Epilogue below on codification explained as being about the crafting of sovereignty.

[106] See Zimmermann (n 71) 396 (discussing the proposed code against the 'historical conditions responsible' for codification understood as 'historical phenomenon originating in the 18th century, and implemented from the end of that century onwards', and concluding that 'the auspices for a European Code of Contract Law, let alone a Civil Code, are far from ideal. There is no common language in which it could be drafted. There is no Supreme Court in private law matters which could effectively ensure its uniform application. There is not yet a sufficiently strong European legal scholarship that could sustain it . . . there is not yet a strong feeling of European identity (comparable to the feeling of national identity in the 19th century) that would give wings to such endeavour. And there is no sense of crisis that would make a codification appear indispensable').

[107] For a synthesis of writers who adopt these views, see the critical analysis of, respectively, Zimmermann (n 71); and Michaels (n 22).

[108] On codes as constitutions, see, eg, Mengoni (n 19): 'Nel modello di costituzionalismo europeo-continentale, di matrice francese, la positivizzazione dei diritti fondamentali non produsse una codificazione del tipo della Costituzione americana, la prima grande codificazione moderna, bensì il codice civile, ossia la codificazione delle libertà borghesi e dei rapporti di libero mercato nella forma di diritti civili-privati', citing Tarello (n 44) 561; G Cornu, *Introduction, les personnes, les biens* (Paris, Éditions Montchrestien, 10th edn, 2001) n 257 (*constitution civile*); J Carbonnier, 'Le Code civil' in Pierre Nora (ed) *Les Lieux de mémoire* vol 1 (Paris, Éditions Gallimard, 1997) ('la véritable constitution de la France, c'est le Code civil. En lui sont récapitulées les idées autour desquelles la société française s'est constituée au sortir de la Révolution et continue de se constituer de nos jours encore, développant ces ideées, les transformant peut-être, sans avoir jamais dit les renier'). On the concept of economic constitution in relation to private law and on the idea of a European Civil Code as economic constitution, see recently H Collins, *The European Civil Code: The Way Forward* (Cambridge, Cambridge University Press, 2007) 91 et seq and 210.

the project of the rational achievement of a set of contingent economic objectives in constitutional mode. I propose re-reading a solid and consistent line of scholarship on codes as economic constitutional phenomena in light of the perspective on administrativisation that I have put forward.

In the writings that propose to understand codes as constitutions, codes are presented as vehicles for the delivery of substantive economico-political statist ideologies. The passage by Wieacker above quoted indicates that codes are about imposing contingent ideological agendas – for example, throughout most of the nineteenth century, the codes tended to prioritise bourgeois concerns over social concerns related to the labour movement (the so-called 'bourgeois codes'). Moreover, codes are about instrumentalising exclusionary choices, that is, excluding whilst including ideological perspectives – the workings of the administrative machinery are about implementing the preferred ideological agendas.

In terms of implementing ideologies (lassez-faire, liberist etc), codes are 'objects' whose instrumental power lies in constituting 'subjects' of (constitutional) law. They are administrative structures that are rationally geared towards constituting *constitutional* rights and duties.[109] Constitutional rights are then a complementary way to do the ideological job, with codified norms (rights and duties) being transfer rules for (constitutional) values.[110] For example, the bourgeois codes constituted absolute contractual and property constitutional freedoms.

Being a regulatory tool aimed at conforming market behaviour towards a set of pre-determined ideological objectives, the code is, materially speaking,[111] about entrenching an *economic* constitution, that is, about creating a particular kind of market system as a matter of constitutional practice.[112] This is because the state via the code constitutes rights and duties for citizens that apply in the mode of a material constitution. All comes full circle. The code qua economic constitution[113]

[109] A major obstacle to not seeing the code as an administrative tool and as an economic constitution rather than just a technique of organisation of private law rules is the public/private divide. I am deliberately overcoming it, in line with studies that have previously done so, eg, Mengoni (n 19) (in relation to the conception of codes as constitutions).

[110] On norms as rules 'transferring' values see eg N Reich, 'Balancing in Private Law and the Imperatives of Public Interest' in Brownsword, Micklitz, Niglia and Weatherill (n 32) 221, 227.

[111] 'Material' in the sense of the thesis 'code qua economic constitution' as opposed to the other conventional explanations of the codification phenomenon as 'national' or 'rational'.

[112] *cf*, eg, Caroni (n 80), 337, 348–49 ('diritto costituzionale succube di quello privato; accessorietá della costituzione; valenza costituzionale dei codici civili') and calling for further analyses of the complex constitutional mechanisms set in place by civil codes; Tarello (n 44) (drawing a parallelism between civil and constitutional codification).

[113] See Zimmermann (n 71) 389–90 (arguing that, at the 'supranational level', 'we no longer need a civil code' for the purposes of the 'constitutional function', as this is discharged at the national level, but, at n 120, distinguishing the case of a European civil code understood as 'economic constitution' as defended by Collins (n 108), that is, understood as 'useful device to contribute towards an integrated civil society out of which a common European identity could be constructed', citing at 2 the work of Collins (n 108)). I understand modern civil codes to be economic constitutions regardless of whether they are prescriptive rather than instructive (for this opposition, see Zimmermann (n 71) 373, arguing that 'the European Civil Code' envisaged by Collins is not a codification in the technical sense of the word: it is conceived as a framework of normative standards). It is, of course, a problematic qua contested economic constitutional project that we are talking about – on 'de-constitutionalisation' and 're-constitutionalisation', see ch 3 and the remainder of this chapter.

is then *constitution civile*[114] because, in implementing an economic 'plan', it becomes a 'law that can channel, facilitate, steer and reinforce social practices regarding market relations', including 'legal guarantees' and 'concepts provided by private law regarding property, contract and persons'.[115] Materially, such social practices are 'constitutional', whatever the degree of command and control and of the facilitation of market processes that they may embody, depending on the foundational policy choices that shape them contingently.[116] One can state this in relation to all modern codes insofar as they have, to whatever extent, been genuinely about implementing a market economy. Enacting the 1804 *Code civil de français* meant creating the conditions for institutionalising a constitution in all but name, the codification of the bourgeois freedoms, effectively creating a market system based on absolute property rights and contractual freedoms.[117] This is equally true of the codification chapter in Piedmont, with the code being considered, in the remarkable words of Federico Sclopis in 1864 with regard to the codification episode,[118] 'the cornerstone of the social edifice' (*Chiave dell'edificio sociale*), which, in the words of Pio Caroni, meant 'volendosi così specificare le diverse modalità attraverso le quali si coglieva la centralità della società-mercato e l'accidentalità dello stato',[119] that is, the codification of the belief in a minimal constitutional state based on the centrality of the market-society and the limited role of the state. The BGB followed a distinctive set of substantive, constitutional objectives, labelled by Wieacker as 'liberist'. In managing to monopolise the private law field, codes (*code corpus*) have been ways to tame, through private law codes operating as a *constitutional* vocabulary, major ideological tensions such as those of feudalism versus liberalism,[120] authoritarianism versus liberalism, liberalism versus republicanism,[121] corporativism and liberalism. For example, applied to both patrimonial law and family law (eg, the introduction of divorce, restriction of parental powers and equality in interstate succession), the *Code civil* met with resistance after 1804 from ultra-royalists and legitimists (opposing 'the individualist ideas of the Revolution and the Enlightenment' as 'endangering the stability and integrity of the family'), whilst the liberals attacked it for being not

[114] See J Carbonnier (n 108) ('la véritable constitution de la France, c'est le Code civil'; J Chirac (Président de la République) 'Message' in *Livre Centenaire* at 3 ('Véritable constitution civile de la France, le Code Civil . . .').

[115] Collins (n 108) 95 (on the concept of economic constitution).

[116] Contrast Collins (n 108) 95 (arguing that: 'In a market order, a distinctive feature of the laws that assure its functions is their emphasis on the facilitation of individual actions and choices. Command and control is limited in comparison to other kinds of social orders').

[117] See, eg, Gordley (n 10) 459, as discussed above (with the qualification that the modern individualistic principles were enforced only a few decades after enactment of the code).

[118] Federico Sclopis, *Storia della legislazione italiana, III, Dall'epoca della rivoluzione francese [1789] a quella delle riforme italiane [1847], parte prima* (Turin, 1864) 278, quoted in Pio Caroni (n 80) at 348. On functional aspects involved in the civil codes of 1865 and of 1942, see also Nicolò (n 82); Asquini (n 69).

[119] Caroni (n 80) 348–49 (but critically noting the need to also focus attention on the role of social legislation as this existed alongside the codes in the nineteenth century).

[120] For various references to this theme, see Caroni (n 9) 280 (as discussed above).

[121] For both, see (n 79) 54 et seq.

liberal enough in matters of loans at interest or movable property.[122] The currently proposed code is, once more, 'law-form' that tames conflicts by enforcing an ideological plan that stands in continuity with the individualism as initiated with the bourgeois codes.

iii. Code as Legislation Today (Genealogy I: 1814–2014)

The new codification movement flies in the face of a massive counter-codification movement, as developed in the form of national law and European law.[123] The counter-codification movement has taken away private laws from the dogmatics of the free market system (laissez-faire),[124] as incorporated in the 'bourgeois codes' of the nineteenth century and their successors, towards defending a new material constitution based on the variety of new interests that must be regulated by private law (in the logic of the welfarist ways of de-codification). The placing of constitutional charters at the core of the private law system as a result of the politicisation and pluralisation of private law has reduced the rank of civil codes and made private law serve its new substantive objectives. De-codification designates the ways in which scholars and judges have faced the challenge of incorporating into the private law system (weakly understood) a pluralistic economic constitution open to conflicting values and the work of mediation of legal actors (in the logic of 'weak constitutionalism').[125] Whereas codes were intended to be centralising tools monistic in both substance (ideological) and structure (administration), de-codification is open to the plurality of often conflicting values implied in the welfare paradigm and relies on a variety of non-hierarchical implementing tools, including the positioning of any judge (including ordinary courts, not necessarily the Constitutional Court) as an active mediator of social conflicts.[126]

The move from the European Commission is 'counter-counter-movement' as it goes towards accommodating a new dogmatic – that of market libertarianism – in old clothes (those of codification). We are witnessing the repetition of an old pattern, with its usual pretense of naturalness and neutrality as captured in these words:

> [L]e caractère cyclique de codifications – la loi de l'éternel retour de la codification, comme enterprise de mise en ordre et d'intelligence du droit par l'écriture.[127]

[122] For this account, see J-L Halpérin, *The French Civil Code* (London, UCL Press, 2005, translated by Tony Weir) 56 et seq.

[123] For the analysis of the counter-codification movement, see above, ch 2.

[124] On laissez-faire in relation to the BGB, see, eg, Reich (n 110); in relation to the Italian Civil Code, see Niglia (n 2) (formalism in relation to Articles 1342–43 Italian Civil Code on standardised terms).

[125] The de-codified ways of private law revolve around interpretative operations that balance the conflicting values in open interpretative contexts, that is, arm's-length interpretation; the codified ways of private law (*code corpus*) instead revolve around disciplinary impositions of centralised economico-constitutional agendas that aim at excluding conflicting values.

[126] On values and institutions typical of the welfare paradigm of private law, see above, ch 2.

[127] Rémy (n 51) 99, 118.

C. Code as *Nomos-and-Thesis* Phenomenon: Between Jurisprudence and Legislation

i. Structure (Vocabularies) and Substance (Positions)

The impetus to merge principles and *acquis* may have come from the new 'sovereign'; however, the Commission's intimation merely reiterates an old pattern, that is, the canonical act of appropriation of the work of scholarship ('officialisation') for the purpose of implementing a contingent market economic (libertarian) agenda. At the same time, the structures of European scholarship are largely 'ready' for the codification move. The intensity of the convergence of legislative and jurisprudential vocabularies over the remaking of a *code corpus* is considerably higher if contrasted with the past episodes of concretisation of the *code corpus* plan.

The contemporary codification strategy is being implemented by the legislature in stronger terms than in the past, if one thinks of the *Code civil* and the conflicting rationales behind it. On the one hand, the European Commission documents surrounding the CFR project are univocal, reflecting a mastery of technocratic craft in portraying the objective of achieving an administrative hierarchy (the code proposal being depicted as 'self-standing' and 'comprehensive') and the inclusion of economic constitutional materials in as detailed a form as possible.[128] Here is a legislature that produces narratives consistently holding that the code being enacted is: 'self-standing and comprehensive'; pursues total harmonisation; is committed to overcoming fragmentation; firmly manifests its belief in market libertarian objectives; commands the judge to adopt an autonomous interpretation of the CESL Optional Code, forbidding interpretation based on national law; and placing freedom of contract as the only overarching value at the core of the proposed *CESL*.[129] On the other hand, to give an historical example, one finds 'less perfect' craft coming from the insiders to the legislative process behind the *Code civil* – Portalis' *Discourse* statements are certainly less regimented, considering for example the statement that the judge enjoys some scope for interpretation within the principles set out in the code by the legislature.[130] These were times in which the opposite sensibility was present, as one can evince from the opinion of the *Tribunal d'appel de Lyon* participating in the consultation regarding the Code and writing in its *Observations*: 'La loi commande: elle n'est pas faite pour instruire; elle n'a pas besoin de convaincre.'[131]

Considering that legislatures can construct codes that are more or less 'open' depending on how much discretion they expect from the jurisprudential forces (a lesson learnt from previous codification experiences), it is significant to note that

[128] See above, ch 1.

[129] See respectively at Arts 4(1), 4(2) and 1(1) CESL.

[130] Portalis (n 28).

[131] Quoted in F Gény , 'La Technique législative dans la codification civile moderne (a propos du centeraire du code civil)' in *Le Code Civil Livre du centenaire* (Paris, Dalloz, 1904) 989, 1012.

out of the present European codification episode comes a code-text that embodies a kind of legislature's closure that more closely resembles the BGB than the *Avant-project Huber* of a Code for Switzerland.[132] François Gény held the BGB to be , in contrast to the *Avant-project Huber* ('le cadres aisés et souples des Projets suisses'),[133] a cluster of 'dispositions, strictement pesées, rigoureusement enchînées e se tenant en échec les unes les autres', so much that 'on a besoin d'une réflexion intense e de tout un travail de l'esprit pour eu pénétrer le sens'; 'une fois en possession du contenu plein . . . on se sent établi sur un terrain treés ferme que donne à l'activité pratique une sécurité presque absolue', although 'on peut selement regretter que ce dernier avantage ne soit acquis qu'au prix d'une tendance à l'abstraction'.[134]

Here, no doubt in a similar fashion to past codification episodes during the period of the triumph of the *code corpus* model (roughly 1850–1950), the state of scholarship is a key factor towards determining this 'closed' kind of legislative technique being implemented at the EU level (*code corpus*) as opposed to weaker codification forms. Alongside the discursive structures considered above in section I.A, also at work is the continuing shift of legal science towards economic objectivisation that increasingly affects private law.[135] Neo-pandectistic and neo-positivistic thinking married with an ideological legislative's economic agenda (as discussed in chapter one) proves this. Equally, a certain interpretation of 'law and economics' enters jurisprudence as privileged methodology, for whoever wishes to uphold the policies that are currently the primary pre-occupation of the Commission must find comfort in such 'law and economics' positions.[136] The praise of private power and related contractual freedoms understood in absolute terms in certain jurisprudential strands[137] go in the same direction. And the vocabularies that understand private law in terms of regulation and pluralisation, including the deployment of alternative methods of resolution (depoliticised)[138] and the practice of de-institutionalised private choice,[139] may be perceived as creating the same effect. Overall, scholarly structures are more ready for the making

[132] *cf* ibid 1034–35, contrasting the Avant-project Huber with the BGB. On legislative techniques in general, see ibid 1032–38; on the contingency of the issue of the extent to which legislation should try to contain or to extend customs or *le libre appréciation du juge*, considering that it all depends on 'inclications populaires, la situation du Corps judiciaire et la confiance qu'il inspire, dans l'importance qu'on attaché à la certitude du Droit au point de vue de la sécurité des affaires, toutes considérations variables suivant les temps e les lieux', see ibid 1033.

[133] ibid 1036.

[134] ibid 1035.

[135] Note the parallel development in international law: M Koskenniemi, 'Hegemonic Regimes' in MA Young (ed), *Regime Interaction in International Law: Facing Fragmentation* (New York, Cambridge University Press, 2012) 305, 307 et seq (discussing economics as the ground for justifying action).

[136] *cf* F Larouche and P Chirico (eds), *Economic Analysis of the DCFR: The Work of the Economic Impact Group within CoPECL* (Munich, Sellier, 2010). See above, ch 1.

[137] See above, ch2 (on the CESL).

[138] For analysis of this practice, see H Micklitz, 'Monistic Ideology versus Pluralistic Reality: Towards a Normative Design for European Private Law' in Niglia (ed) (n 24) 29.

[139] For an analysis of this practice, see J Smits, 'A Radical View on Pluralism' in Niglia (ed) (n 24) 161 et seq, which I understand in terms of defending the idea that law should be made 'free' from the processes associated with institutions, as discussed at ch 2 above (see also Niglia (n 32) at 133 et seq).

of a *code corpus* than has been the case for previous *code corpus* phenomena, such as the *Code civil*, considering that it took more than 'successive days in a series of concentric circles radiating out from Paris, each a day's ride further than the last', as provided for in its Article 1, for the Code to be really implemented.[140]

From this vantage point, and looking at the content of the codified rules (ideological positions), the policy choices that lie behind the proposed code are *also* jurisprudential choices. The proposed code's extended version, the CFR, is an attempt at a new form of political government – a projected regulatory intervention with ideological focus (an economic constitution of a market libertarian kind) and a studied range of agents and tools for regulatory implementation (administrativisation centred on model rules and principles, judges being under an obligation to interpret them according to an 'autonomous' mode of reasoning). Equally, the proposed code's shortened version, the *CESL*, is about instantiating an optional regime as a first step in the implementation of the market libertarian agenda and the related empowerment of private parties to deliver that agenda – with judges being required to implement the 'self-contained' (autonomous from national legal systems and traditions) rules and principles of the CESL only, that is, being 'forbidden' to use national law, in a similar way to that in which the *Code civil* forbade the use of material outside the Code in its Article 4.[141]

Let me now discuss more the dual character (both jurisprudential and legislative) of the codification phenomenon historically and present, that is, the complexity of the respective vocabularies and their intersections in the making of a European *code corpus*.

ii. 'Osmosis': Jurisprudential Vocabularies as Legislation

The 'sovereign's decision' to codify and thus to entrench an economic constitutional plan encounters a barrier – that of the state of the art of jurisprudence, more or less geared towards the codification move and thus making the decisionist move more or less possible.[142] Correspondingly, jurisprudence, if orientated towards codifying the law, encounters a limit in terms of the extent to which the legislature is committed to officially codify the law, if at all[143] (for example, the project for an Italian Code of Commerce as elaborated by the jurisprudential forces was halted by political contingencies).[144] Both dimensions shape each other – the decisionist act materialises through jurisprudential material being

[140] Glenn (n 73) 66; Gordley (n 10) (the Code not as instantly implemented, but as a reference point for the re-organisation of jurisprudence in France in the period 1804–50).

[141] But with a heavy sanction – Art 4 *Code civil* reads: 'The judge who refuses to judge, under pretext of the silence, obscurity or insufficiency of the law, will be subject to prosecution for denial of justice.'

[142] See the three examples given at the start of this chapter.

[143] Savigny (n 5) 35: '[W]ith such a number of authors and such a rapid succession of books and authorities, no particular book can preserve a predominant and lasting influence otherwise than through the authority of the state.'

[144] Asquini (n 69) 253.

re-arranged via the codification work (as per the prohibitions on interpretation contained in Article 5 *Code civil*); the jurisprudential work materialises through creating code-like structures (systematisation,[145] coherence and neutralism, as well as completeness and autonomy) that the sovereign in turn needs to rely upon to construct his own decision. For example, legal thought on individualism and related 'will theories' translated into the legislature's plan to establish a constitutional order qua 'gouvernement de la liberté', as was the case for the *Code civil*.[146] The *Code civil* incorporated compromises over political material as re-elaborated in the juristic language of the code-projects, in relation to what to accept and what to reject of the Revolution, including tensions between Napoleonic authoritarianism and revolutionary principles.[147] The code is a hybrid – a decisionist re-creation of jurisprudential material and a jurisprudential re-creation of decisionist material.[148] One cannot really make the argument that there was ever a stark distinction between 'legislation' and 'jurisprudence' in codification phenomena, a position that was never really believed by the insiders[149] (recall the image of the committee of the *Code civil*, with the Emperor sitting close by the jurists) as both are 'sovereigntist' in instantiating decisionism and 'jurisprudential' in materialising decisions via re-arrangements of legal material. The work of the jurisprudential forces is about constructing the building blocks for the purpose of the preferred administrative and constitutional strategy. The jurists, whether directly employed in the administration,[150] or participating in the committees and consultation proceedings that led to the code, are the most visible forms in which sovereignty and juristic work have gone hand in hand in the centralisation of private law, as built over the course of the eighteenth and nineteenth centuries and part of the twentieth century. The science of law and the science of legislation each have a

[145] On systematic beliefs even in France, see Halpérin (n 79) 43, 46: 'C'est le mythe codificateur, insistant sur la complétude du Code, qui a créé dans nos esptis la conviction que le texte de 1804 était un "système" en soi.'

[146] F Ewald, 'Rapport philosophique: une politique du droit' in *Livre Bicentenaire* (n 51) 76, 95.

[147] See Halpérin (n 79) 43, 50 et seq (considering the Napolenic Code as having partly accepted and partly rejected the tenets of the Revolution, and noting the related conflicts within the jurisprudential forces as emerged in the three code-projects proposed by *Cambacérès* to the revolutionary assemblies, the 'private' project of *Target* and the project of year IX by *Tronchet*, *Portalis*, *Bigot de Préameneu* and *Maleville* (which was not identical with the finally approved code).

[148] From the vantage point of the reconstruction that I am proposing, one must admit that many of the questions raised in scholarship about the codification phenomenon are less relevant than one might think. Whether a modern code is a consolidation act (re-statement of past law) or a 'new' law (original) is a question that need not be posed, for a code is both (see Portalis (n 28): 'The Codes of nations are the fruit of the passage of time; but properly speaking, we do not make them'). The question of the authority of the so-called private or non-legislative codifications (which I understand to be codifications not yet formally 'appropriated' by the sovereign) has no real reason to exist independently of the question regarding the authority of codifications as appropriated by the sovereign (that is, the authority of jurisprudence as co-constitutive of codification), an issue to which I will return in the conclusion to this chapter (however, for the opinion of 'non-legislative codifications' as embodying legal authority, see Jansen (n 2)).

[149] At any time that scholarship emphasises the many failures of codification episodes to bring about 'closure' (see now Glenn (n 73) 65–69), in my view scholarship offers evidence to support my argument.

[150] Tarello (n 44) (discussing the nineteenth century).

logic of their own[151] but both operate in the same terrain – the code is, deep down, 'instrument de révélation du Droit objectif' (both centralising legislative instrument *and* 'revealing' the law on the ground).[152] There is a contingency in determining the 'space' of the legislative technique in that terrain[153] and, on that basis, the greater the determination of the legislature to give room for jurisprudence to operate, the higher the possibility for jurisprudence to take on that task to a greater extent than it would have done were the legislature to make the opposite decision – and vice versa. Thus, in the perception of dominant writers, it was felt that the legislator drafted the BGB with the intention of making the judge a *Subsumtionsautomat* (*bouche de la loi*), whilst, according to Gény, the authors of the projects of a Swiss code aimed at allowing for more discretion to be available to the judge.[154] In turn, jurisprudence itself co-determines the legislative choices. Thus, the BGB was followed by a massive positivism in the first two decades, albeit with counter-trends in areas such as: the circumvention of the limitations of the law of delict at paras 823 et seq BGB in not protecting the patrimony as such via contractual liability; damages of the object possessed and *Verkehssicherungspflichten*; and, as to the law of contract, *clausola rebus sic stantibus*; *doli generalis*; *culpa in contrahendo*; positive breach of contract and third party loss.[155] Equally, in France, it took a few decades for private law jurists to adopt exegetic approaches following enactment of the 1804 *Code civil des français*. Another way in which jurisprudence determined the overall legislature's position was through a certain degree of arbitrariness in the way in which the jurists of the committees appointed for drafting codes identified the legal material to deploy for that purpose, as also shown by the contradictory passages of the *Discours Preliminaire* in support of the *Code civil*.[156] From this vantage point, certain codes have been rightly labelled *code corpus* (codes understood 'as complete as possible *corpus* of precise and detailed norms regarding all the institutes of the law, inspired to the rigorous technicalities as practiced by the experts'),[157] for, in embodying the strong version of the

[151] Gény (n 131) 990 et seq.

[152] ibid 1033 (referred to as 'la Loi écrité').

[153] As discussed above at c.i.

[154] Respectively R Zimmermann, *Roman Law, Contemporary Law, European Law: The Civilian Tradition Today* (Oxofrd Oxford University Press, 2001) 55; Gény (n 131) 1035 (according to whom the then Swiss code project did little to help 'penetrate' the details of the legal system, for 'il faut compter, pour le mettre en oevre, sur la sagacité et l'habilité personnelles d'un pouvoir exécutif ou judiciare se haussant sans cesse jusqu'à la création du Droit').

[155] *cf* Zimmermann (n 154) 55 et seq (criticising, on the basis of the law of delict, the belief that the early years of the BGB were just characterised by positivistic narrowness in the practice of the Imperial Court; the same applies to the law of contract, at 80 et seq).

[156] Portalis (n 28). For example, note the reading of Portalis' work in Van Caenegem (n 2) 8–9 (code civil rules as not new rules, but as the result of 'the experience of centuries'; Portalis as 'conservative' but arguing that 'in Portalis' theoretical work, natural law plays a very important part', against the background consideration of the innovative orientation of natural law during that period, that is, : 'During the Revolution, natural law was constantly invoked to justify new rules and institutions').

[157] On *code corpus* versus flexible code, see (n 82) 240, 241 (arguing in the 1960s for the need to revitalise the polemic ('le polemiche') around codification as developed before the making of the 1865 Italian Civil Code, a code that Nicolò believes to have been characterised by a substantial consensus over the need to base it on the *Code civil*, and the pre-unitary codes, as the best way to unify private law

codification phenomena (eg, BGB), they worked as crucial material for the organisation of the centralised body politic in modern times. In other words, and to paraphrase Paolo Grossi's note on law's pluralism as *carnalità*, the *code corpus* worked as the artificially created *carnalità* of the law of the state in the sense that the state could come into 'existence' as a 'constitutional entity' thanks to *that* body of rules (complete, systematised and autonomous). Jurists and judges acted as key administrative-constitutional actors in writing the script of the *code corpus*. The consciousness of the sovereign in portraying himself as an ideal kind of administrator, manifested in the making of a code, is another sign of this phenomenon, seen from the perspective of the sovereign himself. From this vantage point, the famous quote from *Napoléon* needs be cited in full rather than abridged:

> Ce que rien n'effacera, ce qui vivra éternellement, c'est mon Code civil. Ce sont les procès-verbaux de mon conseil d'État; ce sont les recueils de ma correspondance avec mes ministres; *c'est enfin tout le bien que j'ai fait comme administrateur, comme réorganisateur de la grande famille française.*[158]

This is why one can say that sovereignty is re-created via the process of codification. Whenever anything (any 'entity') as close as possible to a *code corpus* manages to be devised and successfully implemented, *that* kind of code could well be described in terms of legislation, constitution, administration and adjudication at once without making any real categorical mistake. For example, the judicial decisions that apply Articles 1341-1342 of the Italian Civil Code in order to provide for only a formal protection (a double signature) in contexts of heavy interventionism[159] (with the state heavily involved as it was for a few decades around the second half of the twentieth century in most economic activities from banking to insurance) are no different from acts issued in the context of an administrative-based regime of control of unfair terms and declaring the formal legality of any of the terms included in standard form contracts – which was the case for the 1978 *Loi Scrivener*. Everything that falls into the codification phenomenon, from decisionist (administrativisation, economic constitution) to juristic (systematisation, completeness, coherence and related notions and doctrines) material is intertwined. In the codification phenomenon it is 'osmosis' that reigns supreme, that shapes sovereignty, determining the degree to which a code-form is more *corpus* and less *open*, or vice versa, at every point in time from pre-enactment to enactment and post-enactment.

in Italy, with a view to 'definire che cosa debba rappresentare un codice di diritto privato in una società moderna, se esso cioè debba essere un *corpus*, il più completo possibile, di norme precise e analitiche per tutti gli istituti della vita giuridica, ispirate al rigoroso tecnicismo degli iniziati, o se piuttosto non debba essere un tessuto di princìpi, sui filoni fondamentali della esperienza giuridica, che, per la loro capacità espansiva e la loro flessibilità, possano, attraverso la integrazione di fonti normative a carattere meno impegnativo di un codice (leggi speciali, usi, ecc.), e attraverso il penetrante lavoro dei giuristi, teorici e pratici, che vivono e comprendono quella esperienza, adeguarsi più da vicino al ritmo della evoluzione delle nostre strutture sociali').

[158] CT Montholon *Récits de la Captivité de l'Empereur Napoléon à Sainte-Hélène I* (Paris, Paulin, 1847) 401 (emphasis added), as referred to in Michaels (n 22) 290.

[159] Niglia (n 2).

iii. Code as Legislation and *Jurisprudence (Genealogy II: 1814–2014)*

The contingent political imperatives pursued by the legislature, being a co-product of jurisprudential deliberation (eg, *Cambacérès* code-projects closer to revolutionary principles than the *Portalis* project), were more or less realised depending on the extent to which the jurisprudential forces favoured the highly technical discourse of individualism (what Coing labelled 'deductive-axiomatic system of thought' revolving around the protection of atomistic individual rights) over opposing forces that instead favoured an understanding of law as revolving around sociality. By sociality is meant, to put it in the vocabulary of Savigny's *Vom Beruf*, the scientific character of law inherent to its social function; the spontaneous production of law via customs; the history of Roman law until classical age as 'organische Entwicklung';[160] and, in the words of Gurvitch's *L'idée du droit social*, 'le droit social est un droit de communion' . . . 'integrant d'un façon objective chaque totalité active reélle'.[161] The vocabulary of sociality was coined just a decade after the enactment of the *Code civil*, in Savigny's *Vom Beruf* (1814),[162] a work that did not just play a role in stopping the adoption of the *Code civil* in the then Germanic states but that also created the private law vocabulary alternative to the individualistic-orientated rationalist vocabulary of the codifiers – initiating a struggle of vocabularies and beliefs that has characterised the development of private law ever since, as it transfigured from the defence of feudal prerogatives into mature 'social law' (equality, solidarity) starting in the second half of the nineteenth century. The more juristic thought was conquered by the intensity of technical discourse around the individualistic model of private law, the wider the consciousness of the code became as a powerful object worthy of disciplined application by judges and jurists (objectification), and the higher the state-driven normalisation of private law (private law no longer 'spontaneous',[163] but controlled by state strucures) and vice versa. Technicalisation (in the form of exegesis and/or of Pandectistic thinking) prevailed in France, Germany and Italy in the period 1850–1950, the highest point in the modern history of the code-form in that the consciousness of the *code corpus* came to dominance. Before that, France (despite the code) saw the persistence of arm's-length interpretation, as was the case in Germany and Italy before the respective legislatures enacted codes, and until the turn to exegesis in France, and to Pandectistic thinking in Germany first and then Italy. Counter-movements vis-à-vis the practices of intense technicality

[160] Savigny (n 5). For this reconstruction, see Solari (n 4) 235 et seq. Contrast Savigny *System des heutigen römischen Rechts* (Berlin, Aalen: Scientia-Verlag, 1840–1849) (understood as having restored the unity of private law around individualism, despite this being at odds with the sociality premises of the historical school as devised by Savigny himself, as noted by Solari (n 4) 261).

[161] Georges Gurvitch, *L'idée du droit social. Notion et Système du droit social Histoire doctrinale depuis le 17 siècle jusqu'à la fin du 19 siècle* (Amsterdam, Scientiz Verlagalen, 1972) 15 et seq.

[162] For the pastness of this vocabulary, see Tarello (n 44); Wieacker (n 27). On Savigny's thought as being not just 'conservative' in the perception of academic writers, see Solari (n 4). In any case, on the transformation of Savigny's thought in relation to law and sociality over the subsequent decades and on a shift towards individualism in his later work, see Solari (n 4).

[163] P Grossi, *Universalismo e particolarismo nel diritto* (Napoli, Editoriale Scientifica, 2011) 7.

of the individualist vocabulary emerged in turn as the rise of the *code corpus* consciousness took place. These counter-movements took on the task of de-objectifying the consciousness of the *code corpus* (arguments from no coherence, gaps, ambiguities, contradictions in the grammar of the code)[164] as a way to re-orient the law away from the axiomatic-deductive modes of operation on which the individualistic model of the bourgeois codes was based and towards a more social law, pursuant to an understanding according to which individuality and sociality concerns needed to be balanced out. Shifts towards the social took place that affected and changed the *Code civil*[165] and the BGB,[166] and were a motivating factor in replacing the Italian Civil Code of 1865 with the Italian Civil Code of 1942 (interventionism).[167] This occurred in relation to key sectors of private law (from family law to patrimonial law),[168] but always in the shadow of the individualistic logic, which constrained and complicated those shifts immensely, sometimes making it practically impossible for long decades the work of those jurists and judges committed to pursuing socially orientated justice – eg, worker's rights as individual debtors' rights rather than as collective rights; contractors' rights understood as individual claims rather than related to the circumstances of standardised contracting;[169] product liability fault-based as opposed to strict liability; property as an absolute right as opposed to a fragmented, plural and contingent set of property rights. Herein lies the link between code-form and code-substance, showing how the former determined the latter insofar as substantive law embedded in the code-form could be studiously shielded from changes attempted by those jurists and judges who acted in disenchanted mode and who resisted the allure of the language of the *code corpus*. After the mid-twentieth century, the de-codification summarised in chapter two took place, with the jurisprudential forces massively opting out of intense technicality and the enchantment of the objectified law through the shifting of private law towards pragmatic conflict resolution techniques (resolving social conflicts, balancing individual and collective claims). The return of intense technicality within the new codification movement, via strong systematisation and associated techniques (coherence, completeness, neutralism) around a renewed version of the individualistic paradigm (individual choice as an opt-in term insulated from control of unfairness; obliteration of control based on constitutional mandatory rules; individualistic and not social principles as overarching code norms) as incorporated into the proposed European *code corpus* is a sign of the sustained conceptual and substantive power over the last two centuries of the individualistic model within the private law discourse. It also demonstrates how the tensions between individualism and sociality in the organisation of private law have never really been resolved, considering that pri-

[164] For example, see Gény (n 85).

[165] Halpérin (n 79) 54 et seq (on the *Code civil*: 'libérale puis républicaine').

[166] For socially orientated interpretations of law as developed following the enactment of the BGB, see, eg, Haferkamp (n 33); Zimmermann (n 154).

[167] See above in this chapter.

[168] For discussion, see above in this chapter.

[169] Niglia (n 2).

vate law as a field remains divided between the forces that keep re-proposing the individualistic model and those that articulate the living law of sociality as constituted first nationally and then re-constituted in the context of Europeanisation.

Incidentally, it emerges that, retrospectively, codification is the embodiment neither of the will of the sovereign nor of economic structures,[170] abstractions that need to be 'filled in' by taking into account the perspective of jurisprudential material. In my view, the role of politics and economics has been overemphasised in the context of studies only focused on the legislative side of developments, conquered by the ethos of the 'mythe codificateur, insistant sur la complétude du Code'.[171] It is jurisprudence that has been material to those changes as willed by the legislature, contributing to shaping and to elaborating political and constitutional consciousness. In nineteenth-century France, it was jurisprudence (commentators and judges) that, a few decades after the enactment of the *Code civil*, moved away from natural law and embraced individualistic principles of freedom of contract and absolute property rights, in connection with broader political ideas of egualitarianism and of republicanism, the latter ideas being unable to change the law on their own via their alleged incorporation in the Code.[172] Later on, it was jurisprudence that then moved towards embracing free law in a distinct climate (monopoly capitalism)[173] in which the code-form started to be heavily criticised in particular by the social jurists.[174] Even the Code itself mutated, becoming less liberal and more republican (a 'third code').[175] To return to today, it is in relation to a certain state of jurisprudence (new forms of strong systematisation, aspiration to coherence and order in private law; rising consciousness of an individualistic and market orientated law-market) that the new codification project is being pursued. Because of this, we should not talk of superstructure,[176] but of complex structures out of which the codification phenomenon develops and among which jurisprudence plays a fundamental role. For, historically, scholars and judges[177] have been actors in a script whose context has been accurately described by socio-economic writings.[178] But it has been a 'mistake' to have played down the role of jurisprudence in writing the script itself. To contribute to a new discourse aimed at definitively overcoming that 'mistake', the hybrid view of codification phenomena that I am proposing has emphasised the fundamental role

[170] See Varga (n 75), as discussed, in this chapter.

[171] Halpérin (n 79) 46.

[172] For a critical discussion on the role of republicanism and the principle of equality, see Gordley (n 10) 484 et seq.

[173] As discussed above in this chapter.

[174] See, eg, Gény (n 85). See also Marie-Claire Belleau, 'The "Juristes Inquiets": Legal Classicism and Criticism in Early Twentieth Century France' (1997) 2 *Utah Law Review* 379.

[175] Halpérin (n 79) 54–56 (in the decade up until 1880, 'un deuxième code un peu plus liberal'; from 1880, 'un troisième Code civil, authentiquement républicain').

[176] Varga (n 75) 290: 'Modern codification as a new type of formal rationalization of the law was brought about by bourgeois revolution, when the new political establishment permitted the formation of a superstructure reflecting the needs of the economic structure.'

[177] When participating in consultations around a code-project or when implementing, or rebelling against, a code.

[178] See the works of Varga (and Weber) as discussed above in this chapter.

played by jurisprudence both historically and in regard to the present codification phenomenon. From this vantage point, one can better understand the opinion that sees a code as *cité millénaire* in the context of which one must unveil 'des pieces distinctes, des strates diverses et des tensions transversales'.[179] This is because, from the perspective that I am defending in this book, the *code corpus* project should be seen as the product of the modern engineering of the jurisprudential forces (more *città moderna* and less *città millenaria*) in their engagement with the task of organising collectivities as re-defined by modernity, when:

> [I]n un crescente incessante che si avvìa nel Trecento e si compie nella fine del Settecento con la rivoluzione francese, si fa sempre più massiccia la presenza di quel soggetto politico teso a controllare almeno tutto il complesso reticolato sociale e che noi siamo soliti qualificare come 'Stato'.[180]

Seeing jurisprudential material behind the European code allows us to move on to the next step of the argument – to discuss further the role of jurisprudential material in producing and perpetuating the code idea, abstracting from the decisionist moment, to which this section has also been dedicated. Let me now focus on the jurisprudential side of the decisional moment behind codification in order to emphasise its internal, contested character.

D. Divided *Nomos*: Jurisprudence versus Jurisprudence

Based on the discussion in the above pages, the role of jurisprudential forces in codification phenomena past and present is remarkable. The myth of legislative omnipotence has made it almost impossible to see beyond the legislative level of analysis. It has taken two full centuries for studies to start surmounting this barrier and to shed light on the jurisprudential side of the phenomenon.[181] In incorporating the view from jurisprudence, the new reading that this book is proposing opens up the possibility of gaining a real understanding of what is at stake by looking closer at the jurisprudential structures as landscapes of contestation, resembling the features of past episodes of codification as discussed in the preceding pages. The unresolved tensions between individualism and sociality as the key vocabularies that characterise private law in the modern age (the last two centuries) re-emerge. The current European codification process is a chapter of that history.

[179] Halpérin (n 79) 45 and 46 (for 'città millenaria', see G Alpa, *La cultura delle regole. Storia del diritto civile italiano* (Rome, Laterza, 2000) 307).

[180] Grossi (n 163) 20–21.

[181] See the Prologue and also this chapter. But see, eg, Caroni (n 9); P Ungari, *L'eta' della codificazione. Lotta per la codificazione e scuole di giurisprudenza nel Risorgimento* (Napoli, Edizioni Scientifiche Italiane, 1967) (civil codifications in the context of nineteenth-century Italy's *Risorgimento* were the result of a 'struggle among real forces, whose substantial harshness vanished thereafter in memory', as quoted, and commented upon, in F Ranieri, 'Savigny e il dibattito sulla codificazione' in F Ranieri *Das Europäische Privatrecht des 19. und 20. Jahrunderts. Studien zur Rechtsgeschichte und Rechtsvergleichung* (Berlin, Dunker und Humblot, 2007) 1290.

The proposed code is nothing but the product of the work of key strands of scholarship that have managed to regain dominance, lost in circumstances of de-codification, through cooperation with the European Commission.[182] At the same time, and looking at the juristic side of the phenomenon more closely, the codification process is encountering dissent from within, coming from strands of scholarship that draw upon the national experience of de-codification. A polarisation of jurisprudential positions is taking place. This polarisation can be described as focusing on the extreme poles of a continuum of jurisprudential positions that increasingly emerges from the impact of the work of the codifiers on the structures of European private legal thought.

On the one hand, there are the jurisprudential forces that tend to conceptualise private law via the formalistic modes of systematisation, coherence, completeness and neutralism (the 'high technicality' typically embodied in the individualistic vocabulary) and that see codification as the obvious 'final step' in their exercise. This kind of technical approach has already influenced judicial decisions whenever Supreme Courts (Sweden and Spain)[183] or Opinions of Advocate Generals of the CJEU have referred to the DCFR as doctrinal authority in support of their arguments.[184]

On the other hand, there are the jurisprudential forces that adopt a more pragmatic approach that stays as far away as possible from the conceptual apparatus built around the centralising ethos of the codifiers. These are forces that, in terms of their structure, have developed before and independently of the new codification episode. They operate out of a consciousness of pluralisation and fragmentation,[185] their structures having developed through the de-codification movement of law – that true constitutional transformation of private law around socialisation that has given birth to the materialisation paradigm of private law. The driving ethos of these forces is their commitment to the synthesisation of conflicts. When it comes to the Directives, these jurisprudential forces consciously act as a constructive interaction between the national and the supranational level rather than attempting to obliterate the former for the sake of unilaterally superimposing the supranational dimension of law. In chapter two, I have considered their most advanced output, that is, the practice of (high-intensity) constitutional synthesisation before the European courts, and their less advanced, yet no less important, output, that is, the practice of low-intensity constitutional synthesisation. In both, the European individualist vocabulary is constantly combined with, and synthetised with, the social vocabulary coming from the history of the materialisation of private law as made nationally. It is exactly this living European private law that is now threatened by the European move towards codification, causing critical reactions. The key critical points currently raised against the

[182] For the phenomenon of the interaction between juristic work and the functioning of the EU bureaucratic machinery, *cf* Vauchez and de Witte (n 2).

[183] See above, at ch 3.

[184] See, eg, Advocate-General Opinion in Case C-412/06 *Annelore Hamilton v Volksbank Filder eG* [2008] ECR I-02383 [24].

[185] See above, chs 2 and 3.

codification move, as described in chapter three, articulate positions that come from this history of the socialisation of private law. Such critical points are: supporting the idea that as many principles as possible, derived from national traditions of private law, and in particular a range of 'social principles', should be included in a code ('open code');[186] the trust in the deployment of balancing techniques for applying those principles,[187] the objections to the CESL Optional Code as entailing a dangerous shift towards social dumping, and the related argument that national mandatory rules should apply to transnational sale contracts.[188] All these points are, deep down, about defending the strategy of an inclusive private law that incorporates in the European dimension the social values as developed nationally around the techniques of conflicts' synthesisation. The work of Collins is, in my view, another example of how scholarship that is critical of the move towards codification incorporates this wider sensibility, a work that comes from an 'outsider' to the civilian experience, a common law lawyer who, however, engages explicitly with civilian developments in their de-codified shape.[189] In putting forward the proposal for a European code of principles, that is, no 'real code',[190] Collins is, broadly speaking, defending the viewpoint of a private law based on a framework of principles or 'loose collection of principles', which overlaps with the living civilian experience of constitutional synthetisation coming out

[186] See M Hesselink, 'If You Don't Like Our Principles We Have Others' in Brownsword, Micklitz, Niglia and Weatherill (n 32) 65 ('it is doubtful that European private law (or indeed any other part of European law) should be based on a closed system of values at all' and noting how 'the old paradigm of private law as an autonomous, self-contained value system . . . has long been superseded, both in theory and practice') and 69 ('any limitative list of values that should guide the interpretation seems undesirable. Maybe the best we can hope for now is a much less ambitious and more general, inclusive, and open-ended list of values that could inspire the interpretation and further development of the DCFR'); Collins (n 108) 189 (proposing the idea of a European civil code not meant to be 'complete', allowing for national private law systems to remain in place). I understand Michaels to be thinking along these lines when he reminds us of further 'alternative conceptions' of a code (Michaels (n 22) 293–94), which he classifies as 'political' (citing U Mattei, 'Hard Code Now!' (2002) 2(1) *Global Jurist Frontiers* 1535; Collins (n 108)) or as 'post-modern' conceptions (citing F Zenati-Castaing, 'L'avenir de la codification' (2011) 63(2) *Revue Internationale de Droit Comparé* 355, 366 et seq and 373 et seq). Note that the Optional Code at Article 4 states that the interpretation of the CESL should be autonomous and in accordance with its objectives and the principles underlying it, without recourse to the national law that would be applicable in the absence of an agreement to use the CESL, or to any other law, which is aimed at barring the interpreter from relying on any source of law outside of the code, in line with the stated claim that the Optional Code is 'self-standing' and 'comprehensive'.

[187] D Kennedy, 'A Transnational Genealogy of Proportionality in Private Law' in Brownsword, Micklitz, Niglia and Weatherill (n 32) 185; Reich (n 110); L Niglia, 'Taking Private Law Seriously–Of Balancing and the Jurisprudence of the Court of Justice of the European Union' in L Niglia (ed), Symposium 'Balancing in European Law' *Cambridge Yearbook of European Legal Studies* (2014); L Niglia, 'Constitutionalising Private Law' (2014 essay, on file with author).

[188] Respectively, see the discussion on points of resistance vis-à-vis the proposed code regarding 'principles', mandatory rules and 'choice', as discussed above in ch 3.

[189] *cf* Collins (n 108) 106–08 (considering the *BVerfG* saga on the *Bürgschaft*) and 252–55 (considering the engagement of the *BVerfG* with human rights in private law cases).

[190] Zimmermann (n 71) 373, n 28 (commenting on Collins (n 108), arguing that modern codes are prescriptive and that therefore a codification conceived as a 'framework of normative standards' rather than a complex body of detailed rules' and as 'directive' is not a 'codification in the technical sense of the word').

of the courtrooms.[191] Collins' view is about re-enacting a position that is critical of a *code corpus* that has always been present in private law debates on codification. Specifically, arguments for 'legislation by principles' in private law matters belong to radical *European* private law positions that have always resisted codification and that have placed faith in the practice of principled balancing.[192] From this

[191] For a depiction of this ideal, see Collins (n 108) 189 (a European civil code should not be the 'sole source of private law' as 'national private law must continue') and 136 (a European civil code should be 'an agreement of principles as a symbol of solidarity among the peoples of Europe'). In my view, a European civil 'code of principles', understood as a 'framework of normative standards' (rather than 'complex body of detailed rules) and as not comprising 'the sole source of private law' (at 189) would be meaningless insofar as it would simply at best re-state the characters of the living law as described in ch 2 and at worst betray them. This position must conflate with my arguments based on the value of the living law (but contrast Collins (n 108) 133–34, commenting on the failings in the current, Directive-based system of full harmonisation and arguing that 'the promise of a European Civil Code is that it would tackle these flaws in the European harmonization measures'), that is, it is about defending the idea of a private law order based on conflicting principles open to the work of balancing of the judge. However, overall Collins' book is based on an unresolved tension between the conception of a code that 'must exclude and replace all relevant national law' (at 189, summarising in this way the view of '[m]ost advocates of a project for codification at European level', and referring to J Basedow, 'Codification of Private Law in the European Union: The Making of a Hybrid' (2001) 9(1) *European Review of Private Law* 35, 47) and the acceptance of a private law order based on conflicting principles open to the work of balancing of the judge, the latter being the phenomenon that in this book I have reconstructed in descriptive (constitutional synthesisation as *living* practice) and normative (synthesisation as living *constitutional* practice) terms – a tension which Collins resolves by taking a position that is difficult to reconcile with the conflicting structures of private legal thought as they operate in Europe. Collins' position is otherwise representative of moderate strands of private law scholarship (civilian) that keep defending the possibility of a code of principles as a valuable option. But the structures of the living private law are the product of jurisprudential de-codification and, as such, are inherently pluralist and based on conflicting principles (see, eg, T Wilhelmsson, 'Varieties of Welfarism in European Contract Law' (2004) 10 *European Law Journal* 712; Kennedy (n 187)). To superimpose a code-structure upon them for the purposes of channelling these conflicting principles amounts to attempting to block off the living law. In fact, Collins talks of 'common principles' and of 'core principles' (at 135), which appears to be, from the vantage point of the living law as I understand it, a contradictory statement, for either principles are understood to be conflicting or they are held to be 'common'. I find the position of Hesselink (n 186) 66 more straightforward, for, in questioning the need even for a flexible code, he appears not to lose sight of the de-codified, pluralistic state of the art that characterises the living private law: 'it is not clear that European private law needs a limited set of officially recognised private law principles or values *or even a more flexible and open-ended canon*. However, to the extent that there will be such a set or canon – and the European institutions have reiterated that there will be one – it is, of course, crucial that this set be well balanced. A more inclusive European canon of fundamental private law values would include, at least, values almost universally cherished such as dignity, equality and solidarity which are currently excluded from the list' (emphasis added).

[192] For example, in Italy, see S Rodotà 'Ideologie e tecniche della riforma del diritto civile' in *Rivista del Diritto Commerciale* (1967), Part I, at 84 (arguing for the virtues of legislation by principles and general clauses such as Article 2043 of the Italian Civil Code on tort liability). For a re-statement of the argument in favour of a 'legislazione per principi', 'uno strumento forte nei principi di riferimento e flessibile nell'applicazione', 'una interpretazione e concretizzazione delle clausole generali' in the light of values and principles contained in the constitutional texts, in a changing European constitutional framework (Charter of Fundamental Rights and Constitutional Treaty), see Rodotà (n 12) 183 et seq. Note Nicolò (n 82) 243 ('Se il codice rinunzia alla pretesa di definire e regolare tutto, con disposizioni troppo precise e analitiche, se esso tende ad essere un'articolazione di princìpi e di regole di ampio respiro, su cui la dottrina e la giurisprudenza possono lavorare con un apprezzabile margine di libertà, sì da attuare in concreto quella che a molti sembra debba essere la funzione creativa della interpretazione, la stabilità di un codice è in definitiva assicurata, e lo dimostra in modo chiaro il felice destino del codice Napoleone'). See the discussion of the work of S Rodotà, in relation to the European debate on private law, in S Patti, *Diritto Privato e Codificazioni Europee* (Milan, Giuffrè, 2007) 37 et seq. On France and Germany, see, recently, the analyses of Kennedy (n 187) and of Reich (n 110).

vantage point, the struggle over codification at root manifests entrenched positions in the private law discourse about the fundamental dividing issue – what kind of private law one prefers, whether *nomothetic* (codified) or *nomo*-centred (de-codified), respectively, whether systematised *or* pragmatic.[193] Recent developments confirm that the question that Wieacker posed decades ago remains both valid and unresolved, that is:

> [I]s the primary task of private law to provide a technique for solving problems or to construct intellectually and logically coherent doctrinal structures?[194]

Turning to the ideological implications of the jurisprudential divide and recalling that the proposed European code is an economic constitution in-the-making, one must acknowledge that, deep down, all the scholarly conflicts also pertain to contestation over Europe's material constitution. This is because they are about defending the position that instituting conditions for 'social dumping', opting for the dominance of market principles over social principles and favouring the sacrifice of protectionist standards via sheltering the opt-in clause from the scrutiny of fairness *ex* the Unfair Terms Directive is not acceptable according to readings that cling to social constitutionalism as constituted in national private law welfarist orders. *Weltanschaung* explains the predicament of the present codification phenomenon if one plays down conventional ideas and concepts, as one should.[195] The jurisprudential forces that oppose the move towards codification on these grounds are simply re-activating the kind of interpretative patterns typical of constitutional jurisprudence as it takes place nationally, as a result of politicisation and pluralisation, for they propose a rebalancing of the market system with 'social oil', to put it in Gierke's famous words. They resist codification because they claim that it is the kind of law (de-codified) in vogue in their own countries, based on socially orientated market economies (variety of social capitalism) that are worthy of being defended, rather than market libertarianism. If the European code is *constitution économique* that attempts a new revolutionary arrangement for private law[196] around the agenda of market libertarianism, then there are jurisprudential forces that oppose it on the ground of the value of a more inclusive and participatory type of market economic system[197] – the one implemented through specific techniques, such as balancing,[198] and substantive values, such as those incorporated into (national) mandatory rules as deployed in non-codified (common law jurisdictions) or de-codified (civil law jurisdictions) environments. From this vantage point, the jurisprudential forces in favour of codification effectively work towards dismantling the private law material constitution that results out of the

[193] See respectively above at ch 2 (strong systematisation) and ch 4.

[194] Wieacker (n 27) 487. Wieacker framed this question in the terms of a European, as opposed to just a German, private law discourse.

[195] I am referring to the conventionalist views about codification such as nationalism or culturalism, as discussed above in this chapter.

[196] On codification understood in terms of 'revolutionary transformation', see Caroni (n 30) 855 et seq, as cited in Zimmermann (n 71) 369.

[197] See above, ch 3 on 'de-constitutionalisation' and 're-constitutionalisation' as entailed in the move towards codification.

[198] Kennedy (n 187); Reich (n 110).

operations of the living European private law; that is, they work towards both de-constitutionalising and re-constitutionalising private law.[199] Some do so more consciously, insofar as they adopt 'law-market' or constitutional economics or ordo-liberal approaches (as discussed in chapter two), than others, such as those adopting conceptual formalism.[200]

II. CONCLUSION

From the preceding pages, it emerges that behind the European codification episode is a new chapter of an old story: the workings of Western private law jurisprudence creating a highly specialised set of discursive patterns that are continuously re-enacted and re-edited (re-assembled)[201] and never completely re-made;[202] the legislature in turn taking advantage of those predicaments in which the law happened to lend itself to being crystallised in code format by making the law appear as if it were 'in its entirety' (that is, the dogmas of completeness and coherence of the code) the result of legislative craft; deeply divided structures of jurisprudence, for, as typical of past codification phenomena in modern times, points of resistance vis-à-vis a code are deep down not just struggles against the legislature, but also, and more fundamentally, internal struggles that deeply divide the jurisprudential forces as to the method for organising private law (monistic or pragmatic); the non-technicality of the jurisprudential dispute, for at stake is a true constitutional struggle over who should have the ultimate say on private law determinations – whether the upholders of the code-project and the ideological plan that it incorporates *or* those who believe in the pluralist art of balancing conflicting constitutional values as practised in the context of the living law;[203] the contingency of the codification project on the outcome of these struggles among the jurisprudential forces, for history teaches that a code manages to be implemented only against the background of a substantial consensus of the surrounding jurisprudential forces.

[199] See above, ch 3.

[200] See above, section I.

[201] On 'assemblage', see above, ch 1.

[202] See A Bürge, *Das französische Privatrecht im 19. Jahrhundert zwischen Tradition und Pandektenwissenschaft, Liberalismus und Etatismus* (1991) as interpreted by Gordley (n 10) 461–62 in relation to the so-called individualistic principles as incorporated in the *Code civil*, arguing that 'Bürge was correct to think that there is nothing modern or individualistic about them' and that the individualistic principles via will theories were then developed in later decades; Caroni (n 9).

[203] For more discussion on this, see L Niglia, 'Constitutionalising European Private Law' (essay 2014, on file with author).

Epilogue

I. OF CODIFICATION AND CRITIQUE

THE CRITIQUE OF codification in this book is comparatively and historically orientated, centred as it is, first, on an understanding of modern codes less as mysterious[1] or sacred texts,[2] and more as contingent governmental tools for market ordering with pretense to arrange a total, centralised and ideological administration of private law relations and, second, on the related understanding of codes as epistemic tools crafted by certain strands of jurisprudential forces contested by others, given that the constitutional material implied in code-projects has always given rise to controversy over how to settle the underlying social conflicts. Thus, the dynamics of laissez-faire versus feudalism affected the making of the *Code civil* and of the Prussian Civil Code. whereas capital versus labour dynamics affected codification episodes from the second half of the nineteenth century onwards and, ever since the illusory coherence of the individualism of the bourgeois codes was dispersed, as awareness of social conflicts arose,[3] contestation has characterised the ways in which the complex relationships between individual and social values are arranged in matters of patrimonial law (contract, tort, property, restitution) and in matters of family law. Codification has been a vocabulary context through which the contestation patterns were framed for a long time until the jurisprudential forces gave way to the de-codified modes of administering the private law world. It has been another sign of the

[1] C Donahue, 'Private Law without the State and During its Formation' in N Jansen and R Michaels (eds), *Beyond the State: Rethinking Private Law* (Tübingen, Mohr Siebeck, 2008), 121, 129 (arguing that it is 'something of a mystery' why the *Corpus iuris civilis* could become such a 'popular teaching book'), an opinion criticised by N Jansen, *The Making of Legal Authority: Nonlegislative Codifications in Historical and Comparative Perspective* (Oxford: Oxford University Press, 2010) 29 and 45, also in relation to modern codes.

[2] On codes as 'sacred texts', see G Fletcher, 'Three Nearly Sacred Books in Western Law' (2001–02) 54 *Arkansas Law Review* 1 as inter alia referred to in R Michaels, 'Code vs Code. Nationalist and Internationalist Images of the Code Civil in the French Resistance to a European Codification' (2012) *European Review of Contract Law* 277, 294 ('What we see is reminiscent of a religious war. Different sects within the same religion (the civil law) fight aggressively'), but one must agree with Michaels, for controversies around codification are no less contentious and divisive than religious issues have historically proven to be.

[3] See the works of F Gény (France), S Rodotà (Italy) and F Wieacker (Germany), as cited in previous chapters.

success of the codification phenomenon that, despite the turn towards de-codification, the code (*corpus*) vocabulary has not collapsed in its entirety.[4]

It is that historically formed vocabulary that re-emerges today in the contingent proposal of a *code corpus*.[5] The new code-project belongs to that history, as evidenced by this book's critical description of the codification phenomenon as the product of jurisprudential work, with an analysis of the phenomenon through the looking glass of jurisprudence – a methodological tool that is superior to concentrating analysis only on the legislative side of things, in that it enables a better understanding. Thus, insofar as jurisprudence actively participates in the design of the new code-project, it is a truly governmental force, and insofar as jurisprudential forces of a different kind resist the move towards codification, they question the project of establishing a libertarian market order as implicated in the proposed code. Contestation concerns form, that is, techniques at once both legislative and interpretative, but it also concerns substance, that is, the decision regarding which material constitution to conjure up. At all levels, the code-form is a manifestation of these deeper struggles.

Of this comparatively and historically orientated analysis, one must now closely consider two features that have always characterised codification episodes in modern times and that pose key questions in relation to the new codification phenomenon.

A. Between Codification and Statehood

Let me return to the conception of a code as national, rational and natural law.[6] I have argued that, although this conception is a perspective worthy of respect in terms of analysing the codification phenomenon, over-emphasising its explanatory role offers little help if one wishes to really understand the phenomenon. One must recall that, in being tools for framing material constitutions, codes as epistemic material have contributed to giving rise to state-based centralised structures of government in the nineteenth century,[7] in the context of the complex interactions between legislative and jurisprudential levels. [8] In other words, codes have played a key role in *étatisation*[9] and they have played that role in contexts of

[4] See N Irti, *L'etá della decodificazione* (4th edn, Milan, Giuffrè, 1999), who maintains a belief in an 'exegesis'-orientated approach to interpretation, a position criticised by P Grossi in P Cappellini and B Sordi (eds), *Codici. Una Riflessione di Fine Millennio* (Milan, Giuffrè, 2002) 27, according to whom the interpreter 'non potrà limitarsi ad esercitare il suo sapere su un *testo,* all'interno di *quel* testo come un universo senza finestre; egli dovrà anche aver coscienza che quel testo incarna uno schema ordinativo della realtà e dovrà preoccuparsi di collocare quel testo nella vita del diritto, lui che è il mediatore fra quel testo rigido e, come testo definito, sempre più avulso dalla continuità del divenire sociale, e il divenire stesso cui il testo è destinato e vocato'.

[5] See chs 1 and 4

[6] For discussion, see Cappellini and Sordi (n 4).

[7] For a discussion on such administrative and economico-constitutional structures, see ch 4.

[8] See ch 4.

[9] P Glenn, *The Cosmopolitan State* (Oxford, Oxford University Press, 2013) 12 (on *étatisation*) and 65 et seq (on code of private law as an 'irresistible model of state construction').

idealisations about nationhood, identity and related rationalising schemes that are supposed to fit the agenda of state unification, in a lineage of writings that precedes and succeeds those of Savigny and of Thibaut of 1814. Today, as the codification project is being re-proposed, the question arises as to whether the making of a code via the official enactment of binding legislation (*ratione imperii*) and via framing based on congenial structures of jurisprudence (*imperio rationii*) equally implicates the production of state structures at the EU level – in other words, whether the enactment of code structures would be bound to replicate the national state structures at the supranational level, turning the supranational into a statist entity. Would the enactment of a code entail the re-production of state-like centralised governmental structures at the EU level? This is an important question to investigate both in the private law realm[10] and in relation to the rising literature that argues that the EU is increasingly becoming state-like[11] in terms not only of its incredible array of competences but also in the deeper terms of the argument whereby disciplinary structures resembling those of state government are developing at the EU level in relation to the Economic and Monetary Union governance. On the basis of the analysis of this book, enacting a European code would certainly entail the creation of a major – if not the major – building block for pushing further the transformation of the EU into a state-like entity. Let us recall that a *code corpus* implies the setting-up of an administrative apparatus with its own ideological outlook, that is, it is a structure of *étatisation*. Private law would once more become the engine for centralised state-like sovereignty structures, as opposed to 'weak sovereignty' typical of the history of private law of the second half of the twentieth century. That is, enacting a *code corpus* as embodied in the European proposal would be about re-creating strong forms of sovereignty against domestic contexts which widely practise weak and shared forms of constitutional engagements[12] and, therefore, 'weak sovereignty' as the preferred engine for the governing of polities, including matters of private law. As a result, the responsibility entailed in the choice for codification or otherwise, that is, for turning Europe into a state rather than keeping it in its 'supranational' condition,[13] lies with the jurisprudential forces themselves and cannot be attributed externally to 'the legislature'.

B. Between Codification and Authority

There is then the problem of the authority of a code, that is, what is the authority of a code and, more specifically, of a European Civil Code? The two questions are related, but for the purposes of analysis need be kept separate.

[10] See, eg, R Zimmermann, 'Codification. The Civilian Experience Reconsidered on the Eve of a Common European Sales Law' (2012) 8(4) *European Review of Contract Law* 367.

[11] D Chalmers, 'The European Redistributive State and a European Law of Struggle' (2012) 18 *European Law Journal* 667.

[12] On the parallelism between 'weak constitutionalism' and 'weak systematisation', see above, ch 4.

[13] On 'supranationalism' and 'statehood' in European integration *cf* JH Weiler, *To Be a European Citizen: Eros and Civilization* (Toronto, Toronto University Press, 1998).

I have explained that codification is a dynamic and never-static phenomenon, for, to exaggerate, there is never a well-defined code-text, but always interpretations of it and perspectives on it – and struggles. Understanding a code is about capturing these perspectives, and capturing them is about detecting struggles as well as participating in them. Authority is relative to which forces manage to affirm their viewpoint relative to any of the conflicting viewpoints. From this vantage point, codification is, at root, a contingent phenomenon.[14] A code, once enacted, may enjoy weak authority or no authority at all in being highly contested and resisted, depending on the degrees of contestation and resistance that surround the code-product. For example, the *Code civil* in the first decades of the nineteenth century was less code-in-action and more code-in-the-waiting, as a result of the stalemate in the application of its articles in the courtrooms, given that many judges chose not to apply the code 'faithfully', but to continue to apply the Roman law-based jurisprudential material. But a code may enjoy stronger authority whenever it can count on a substantial jurisprudential consensus, as was (according to some readings as referred to above) the case for the BGB, at least until the second decade of the twentieth century. And there are significant variations on this theme, considering that some institutions and norms within the code might enjoy stronger authority than others, creating conflicting patterns of enforcement of a code. For example, major parts of the *Code civil* might have started to be fully enforced from the mid-nineteenth century, but it then took a few decades for key norms such as Articles 1382 et seq of the French Civil Code, and specifically the requirement of faulty liability, to be played down in those product liability judicial decisions based instead on strict liability.[15] The configuration of key institutions of private law has been heavily affected by the power of the *code corpus* vocabulary relative to the counter-argument that certain code-based doctrinal constructions should be avoided altogether in disputes that manage to outlive the fall of the centrality of the code (de-codification), as can be seen in relation to major doctrinal constructs aimed at circumventing the perceived limitations incorporated in various relevant articles of codes.[16] Examples of such doctrinal constructs include: standardised contracts in relation to Articles 1341 and 1342 of the Italian Civil Code; guarantees held not to be unilateral obligatory relations with regard to paras 765 *et seq* BGB; contractual liability and *Verkehssicherungspflichten* in relation to paras 823 *et seq* BGB; and *clausola rebus sic stantibus*, *doli generalis*, *culpa in contrahendo*, positive breach of contract and

[14] On the possible compatibility between arguments from normativity and from contingency, see L Niglia, 'Pluralism in a New Key – Between Plurality and Normativity' in L Niglia (ed), *Pluralism and European Private Law* (Oxford, Hart Publishing, 2013) 249.

[15] See above, at ch 1.

[16] On the argument about the practices of 'circumventing' the 'unsatisfactory provisions' of the law of delict *ex* para. 823 et seq BGB, in relation to the role of the Germanic Imperial Court in the first two decades of the twentieth century, see R Zimmermann, *Roman Law, Contemporary Law, European Law: The Civilian Tradition Today* (Oxford, Oxford University Press, 2001) 55 et seq, as discussed above in ch 4.

third party loss in relation to various other BGB rules.[17] Overall, there is no such thing as 'the authority' of a code independently of perspectives and struggles, an 'error' of the positivistic views of codification as legislation and one no less enforced by historically orientated views.[18]

What lessons can be learnt from this historical pedigree on code and authority with regard to the European codification experiment? In relation to the question of the authority of a would-be European civil code, including the problem of the authority of the DCFR as code-text understood as private codification,[19] one must look seriously into the structural features of the private law world in order to answer it. The authority of private law based on the patterns of constitutional jurisprudence, that is, the national level in its interaction with the European level (composite constitutionalism),[20] is other than, and alternative to, the market-orientated constitutional character of the would-be European code. The issue of authority turns into an inquiry on the contingency of jurisprudential material. There is no authority in a code-text other than that conferred upon it by the historical circumstances and, in present terms, they are about the conflict between those who uphold the code and its values, and those who resist it on the basis of the constitutional pluralist heritage; between arguments for decoupling private law from its constitutional, and related political, constitutive dimensions[21] towards re-constitutionalising it around market holism, and arguments in defence of the existing constitutional and political structures of private law. Private law is *crocevia* of the many projects of normativity as produced by the insiders, legislators, jurists and judges,[22] and its normativity consists of their accumulated impact. If law moves the world, it does so through its capacity for generating and projecting on society normative materials of this kind. And one must note the extraordinary character of the proposed code, it being decoupled from polity structures that ensure a degree of social legitimacy, which certainly places it beyond the

[17] See respectively L Niglia, *The Transformation of Contract in Europe* (The Hague, London, New York, Kluwer Law International, 2003) (on standard contracts); L Niglia, 'The Non-Europeanisation of Private Law' (2001) *European Review of Private Law* 575 (on guarantees, indicating resistance of certain Germanic courts vis-a-vis applying the Doorstep Directive's right of cancellation to guarantees on the basis of the argument that guarantees are, under the BGB, unilateral contracts) and Zimmermann (n 16) 55 et seq and at 80 et seq (synthesising debates on each of the remaining doctrinal constructs).

[18] But in the context of legal historical analyses, see the more nuanced position of Zimmermann (n 10) 378 ('The codifications are acts of legislation and thus derive their authority from the state', but arguing that: 'Unlike most individual statutes on taxation, trade or agriculture, however, they have not been written by members of Parliament, nor even usually by government officials, but by distinguished experts from legal practice or legal scholarship').

[19] This notion comes from FC von Savigny, *Vom Beruf unserer Zeit für Gesetzgebung und Rechtswissenschaft* (Heidelberg, 1814); translated as *Of the Vocation of Our Age for Legislation and Jurisprudence* (London, Littlewood & Co, 1831, translated by Abraham Hayward) 35 (arguing in relation to codes that 'a work of the kind might be accomplished by private jurists, without requisition or confirmation on the part of the state. This was often the case of the old German law, and we should have a great deal of trouble to make our forefathers understand that difference between a law book, as a private production, and a real code, which we consider so natural and necessary'). My own view on this notion in relation to modern times is implicit in ch 4 above.

[20] See above, at ch 2.

[21] On the interface between constitutional and political structures, see above, ch 3, at Section I.C.

[22] See above, ch 4.

normality of constitutional developments. Indeed, the individualist core of the proposed codification agenda threatens the sustainability of the existing structures of social legitimacy.

If the code is a force that constitutes (state) authority by selectively excluding whilst including legal material in substantively contested mode,[23] and if the proposed European code is no less forceful in that sense, as in my view is the case, then we must address the question of the legitimacy of that force rather than leaving it to the evolutionary progress (or, should I say, regress)[24] of the underlying forces. There is a normative question inherent in the problematic, with normativity indicating the constitutional struggles that underlie the move towards codification concerning the problematic placement of private power beyond the reach of constitutional politics as drawn by the living law. This is because those who cling to a constitutionally justified normativity, such as that of the existing structures of European private law, talk the language of loyalties and of communities, a language that is in turn unknown to those who pursue the individualist project.[25] The problem of the proposed code is that it is about de-constitutionalisation in the specific sense of aiming at de-socialising law, reversing the late modern revolution of the past few decades revolving around the socialisation of the state and the related *étatisation* of society.[26] It is a true political act that is being proposed, despite the apologetic pretense at neutrality.

II. OF CODIFICATION AND ITS POVERTY

Franz Wieacker held that: 'The disappearance of the liberal economy involved the collapse of its greatest juristic creation, a unified private law.'[27] Wieacker's words are a synthesis of reflections shared by jurists showing the same kind of sensibility, for example, by Georges Gurvitch in the early 1930s:

> Fixés par . . . le Code, encore plus ou moins stables dans la deuxième moitié du XIXe siècle, le vieux cadres juridiques ont craqué et continuent à se désagréger de jour en jour; les cadres nouveaux sont encore dans le devenir et on n'en aperçoit que les premières ébauches.[28]

[23] To adapt the vocabularies of Niklas Luhmann, *Theory of Society*, vol 1 (Stanford, Stanford University Press, 2012, translated by Rhodes Barrett) 281 et seq and of Glenn (n 9) towards contextualising the operations of 'inclusivity' and 'exclusivity' in relation to the wider legitimacy question of the authority of state structures thus produced, as discussed above, in ch 3 (deconstitutionalisation, reconstitutionalisation) and in the remainder of this chapter. On exclusion and inclusion as related to normativity rather than just the 'logic of evolution', see Niglia, 'Pluralism in a New Key – Between Plurality and Normativity' in Niglia (n 14).

[24] See above, ch 2.

[25] See B. Lurger, 'A Radical View of Pluralism?' in Niglia (ed) (n 14) (criticising the position of J Smits 'A Radical View of Pluralism' in ibid).

[26] Above, at ch 2.

[27] F Wieacker, *A History of Private Law in Europe* (Oxford, Clarendon Press, 1995) 431.

[28] Georges Gurvitch, *L'idée du droit social. Notion et Système du droit social Histoire doctrinale depuis le 17 siècle jusqu'à la fin du 19 siècle* (Aalen, Scientiz Verlag alen, 1972) 1, including the consideration that: 'Des institutions inédites e imprévues, insaisissables pour la pensée juridique traditionnelle, surgissent de tous côtés, avec une spontanéité élémentaire et toujours grandissante.'

Ever since, pluralisation and fragmentation have been firmly at the core of national private law. We are witnessing the attempt to re-constitute the continental unity of private law in an age that has restored the fortune of the market economy with a strong market libertarian ethos behind the proposed European code. But that re-constitution only represents one 'view of the cathedral'. There is another contending view that comes from the forces that understand themselves as being constitutional in that they aim at delivering the wider range of sociality objectives to which national constitutions have made us accustomed. I consider among these forces those voices that articulate the need for a wider range of principles than those contained in the DCFR, a proposal sometimes articulated in the opinion that those principles should be incorporated into a flexible and open code of principles. These are voices that re-instate a discourse about private law that has a long pedigree, revolving around a controversy among scholars on the option for codification or for legislation based on principles.[29] It is about Europeanising a dilemma that has always been present in national private laws.[30] The European codification process is about deep movements of forces clashing over form and substance at once. Let me re-visit the sociality position for the purpose of understanding the present codification phenomenon better by going back, once again, to the *Kodifikationsstreit* and in particular to Savigny's work.

* * *

The struggle for the configuration of private law as it emerges with regard to the new codification episode resembles the struggle between Savigny and Thibaut in at least one respect. Savigny opposed Thibaut on the then codification enterprise, the *Code civil* and its embodiment of mature rationalist legal thought as developed over the eighteenth century,[31] on the basis of his idea of law as sociality rather than just individuality. Although Savigny eventually succumbed to dogmatic rationalism in his subsequent work, the *System des heutigen römischen Rechts*, with the re-composition of the civilian system around the individual, including family law,[32] it remains to his credit to have introduced the problematic of conflicts in private law,[33] the idea that conflicts between individuality and sociality (particularity versus universality, *diritto soggettivo*/'subjective right' versus *diritto oggettivo*/'objective right') should be resolved within the private law dis-

[29] For a re-statement of that debate, see S Patti, *Diritto Privato e Codificazioni Europee* (Milan, Giuffrè, 2007) 37 et seq (discussing and contrasting the positions of Stefano Rodotà and of Justus Wilhelm Hedelmann) and above, at ch 4.

[30] For the Italian version, see S Rodotà, 'Ideologie e tecniche della riforma del diritto civile' (1967) *Rivista del Diritto Commerciale* I, 84; S Rodotà, 'Il Codice civile e il processo costituente europeo' in V Roppo (ed), *A European Civil Code? Perspectives and Problems* (Milan, Giuffrè, 2005) 183 et seq.

[31] G Tarello, *Storia della Cultura Giuridica Moderna. Assolutismo e Codificazione del Diritto* (Bologna, Il Mulino, 1976); G Solari, *Filosofia del Diritto Privato. Volume II. Storicismo e Diritto Privato* (Turin, Giappichelli, 1971, 1st edn 1940).

[32] Solari (n 31) 256 et seq.

[33] ibid 300: '[F]u merito particolare del Savigny avere primamente rilevato il valore del conflitto e la necessità di risolverlo in seno al diritto privato'.

course, anticipating the terms in which juristic thought placed itself in relation to the broader range of social and political conflicts to come. What followed is a story that I have re-told when discussing the European codification proposal,[34] a variation on the original Savignyan theme as transformed over the following decades in relation to the changing historical conditions. It is the story of how 'the social', thus invented, could be internalised fully over the following decades in the private law discourse, not as a coherent whole (as if a mirror image of the individualistic rendition of the code), but in the form of contingent and fragmented welfarist settlements ('de-codification') in which the struggles between property and collective interests, labour and capital, landlords and tenants, drafters of contracts and adherents, buyers and sellers, and shareholders and managerial interests could frequently come to a resolution via compromising acts (legislative or judicial), never settling issues once and for all.[35]

But this is a story that could be dramatically halted by the move towards codification that, whilst proposed in a space beyond the realm of 'nationalism', embodies and re-deploys once more nonetheless the nineteenth-century individualist ethos in full strength, as discussed in chapters one and two[36] – it being a contingent and contested discursive structure drawing the lines of protection in defence of certain interests over others (drafters of contracts rather than adherents, lenders rather than borrowers, tenants rather than landlords etc)[37] and placing faith in a code-based disciplinary kind of interpretation that accommodates partisan values. It is remarkable how the individualist strands of positivism and historicism are being re-engineered[38] so as to once more pursue those objectives. No doubt, the turn towards private law welfarism cannot claim to have been able to completely break away from the historical past of private law as formed around the nineteenth-century bourgeois codes, as also shown by the persistent polemics against the constitutionalisation of private law that have arisen over the course of the twentieth century and are still in place.[39]

Seen in this light, in an environment in which struggles define the legal consciousness as much as ever, the jurisprudential forces should make a conscious decision as to whether to opt for codification *or* to tackle social conflicts as they take shape in the public arena in the de-codified ways that the living law has accustomed us to. The former is a poor option, for those who propound it end up

[34] See above, ch 2 (on pluralisation, politicisation and constitutionalisation in relation to private law), a story not really taken seriously by both those who keep thinking that the code is still the key feature of national private law in the context of the so-called 'code versus code' debate (for a critical account of these positions, see Michaels (n 2)) and those who uphold the re-codification strategy.

[35] On the role of the legislature and of the judiciary in that respect, see above, ch 2.

[36] See above, ch 1 (on arguments from the 'pyramid of principles and rules' and the ideology of market libertarianism as embodied in the DCFR); and Wieacker (n 27) 431–41 (socially orientated legislation destroying the coherence of the individualistic codes of the late nineteenth century). On 'nationalism' see above, ch 4.

[37] For details, see above, chs 1 and 2.

[38] See above, ch 1.

[39] M Kumm, 'Who is Afraid of the Total Constitution? Constitutional Rights as Principles and the Constitutionalization of Private Law' (2006) 7 *German Law Journal* 341.

with a law that pretends to be universal, but that fails universality, purporting to place all of the law under the ideologically biased category of individualism. This is because what individualistic rationalism does is to leave us with no satisfactory resolution of the societal problems that surround private law. In the words of Gioele Solari:

> Se . . . il razionalismo giuridico aveva elaborato la nozione del diritto soggettivo, esso non riuscì a dare una soluzione soddisfacente del diritto in senso oggettivo, né lo poteva perché dalla negazione di qualsiasi realtà sociale distinta dall'individuo fu indotto a ricorrere alla finzione del contratto per mascherare l'arbitrio degli individui nella creazione della legge, della società, dello Stato.[40]

The socialisation of private law is the story of the repositioning of private law along 'the social', but always in the shadow of the powerful modernist vocabulary of a coherently organised individualism as allegedly shaping the code-form. From this vantage point, codification qua de-constitutionalisation and re-constitutionalisation is at root about de-socialising private law, in the sense of detaching it from the experience of, and the legal narratives about, the collective.[41] At stake is not just the issue of making or not a code, but the defence of the constitutional tradition of private law as developed over the course of late modernity. Expelling the social principles from the DCFR has been less a work of textual, aesthetical rewriting[42] and more an act that challenges the ethical-political-constitutional private law world as reconstituted over late modernity. The struggle for private law as taking place in the shadow of the new codification project is about this basic issue – whether to defend the social-constitutional world of private law or whether to 'abandon' it and exchange it for the *code corpus*. Let me recall some of the comparative and historical aspects considered in the previous chapters in order to stress the importance of this argument.

When the codifiers manage to prevail (without ever silencing the opponents – a lesson from history) and the *code corpus* consciousness becomes the dominant perception of the law (yielding the normalisation effect discussed in chapter one), a disciplinary environment establishes itself that gravely disempowers arm's-length interpretation and that accordingly lowers the intensity of the struggles that characterise the codification phenomenon. This disempowerment sometimes entails bringing the intensity of such struggles to the minimum, the case of the shaping around exegesis of interpretative activities in France from the middle of the nineteenth century onwards, and in Germany and Italy as a result of the influence of Pandectistic thinking from the late nineteenth century onwards. The examples of product liability and of standard form contracts[43] tell us how that happens at the micro-level of piecemeal code institutions and norms. It was in

[40] Solari (n 31) 299.

[41] On 'sociality' (*socialità*) understood in terms of the collective, see eg the legal philosophical considerations of ibid 285.

[42] On aspects related to 'formal presentation' in relation to the codification phenomenon, see Jansen (n 1) 112 et seq.

[43] See above, ch 1.

this climate (about 100 years between the mid-nineteenth century and the mid-twentieth century) that the belief in the code as individualistic law (as coherent, comprehensive and self-standing *code corpus*)[44] could develop in various degrees in France, Germany and Italy (always criticised in socially orientated scholarship)[45] under the powerful influence of Pandectistic thinking as reformulated *inter alia* by Puchta and as imported in Italy in the last decades of the nineteenth century. This was a time in which the code became reified, with the subjects-of-the-law qua makers of the law (jurisprudence) creating the object (the code), but ending up being re-shaped by it insofar as the struggles decreasingly affected the law in operation and the codifiers managed to get as close as possible to their objective of silencing the opponents. As to Italy, as early as 1860, this climate produced the consciousness, represented in the 1860 *Relazione* of the Italian Minister *Cassinis* in support of the First Project of revision of the Codice Albertino, that 'la formula codificata del diritto era stata la vocazione del secolo', 'una condizione dei civili progressi', 'la questione del modo di codificare era già sciolta dal fatto e dal consenso universale' and, later on when a project based on the *Code civil* was drafted, arguing that an Italian civil code could be made by simply 'compiling' it rather than having to 'form it' – conveying the idea of a code as a ready-made entity' on which to cling mechanically.[46] The code thus managed to be perceived as neutral and objective law by many of the legal actors and external observers before being once more attacked for not really being so, that is, for being fragmentary and contradictory and in need of the inevitable role of the judge as gap-filler and as law maker.[47]

The *code corpus* that is being proposed today is born out of a similar structural landscape and it aims at pursuing not only a contested ideological project but also (and relatedly) the de-socialisation of private law, with the objective of alienating private law from the social and thus making it unable to mediate conflicts. For the danger of constructing a law that is structurally unable to tame conflicts may soon be with us, a law that goes around in endless circles without managing to balance and mediate conflicts, with the associated powerful effect of covering up private power as if it were a kind of legitimate realm of autonomy even when what is at work is the exercise of private power in unequal bargaining conditions, as is typically the case for standardised contracts.[48] In this attempt at re-engineering the epistemic structures of private law in such a fundamental fashion, lies the danger of leaving social conflicts unable not only to be intercepted but also to be resolved

[44] To consider 'codes' to be about 'closure' (Glenn (n 9) 63 et seq) and 'reification' (C Varga, 'The Contemporaneity of Lukács' Ideas with Modern Social Theoretical Thought' (2013) 99 *Archiv für Rechts- und Sozialphilosophie* 42, 49) makes sense in relation to the phenomenon of the *code corpus*.

[45] For a synthesis of the relevant literature on socially orientated legal thought, see Wieacker (n 27); Irti (n 4); Tarello (n 31) 69 et seq (on exegesis and then Pandectistic thought defining private law in Italy in the second half of the nineteenth century and in the first decades of the twentieth century).

[46] See Rosario Nicolò, 'Codice Civile' in Francesco Calasso (ed), *Enciclopedia del Diritto*, vol VII (Milan, Giuffrè, 1960) 240, 241–42 (although arguing that, despite the almost unanimous consensus, there was some motivated opposition).

[47] See above, ch 4 and the works of F Gény, R Nicolò and S Rodotà as taking this critical path.

[48] Niglia (n 17).

by the legal mind, placing them at the margins of the operations of a law rendered narrow. For example, through designing a law-codified based on mandatory and default rules detached from, whilst ostracising mandatory and default rules belonging to, domestic constitutional structures.[49] European integration has never attempted a radical 'constitutional' project such as that incorporated into the codification project as pursued by the Commission and its legal brethren. Ironically, it is proposed in the present times of economic and social crisis arguably not seen since the 1930s, characterised by increasing mass social inequalities across and within countries, as they visibly emerge in the shadow of the European financial crisis, and by the need for conjuring up new forms of cross-country solidarities that balance out those inequalities. The code-project strikes one as ignoring and betraying certain deep values that Europe has placed at its core and that should be defended.[50] It is for this reason that the European private law discourse needs to respond to the proposed code-project by an active exercise of legal memory, that is, by reclaiming the virtue of the heritage of values built over the past few decades in the nation state and as transferred on to Europe, and by defending the liaison between private and public, national and European constitutional dimensions[51] that is at risk of being severed by the return of the code-form.

One must end with recalling another 'dispute' over codification, one that is never really mentioned in standard literature, that developed in parallel to that between Friedrich Carl von Savigny and Anton Friedrich Justus Thibaut, in an exchange between Jeremy Bentham and James Madison. Bentham proposed a code for the US in order to win over 'that mass of foreign law, the yoke of which, in the worldless, as well as boundless, and shapeless shape of the common, alias unwritten law, remains still about your necks',[52] a proposal that Madison rejected inter alia with these words:

> With respect to the unwritten law, it may not be improper to observe, that the extent of it has been not a little abridged, in this Country, by successive events. A certain portion of it was dropped by our emigrant forefathers as contrary to their principles, or inapplicable to their new situation. The Colonial Status had a further effect in amending and diminishing the mass. The revolution from Colonies to Independent States, lopped off portions. And the changes which have been constantly going on since this last event, have every where made, and are daily making further reductions.[53]

[49] See above, ch 2.

[50] These tensions emerge, for example, in the arguments put forward in defence of the inclusion of as many as possible of the heritage of private law social principles in the DCFR (as discussed above in ch 2) and in the arguments stressing the close relationship between private law and the values contained in the EU Charter on fundamental rights as opposed to the apology of private law as neutral to values (see, eg, Rodotà 'Il Codice civile' (n 30) 193).

[51] As discussed above in chs 2, 3 and 4.

[52] Letter of Jeremy Bentham to the then President of the United States of America (Queen Square Place, Westminster, October 1811), James Madison, in the passages quoted above at the beginning of ch 1.

[53] Letter *of* James Madison, then President of the Congress of the American United States, *to Jeremy Bentham*, London of 8 May 1816 (Washington), reproduced in P Schoefield and J Harris (eds), *Jeremy Bentham, 'Legislator of the World': Writings on Codification, Law, and Education* (Oxford, Clarendon Press, 1998) 36–37.

To the claims put forward by the codifiers today, one should react with the above words, which signify the unrenounceable role of the wider societal forces in making choices that contribute towards episodes of political emancipation (such as the contingent choices to 'drop', make 'inapplicable', 'amend', 'diminish', 'lop off' and 'reduce' the common law referred to in Madison's quote), a lesson learnt from the history of codification of the last two centuries. Central to the history of private law of the last two centuries is the work of the jurisprudential forces and their ability to engineer political emancipation in certain fragments of time such as, remarkably, those of the last 70 years or so as displayed at the national and at the European level within the paradigm of the socialisation of private law.[54] This history places an immense responsibility on scholars and judges. The return of the idea of a code presents itself as an elegant way in which some may be tempting others to give up that responsibility, consigning law to a reified realm of objective rules and principles of dubious ideological value. The European jurisprudential forces, in facing our troubled times, need be aware of the implications of that move and of the unrenounceable role that history places on them as guardians of the living, plural, constitutional private law.

[54] See ch 2.

Bibliography

T Ackermann, 'Public Supply of Optional Standardized Consumer Contracts: A Rationale for the Common European Sales Law?' (2013) 50 *CMLR* 11

R Alexy, 'Constitutional Rights, Balancing and Rationality' (2003) 16(2) *Ratio Juris* 131

G Alpa, *La cultura delle regole. Storia del diritto civile italiano* (Rome, Laterza, 2000) 307)

—— and M Andenas, *I Fondamenti del Diritto Privato Europeo* (Milan, Giuffrè, 2005)

T Ascarelli, *L'idea di codice nel diritto privato e la funzione dell'interpretazione* (1945) in T Ascarelli, *Saggi Giuridici* (Milan, Giuffrè, 1949) 48

A Asquini, 'Codice di commercio' in Francesco Calasso (ed), *Enciclopedia del Diritto*, vol VII (Milan, Giuffrè, 1960)

C Aubry and C Rau, *Cours de droit civil français* (1869–71)

O Bar-Gill and O Ben-Shahar, 'Regulatory Techniques in Consumer Protections: A Critique of European Consumer Contract Law' (2013) 50 *CMLR* 109

T Barkhuysen and S Lindenbergh (eds), *Constitutionalisation of Private Law* (Leiden, Martinus Nijhoff, 2006)

J Basedow, 'Transjurisdictional Codifications' (2009) 83 *Tulane Law Review* 973

——'The Optional Instrument of European Contract Law: Opting-in through Standard Terms – A Reply to Simon Whittaker' (2012) 8 *European Review of Contract Law* 82

——'The State's Private Law and the Economy: Commercial Law as an Amalgam of Public and Private Rule-Making' (2008) 56(3) *American Journal of Comparative Law* 703

——'Codification of Private Law in the European Union: The Making of a Hybrid' (2001) 9(1) *European Review of Private Law* 35

J Basedow, K Hopt and R Zimmermann, 'Preface' in J Basedow, K Hopt and R Zimmermann (eds), *Max Plank Encyclopedia of European Private Law* (Oxford, Oxford University Press, 2012) v

H Beale, 'The European Commission's Common Frame of Reference: A Progress Report', (2006) 2 *European Review of Contract Law* 303

D Beach, *The Dynamics of European Integration* (Houndmills, Basinkstoke, New York, Palgrave Macmillan, 2005)

——'EU Institutions and ICG Negotiations – How the Negotiation Process Affects their Ability to Gain Influence in ICGs' in P Meertz and F Cede (eds), *Negotiating European Union* (Houndmills, Basinkstoke, New York, Palgrave Macmillan, 2004)

M-C Belleau, 'The "Juristes Inquiets": Legal Classicism and Criticism in Early Twentieth-Century France' (1987) 2 *Utah Law Review* 379

M Bellomo, *L'Europa del Diritto Comune* (8th edn, Rome, Il Cigno Galileo Galilei Edizioni di Arte e Scienza, 1998)

J Bentham, 'Letter to the President of the United States', 1811 in P Schoefield and J Harris (eds), *Jeremy Bentham, 'Legislator of the World': Writings on Codification, Law, and Education* (Oxford, Clarendon Press, 1998)

——'Papers Relative to Codification and Public Instruction' in J Bowring (ed), *The Works of Jeremy Bentham, Volume IV* (Edinburgh, Tait, 1843) 518

L FM Besselink, *A Composite European Constitution. Een Samengestelde Europese Constitutie* (Groningen, Europa Law Publishing, 2007)

R Brownsword, H Micklitz, L Niglia and S Weatherill (eds), *The Foundations of European Private Law* (Oxford, Hart Publishing, 2011)

——'The Theoretical Foundations of European Private Law: A Time to Stand and Stare' in *The Foundations of European Private Law* (Oxford, Hart Publishing, 2011) 171

HE Brandner and P Ulmer, 'EG-Richtlinie über missbräuchliche Klauseln in Verbraucherverträgen. Kritische Bemerkungen zum Vorschlag der EG-Kommission' (1991) *Betriebs Berater* 701

G Brüggemeier, 'Constitutionalisation of Private Law – The German Perspective' in T Barkhuysen and S Lindenbergh (eds), *Constitutionalisation of Private Law* (Leiden, Martinus Nijhoff, 2006) 59

——A Colombi Ciacchi and G Comandé (eds), *Fundamental Rights and Private Law in the European Union*, vol I, *A Comparative Overview* (Cambridge, Cambridge University Press, 2010)

J M Buchanan, *Constitutional Economics* (Oxford and Cambridge, MA, Blackwell, 1991)

JP Burgess, 'Culture and the Rationality of Law from Weimar to Maastricht' in C Joerges and NS Ghaleigh (eds), *Darker Legacies of Law in Europe* (Oxford, Hart Publishing, 2003) 143

A Bürge, *Das franzosische Privatrecht im 19. Jahrhundert zwischen Tradition und Pandektenwissenschaft, Liberalismus und Etatismus* (Frankfurt am Main, Klostermann 1991)

C-W Canaris, *Systemdenken and Systembegriff in der Jurisprudenz* (Berlin, Dunckler und Humblot, 1983)

P Cappellini and B Sordi (eds), *Codici. Una Riflessione di Fine Millennio* (Milan, Giuffrè, 2002)

J Carbonnier, 'Le Code civil' in Pierre Nora (ed), *Les Lieux de mémoire* vol 1(Paris, Éditions Gallimard, 1997)

P Caroni, 'Il codice rinviato. Resistenze europee all'elaborazione e alla diffusione del modello codicistico' in P Cappellini and B Sordi (eds), *Codici. Una riflessione di fine millennio* (Milan, Giuffrè, 2002)

——'Kodifikation' in A Erler and E Kaufmann (eds), *Handwoerterbuch zur Deutchen Rechtsgeschichte* (Berlin, Erich Schmidt Verlag, 1978) 907

——'Codificare su due versanti: quello civile e quello penale. Riflessioni sul mito del codice-guida' in E Tavilla (ed), *Giuseppe Luosi, giurista italiano ed europeo. Traduzioni, tradizioni e tradimenti della codificazione. A 200 anni dalla traduzione in italiano del Code Napoléon (1806–2006)* Atti del Convegno Internazionale di Studi, Mirandola-Modena, 19–20 October 2006 (2009) 347

M Cartabia and JHH Weiler, *L'Italia in Europa* (Bologna, Il Mulino, 2000)

A Carty 'Sovereignty in International Law: A Concept of Eternal Return' in J Hoffman et al eds, Sovereignty (Cassell, 1997) 101–16

C Castronovo, *Problema e Sistema nel Danno da Prodotti* (Milan, Giuffrè, 1979)

A Cavanna *Storia del Diritto Moderno in Europa* (Milan, Giuffrè, 1982–2006)

D Chalmers, 'The European Redistributive State and a European Law of Struggle' (2012) 18 *European Law Journal* 667

D Chalmers, 'Constituent Power and the Pluralistic Ethic' in M Loughlin and N Walker (eds), *The Paradox of Constitutionalism* (Oxford, Oxford University Press, 2008) 313

J Chirac (Président de la République) 'Message' in *Livre Centenaire*

H Coing, *Zur Geschichte der Privatrechtsystems* (Frankfurt am Main, Suhrkamp, 1962)

H Collins, 'The Impact of Human Rights on Contract Law in Europe' (2001) *University of Cambridge Legal Studies Research Papers Series* 8

—— *The European Civil Code: The Way Forward* (Cambridge, Cambidge University Press, 2007)
G Comandé, 'Comparative Remarks' in G Brüggemeier, A Colombi Ciacchi and G Comandé (eds), *Fundamental Rights and Private Law in the European Union*, vol I, *A Comparative Overview* (Cambridge, Cambridge University Press, 2010) 754
G Comparato *Nationalism and Private Law in Europe* (Oxford, Hart Publishing, 2014)
G Cornu, *Introduction, les personnes, les biens* (Paris, Éditions Montchrestien, 10th edn, 2001)
K Cosack in Hans Planitz (ed), *Die Rechtwissenschaft der Gegenwart in Selbstdarstellungen*, vol I (Leipzig, F Meiner, 1923–25) 16
R Craswell, 'Property Rules and Liability Rules in Unconscionability and Related Doctrines' (1993) 60 *University of Chicago Law Review* 1
M Delmas-Marty (ed), *Critique de l'Integration Normative* (Paris, PUF, 2004)
P de Man, *The Resistance to Theory* (Minneapolis, MN, University of Minnesota Press, 1986)
C Demolombe, *Cours de Code Napoléon* (1854–82)
C Donahue, 'Private Law without the State and During its Formation' in N Jansen and R Michaels (eds), *Beyond the State: Rethinking Private Law* (Tübingen, Mohr Siebeck, 2008) 121
J-P Dunand, 'Entre tradition et innovation. Analyse historique du concept de code' in J-P Dunand and B Winiger (eds), *Le Code Civil Francais dans le droit europeen* (Brussels, Bruylant, 2005) 3
M Duranton, *Cours de droit français suivant le Code civil* (3rd edn, 1834)
G Dürig, 'Der Grundgrechtssarz von der Menschenwuerde – Entwurf eines praktikablen Wertsystems der Grundrechte aus Art. 1 Abs. 1 in Verbindung mit Art. 19 Abs. II des Grundgesetzes' (1956) *AöR* 117
H Eidenmüller, *Effizienz als Rechtsprinzip. Möglichkeiten und Grenzen der ökonomischen Analyse des Rechts* (3rd edn, Tübingen, Mohr Siebeck 2005)
——'What Can Be Wrong with an Option? An optional Common European Sales Law as a Regulatory Tool' (2013) 50 *CMLR* 69
——'Recht als Produkt' (2009) 64 *Juristenzeitung* 641
H Eidenmüller, F Faust, H Grigoleit, N Jansen, G Wagner and R Zimmermann, 'The Common Frame of Reference for European Private Law – Policy Choices and Codification Problems' (2008) 28(4) *Oxford Journal of Legal Studies* 659, 665
——'Der Gemeinsame Referenzrahmen für das Europäische Privatrecht – Wertungsfragen and Kodifikationsprobleme' (2008) 63 *Juristenzeitung* 529
——N Jansen, E Kieninger, G Wagner and R Zimmermann, 'Der Vorschlag für eine Verordnung über ein Gemeinsames Europäisches Kaufrecht' (2012) *Juristenzeitung* 269
M Everson, 'The Limits of the 'Conflicts Approach': Law in Time of Political Turmoil' (2011) 2(2) *Transnational Legal Theory* 271
F Ewald, 'Rapport philosophique: une politique du droit' in *Le Code Civil 1804–2004 Livre du Bicentenaire* (Paris, Dalloz, 2004) 76
B Fauvarque-Cosson, 'Faut-il un Code Civil Européen?' (2002) 3 *Revue Trimestrielle de Droit Civil* 463, 480
——'Vers un droit commun européen de la vente' (2012) 188 *Recueil Dalloz* 34
M Fromont, 'Les droit fondamentauz dans l'ordre juridique de la République Fédérale d'Allemagne' in *Recueil d'e'tudes en l'honneur de Ch. Eisenmann* (Paris, Cujas, 1975) 55
G Fletcher, 'Three Nearly Sacred Books in Western Law' (2001–02) 54 *Arkansas Law Review* 1

HG Gadamer, *Wahrheit und Method. Grundzüge einer philosophischen Hermeneutik* (Tübingen, Mohr Siebeck, 1960)
A Gambaro, 'Codici e diritto giurisprudenziale' in P Cappellini and B Sordi (eds), *Codici, Una Riflessione di Fine Millennio* (Milan, Giuffrè, 2002) 507
G Gandolfi, 'Per un Codice Europeo dei Contratti' (1991) 45 *Rivista Trimestrale di Diritto e Procedura Civile* 781
F Gény, *Méthode d'interprétation et sources en droit privé positif. Essai Critique* (2nd edn, Paris, LGD, 1919)
—— 'La Technique législative dans la codification civile moderne (a propos du centeraire du code civil)' in *Le Code Civil Livre du centenaire* (Paris, Dalloz, 1904) 989
F Ghestin, *Traité de droit civil. Introduction générale* (Paris, Librairie Générale de Droit et de Jurisprudence, 1994)
G Gilmore, 'Legal Realism: Its Cause and Cure' (1961) 70 *Yale Law Journal* 1037
HP Glenn, *Legal Traditions in the World: Sustainable Diversity in Law* (4th edn, Oxford, Oxford University Press, 2010)
—— 'Persuasive Authority' (1987) 32 *McGill Law Journal* 261, 263
—— *The Cosmopolitan State* (Oxford, Oxford University Press, 2013)
R Goksor, 'Jurisprudence on Protection of Weaker Parties in European Contract Law from a Swedish and Nordic Perspective' (2006) 6 *Chicago-Kent Journal of International & Comparative Law* 184
F Gomez and JJ Ganuza, 'The Economics of Harmonising Private Law through Optional Rules in Pluralism' in L Niglia, *Pluralism and European Private Law* (Oxford, Hart Publishing, 2013) 181
J Gordley, 'The Myths of the French Civil Code' (1994) 42 *American Journal of Comparative Law* 459
G Gorla Voce, 'Giurisprudenza' in C Mortati and S Pugliatti (eds), *Enciclopedia del Diritto*, vol XIX (Milan, Giuffrè, 1970) 490
P Grossi, *Assolutismo Giuridico e Diritto Privato* (Milan, Giuffrè, 1998)
—— *Universalismo e particolarismo nel diritto* (Editoriale Scientifica, 2011)
S Grundmann, 'The Optional European Code on the Basis of the Acquis Communautaire – Starting Points and Trends' (2004) 10 *European Law Journal* 698, 710
—— 'CESL, Legal Nationalism or a Plea for Appropriate Governance' (2012) 8(3) *European Review of Contract Law* 241
G Gurvitch, *L'idée du droit social. Notion et Système du droit social. Histoire doctrinale depuis le 17 siècle jusqu'à la fin du 19 siècle* (Aalen, Scientiz Verlag, 1972, reprint of 1932)
J Habermas, *Between Facts and Norms: Contribution to a Discourse Theory of Law and Democracy*, W Rehg (trs) (Cambridge, MA, MIT Press, 1996)
HP Haferkamp, 'Bürgerliches Gesetzbuch (BGB)' in J Basedow, K Hopt and R Zimmermann (eds), *Max Plank Encyclopedia* (Oxford, Oxford University Press, 2012) 120
D Halberstam, 'Systems Pluralism and Institutional Pluralism in Constitutional Law: National, Supranational, and Global Governance' in M Avbelj and J Komarék (eds), *Constitutional Pluralism in the European Union and Beyond* (Oxford, Hart Publishing, 2012)
J-L Halpérin, *L'Impossible Code civil* (Paris, Presses Universitaires de France, 1992)
—— 'Le regard de l'historien' in *Le Code civil 1804-2004 Livre du Bicentenaire* (Dalloz, Paris, 2004) 43
—— *The French Civil Code*, T Weir (trs) (London and New York, UCL Press, 2006)
H Hattenbauer (ed), *Thibaut und Savigny. Ihre Programmatichen Schriften* (2nd edn, Munich, Verlag Franz Vahlen, 2002)

N Hartmann, *Il problema dell'essere spirituale* (Florence, La Nuova Italia, 1971)
M Heiddeger, *Die Frage nach dem Ding* (3rd edn, Tübingen, Mohr Siebeck, 1987)
M Hesselink, 'A Toolbox for Judges' (2011) 17 *European Law Journal* 441
——'An Optional Instrument on EU Contract Law: Could it Increase Legal Certainty and Foster Cross-Border Trade?' *European Parliament (2010), Policy Department, PE 425.642*
——'If You Don't Like Our Principles We Have Others' in R Brownsword, H-W Micklitz, L Niglia and S Weatherill (eds), *The Foundations of European Private Law* (Oxford, Hart Publishing, 2011) 59
—— *CFR and Social Justice: A Short Study for the European Parliament on the Values Underlying the Draft Common Frame of Reference for European Private Law: What Roles for Fairness and Social Justice?* (Munich, Sellier, 2008)
—— *The New European Private Law* (The Hague, Kluwer Law International, 2002)
——'The European Commission's Action Plan: Towards a More Coherent European Contract Law?' (2004) 12 *European Review of Private Law* 397
E Hondius, Book Review of Niglia 'The Transformation of Contract in Europe' in (2004) 6 *European Review of Private Law* 855
N Irti, *L'etá della decodificazione* (4th edn, Milan, Giuffrè, 1999)
——'L'etá della decodificazione' *in Diritto e Societá* (1978) 613
N Jansen, *The Making of Legal Authority: Non-legislative Codifications in Historical and Comparative Perspective* (Oxford, Oxford University Press, 2010)
——'Legal Pluralism in Europe: National Laws, European Legislation, and Non-legislative Codifications' in L Niglia (ed), *Pluralism and European Private Law* (Oxford, Hart Publishing, 2013)
—— and R Zimmermann, '"Recasting the Acquis Communautaire?" A Critical Evaluation of the Principles of the Existing EC Contract Law' [2008] *Modern Law Review* 505
—— and R Michaels, 'Private Law and the State' (2007) 71 *Rabels Zeitschrift* 395
C Joerges, 'The Europeanization of Private Law as a Rationalization Process and as a Contest of Disciplines: An Analysis of the Directive on Unfair Terms in Consumer Contracts' (1995) 3 *European Review of Private Law* 175
—— and NS Ghaleigh (eds), *Darker Legacies of Law in Europe* (Oxford, Hart Publishing, 2003)
—— 'On the Legitimacy of Europeanising Private Law: Considerations on a Justice-Making Law for the EU Multi-level System' (2003) 7(3) *Electronic Journal of Comparative Law*, http://www.ejcl.org/ejcl/73/art73-3.html
—— and J Falke (eds), *Karl Polanyi, Globalisation and the Potential of Law in Transnational Markets* (Oxford, Hart Publishing, 2011)
L Josserand, 'La reconstruction d'un droit de classe' *Dalloz*, 1937, *chron* 1
Du Kennedy, 'Comment on Rudolf Wietholter's "Materialization and Proceduralization in Modern Law" and "Proceduralization of the Category of Law"' in C Joerges and D Trubek (eds), *Critical Legal Thought: An American-German Debate* (Baden-Baden, Nomos Verlagsgesellschaft, 1988)
——'Thoughts on Coherence, Social Values and National Tradition in Private Law' in M Hesselink (ed), *The Politics of a European Civil Code* (The Hague, Kluwer Law International, 2006); and in Du Kennedy (ed), *Legal Reasoning. Collected Essays* (Aurora, CO, The Davies Group Publishers, 2008)
——'A Transnational Genealogy of Proportionality in Private Law' in R Brownsword, H-W Micklitz, L Niglia and S Weatherill (eds), *The Foundations of European Private Law* (Oxford, Hart Publishing, 2011) 185

Du Kennedy, 'Three Globalizations of Law and Legal Thought: 1850–2000' in David M Trubek and Alvaro Santos (eds), *The New Law and Economic Development: A Critical Appraisal* (Cambridge, Cambridge University Press, 2006) 19

W Kerber and S Grundmann, 'An Optional European Contract Law Code: Advantages and Disadvantages' (2006) 21 *European Journal of Law and Economics* 215

PF Kjaer, 'The Structural Transformation of Embeddedness' in C Joerges and J Falke (eds), *Karl Polanyi, Globalisation and the Potential of Law in Transnational Markets* (Oxford, Hart Publishing, 2011) 85

M Koskenniemi, 'Hegemonic Regimes' in MA Young (ed), *Regime Interaction in International Law: Facing Fragmentation* (New York, Cambridge University Press, 2012) 305

H Kötz, 'Taking Civil Codes Less Seriously' (1987) 50 *Modern Law Review* 1

M Kumm, 'Who is Afraid of the Total Constitution? Constitutional Rights as Principles and the Constitutionalization of Private Law' (2006) 7 *German Law Journal* 341

K H Ladeur '"We, the European People . . ." – Relâche?' (2008) *European Law Journal* 14

F Larnaude, 'Le Code Civil et la nécessité de sa Revision' in *Le Code civil 1804–1904 Livre du Centenaire* (Paris, Dalloz, 2004) 901

F Larouche and P Chirico (eds), *Economic Analysis of the DCFR: The Work of the Economic Impact Group within CoPECL* (Munich, Sellier, 2010)

M Lasser, 'Judicial (Self-)Portraits: Judicial Discourses in the French Legal System' (1995) 104 *Yale Law Journal* 1325

M La Torre, 'The Poverty of Global Constitutionalism' in L Niglia (ed), *Pluralism and European Private Law* (Oxford, Hart Publishing, 2013) 53

F Laurent, *Principes de droit civil français* (1869–78)

P Legrand, 'Against a European Civil Code' (1997) 60 *Modern Law Review* 44

P Letto-Vanamo, 'Fragmentation and Coherence of Law – A Historical Approach' in P Letto-Vanamo and J Smits (eds), *Coherence and Fragmentation in European Private Law* (Münich, Sellier Europa Publisher, 2012) 151

Y Lequette, 'Quelques remarques à propos du projet de code civil européen de M von Bar' (2002) *Dalloz Chron* 2202

N Luhmann, *Theory of Society*, vol 1, R Barett (trs) (Stanford, Stanford University Press, 2012)

G Lukács, *History and Class Consciousness*, R Livingstone (trs) (Cambridge, MA, MIT Press, 1971)

B Lurger, 'A Radical View of Pluralism?' in L Niglia (ed), *Pluralism and European Private Law* (Oxford, Hart Publishing, 2013) 173

J Madison (letter to Jeremy Bentham, London of 8 May 1816 (Washington)), reproduced in P Schoefield and J Harris (eds), *Jeremy Bentham, 'Legislator of the World': Writings on Codification, Law, and Education* (Oxford, Clarendon Press, 1998) 36

C Mak, Book Review of L Niglia (ed), *Pluralism and European Private Law* in (2013) 51(2) *Common Market Law Review* 717

B Markesinis, 'Why a Code is Not the Best Way to Advance the Cause of European Legal Unity' (1998) 5 *European Review of Public Law* 519

U Mattei, 'Hard Code Now!' (2002) 2(1) *Global Jurist Frontiers* 1535

L Mengoni, *Diritto e Valori* (Bologna, Il Mulino, 1985)

——'L'Europa dei codici o un codice per l'Europa?' (Rome, Centro di Studi e Ricerche di Diritto Comparato e Straniero, 1993)

——'Problema e sistema nella controversia sul metodo giuridico' (1976) *Jus* 3

——'Note sul rapporto tra fonti di diritto comunitario e fonti di diritto interno degli Stati membri' in N Lipari (ed), *Diritto Privato Europeo e Categorie Civilistiche* (Napoli, ESI, 1988) 32

P Mengozzi, 'The Judicial Protection of Individual Rights and the Principle of Proportionality After Lisbon' in L Niglia (ed), Symposium 'Balancing in European Law' (2013–2014) 16 *CYELS* 335

—— 'Il rapporto tra stati e individui nella giurisprudenza comunitaria' in *La Formazione del Diritto Europeo. Giornata di Studio per Alberto Trabucchi nel centenario della nascita Quaderni della Rivista di Diritto Civile* (Padua, Cedam, 2008) 111

E-J Mestmäcker, *Wirtschaft und Verfassung in der Europäischen Union* (Baden-Baden, Nomos, 2004)

R Michaels, 'Code vs Code. Nationalist and Internationalist Images of the Code Civil in the French Resistance to a European Codification' (2012) 8 *European Review of Contract Law* 277

—— 'Why We Have No Theory of European Private Law Pluralism' in L Niglia (ed), *Pluralism and European Private Law* (Oxford, Hart Publishing, 2013)

—— 'Of Islands and the Ocean: The Two Rationalities of European Private Law' in R Brownsword, H-W Micklitz, L Niglia and S Weatherill (eds), *The Foundations of European Private Law* (Oxford, Hart Publishing, 2011) 139

H-W Micklitz, 'The Visible Hand of European Regulatory Private Law' (2009) 28 *Yearbook of European Law* 3

—— 'The Concept of Competitive Contract Law' (2005) 23 *Penn State International Law Review* 549

—— 'The Expulsion of the Concept of Protection from the Consumer Law and the Return of the Social Elements in the Civil Law: A Bittersweet Polemic' in EUI (European University Institute) Working Papers 2012/03

MC Mirrow, 'The Power of Codification in Latin America. Simon Bolivar and the Code Napoleon' (2000) 8 *Tulane Journal of International and Comparative Law* 83

C Möllers, *The Three Branches. A Comparative Model of Separation Powers* (Oxford, Oxford University Press, 2013)

CT Montholon, *Récits de la Captivité de l'Empereur Napoléon à Sainte-Hélène I* (Paris, Paulin, 1847)

VP Mortari, 'Codice (Storia)' in *Enciclopedia del Diritto* (Milan, Giuffrè, 1970) 227

L Muratori, 'Dei Difetti della Giurisprudenza. Trattato' *Venetiis* 1742

R Nicolò, 'Codice Civile' in Francesco Calasso (ed), *Enciclopedia del Diritto*, vol VII (Milan, Giuffrè, 1960) 240

H Nieuwendhuis, 'Fundamental Rights Talk. An Enrichment of Legal Discourse in Private Law' in T Barkhuysen and S Lindenbergh (eds), *Constitutionalisation of Private Law* (Leiden, Martinus Nijhoff, 2006) 1

L Niglia, 'The Non-Europeanization of Private Law' (2001) 4 *European Review of Private Law* 575

—— *The Transformation of Contract in Europe* (The Hague, Kluwer Law International, 2003)

—— 'Standard Form Contracts in Europe and North America – One Hundred Years of Unfair Terms?' in C Rickett and T Telfer (eds), *International Perspectives on Consumers' Access to Justice* (Cambridge, Cambridge University Press, 2003) 101

—— *Trilogy on European Private Law (2006–2010)*:

—— 'Taking Comparative Law Seriously – Europe's Private Law and the Poverty of the Orthodoxy' (2006) 54(3) *American Journal of Comparative Law* 401 (Instalment One)

L Niglia, 'Beyond Enchantment: The Possibility of a New European Private Law' (2009) 28 *Yearbook of European Law* 60 (Instalment Two)

——'Of Harmonisation and Fragmentation – The Problem of Legal Transplants and the Europeanisation of Private Law' (2010) 2 *Maastricht Journal of European and Comparative Law* 116 (Instalment Three)

——'Form and Substance in European Constitutional Law: The Social Character of Indirect Effect' (2010) 16(4) *European Law Journal* 439.

——Review of *The Cambridge Companion of European Union Law (2011) European Law Review* 36 760

——'Of Jurisdictional Balancing' in R Brownsword, H-W Micklitz, L Niglia and S Weatherill (eds), *The Foundations of European Private Law* (Oxford, Hart Publishing, 2011)

——'The Political Foundations of European Private Law: Editorial' in R Brownsword, H-W Micklitz, L Niglia and S Weatherill (eds), *The Foundations of European Private Law* (Oxford, Hart Publishing, 2011) 177

——'Of Constitutionality and Private Consumer Law in Europe' (2012) 4 *Journal of European Consumer and Market Law* 223

——'The Question Concerning the Common Frame of Reference' (2012) 18 *European Law Journal* 736

——(Niglia et al, co-ed) *The Foundations of European Private Law* (Oxford, Hart Publishing, 2011)

——(ed), *Pluralism and European Private Law* (Oxford, Hart Publishing, 2013)

——'The Double Life of Pluralism in Europe' in L Niglia (ed), *Pluralism and European Private Law* (Oxford, Hart Publishing, 2013) 249

——'Pluralism in a New Key: Between Plurality and Normativity' in L Niglia (ed), *Pluralism and European Private Law* (Oxford, Hart Publishing, 2013) 9

——'An Age of European Re-Codification' (essay on file with author 2014–15)

——'Of Complexity and Tradition' (essay on file with author 2014–15)

——(ed), Symposium 'Balancing in European Law' *Cambridge Yearbook of European Legal Studies* (2014) 333ff.

——'Constitutionalising European Private Law' (essay on file with author 2014–15)

——'Taking Private Law Rights Seriously–Of Balancing and the Jurisprudence of the Court of Justice of the European Union' in L Niglia (ed), *Symposium–Balancing in European Law* in *Cambridge Yearbook of European Legal Studies* (Oxford, Hart Publishing, 2014) 394

HC Nipperdey, *Grundrechte und Privatrecht. Eine Universitätrede* in Hans C Nipperdey (ed), *Festschrift für Eric Molitor* (M*ünchen, Beck*, 1962) 17

EA O'Hara and L E Ribstein, *The Law Market* (Oxford, Oxford University Press, 2009)

P Oestmann (ed), *Gewohnheit. Gebot. Gesetz. Normativität in Geschichte und Gegenwart* (Tübingen, Mohr Siebeck, 2011)

——*Rechtsvielfalt vor Gericht. Rechtsanwendung und Partikluarrecht im Alten Reich* (Frankfurt, Klostermann, 2002)

C Offe, 'Europe Entrapped' (2013) 19(5) *European Law Journal* 95

S Patti, *Diritto Privato e Codificatione europea* (Milan, Giuffrè, 2007)

I Pernice and F Mayer, 'De la constitution composée de l'Europe' (2000) *Revue trimestrelle de droit européen* 623

——'Multilevel Constitutionalism in the European Union' (2002) 27 *European Law Review* 511

J-E-M Portalis, 'Discours préliminaire sur le Code Civil' in *Discours, rapports et travaux inédits sur le Code Civil* (Paris, Joubert, 1844)
GF Puchta, *Das Gewohnheitsrecht* (Erlangen, Palm, vol I, 1828; vol II 1837)
L Raiser, *Die Aufgabe des Privatrechts* (Kronberg/Ts, Athenaeum, 1977)
F Ranieri, *Das Europäische Privatrecht des 19. und 20. Jahrunderts. Studien zur Rechtsgeschichte und Rechtsvergleichung* (Berlin, Dunker und Humblot, 2007)
——'L'influence du Code Civil sue les codifications du 19e siècle: Essor et déclin d'un modèle européen' in *Das Europäische Privatrecht des 19. und 20. Jarhunderts. Studien zur Rechtsgeschichte und Rechtsvergleichung* (Berlin, Duncker & Humblot, 2007)),
F Realmonte *Il Problema del Rapporto di Causalità nel Risarcimento del Danno* (Giuffré, Milano, 1967)
N Reich, 'Balancing in Private Law and the Imperatives of the Public Interest' in R Brownsword, H Micklitz, L Niglia and S Weatherill (eds), *The Foundations of European Private Law* (Oxford, Hart Publishing, 2011) 221
——'Pluralism and Private Law in the Union' in L Niglia (ed), *Pluralism and European Private Law* (Oxford, Hart Publishing, 2013) 73
MW Reimann, 'The Historical School Against Codification: Savigny, Carter, and the Defeat of the New York Civil Code' (1989) 37 *American Journal of Comparative Law* 95
——'Product Liability in a Global Context: The Hollow Victory of the European Model' (2003) 2 *European Review of Private Law* 128
——'Comparative Law and Private International Law' in M Reimann and R Zimmermann (eds), *The Oxford Handbook of Comparative Law* (2nd edn, Oxford, Oxford University Press, 2008) 1375
O Remien, S Herrler and P Limmer (eds), *Gemeinsames Europäisches Kaufrecht für die EU?* (Munich, CH Beck, 2012)
P Rémy 'Regards sur le code' in *Le Code Civil 1804–2004 Livre du Bicentenaire* (Paris, Dalloz, 2004) 99
A Riles, 'The Anti-Network' (2009) *American Journal of Comparative Law* 612
S Rodotà, 'Il Codice civile e il processo costituente europeo' in V Roppo (ed), *A European Civil Code? Perspectives and Problems* (Milan, Giuffrè, 2005) 183
——'Ideologie e tecniche della riforma del diritto civile' (1967) *Rivista del Diritto Commerciale* I, 84
——'Il Codice civile e il processo costituente europeo' in V Roppo (ed), *A European Civil Code? Perspectives and Problems* (Milan, Giuffrè, 2005) 183
A Rosas, 'Balancing Fundamental Rights in EU Law' in L Niglia (ed), Symposium 'Balancing in European Law' *Cambridge Yearbook of European Legal Studies* (2014) 348
M Ruffert, *Vorrang der Verfassung und Eigenständigkeit des Privatrechts* (Tübingen, Mohr Siebeck, 2001)
J Rutgers, 'An Optional Instrument and Social Dumping' (2006) *European Review of Contract Law* 199
R Sacco, 'Rapport de Synthése' in *La circulation du smodèle juridique français* (Paris, Journées franco-italiennes, 1994)
——'Legal Formants' (1991) 39 *American Journal of Competition Law* 1
R Saleilles, *Étude sur la théorie générale de l'obligation d'après le premier Code civil pour l'Empire Allemand* (3rd edn, Paris, LGD, 1914; 1st edn, 1889)
—— *De la déclaration de volonté: Contribution à l'étude de l'acte juridique dans le Code civil allemand* (Paris, 1901)

R Saleilles, *De la personnalité juridique: Histoire et théorie* (Paris, 1910)

——'Préface' in F Gény (ed), *Méthode d'interprétation et sources en droit privé positif. Essai Critique* (Paris, LGD, 1919)

R Savatier, *Les Métamorphoses économiques et sociales du droit privé d'aujourd'hui* (2nd edn, Paris, Dalloz, 1959)

FC von Savigny, *Vom Beruf unserer Zeit für Gesetzgebung und Rechtswissenschaft* (Heidelberg, Mohr und Zimmer, 1814); translated as *Of the Vocation of Our Age for Legislation and Jurisprudence*, A Hayward (trs) (London, Littlewood & Co, 1831)

FC von Savigny, *System des heutigen römischen Rechts* (Berlin, Aalen, Scientia-Verlag, 1840–1849)

Ch U Schmid, 'The Instrumentalist Conception of the Acquis Communautaire in Consumer Law and its Implications on a European Contract Law Code' (2005) 1 *European Review of Contract Law* 211

—— *Die Instrumentalisierung des Privatrechts durch die Europäische Union. Privatrecht und Privatrechtskonzeptionen in der Entwicklung der Europäischen Integrationsverfassung* (Baden-Baden, Nomos, 2010)

K Schmidt, *Lex mercatoria: Allheilmittel? Rätsel? Chimäre?* in Junichi Murakami et al (eds), *Globalisierung und Recht* (Berlin, de Gruyter, 2007) 153

AM Slaughter, 'A Typology of Transjudicial Communication' (1994–95) 29 *University of Richmond Law Review* 99

P Schlechtriem, *Restitution und Bereicherungsaugleich in Europa: Eine Rechtsvergleichende Darstellung* (Tübingen, Mohr Siebeck, Volume I, 2001; Volume II, 2001)

H Schulte-Nölke, F Zoll, N Jansen and R Schulze (eds), *Der Entwurf für ein optionales europäisches Kaufrecht* (Munich, Sellier, 2012)

F Sclopis, *Storia della legislazione italiana, III, Dall'epoca della rivoluzione francese [1789] a quella delle riforme italiane [1847], parte prima* (Turin, 1864)

J Smits, 'A Radical View on Pluralism' in L Niglia (ed), *Pluralism and European Private Law* (Oxford, Hart Publishing, 2013) 161

——'Party Choice and the Common European Sales Law, or: How to Prevent the CESL from Becoming a Lemon on the Law Market (2012) 50 *CMLR* 51

——'Private Law and Fundamental Rights: A Sceptical View' in T Barkhuysen and S Lindenbergh (eds), *Constitutionalisation of Private Law* (Leiden, Martinus Nijhoff, 2006)

FG Snyder, *The EU, The WTO and China. Legal Pluralism and International Trade Regulation* (Oxford, Hart Publishing, 2010)

G Solari, *Individualismo e Diritto Privato* (Turin, 1959)

—— *Filosofia del Diritto Privato. Volume II. Storicismo e Diritto Privato* (1st edn, Turin, Giappichelli, 1971, 1940)

A Somek, *Individualism: An Essay on the Authority of the European Union* (Oxford, Oxford University Press, 2008)

E Stein, 'International Integration and Democracy: No Love at First Sight' (2001) 95 *American Journal of International Law* 489

ME Storme, 'The Foundations of Private *Law* in a Multi-level Structure: Balancing, Distribution of Law-making Power and other Constitutional Issues' in R Brownsword, H-W Micklitz, L Niglia and S Weatherill (eds), *The Foundations of European Private Law* (Oxford, Hart Publishing, 2011) 379

Study Group on Social Justice in European Private Law, 'Manifesto' (2004) 6 *European Law Journal* 653

G Tarello, *Storia della Cultura Giuridica Moderna. Assolutismo e Codificazione del Diritto* (Bologna, Il Mulino, 1976)

E Tavilla (ed), *Giuseppe Luosi, giurista italiano ed europeo. Traduzioni, tradizioni e tradimenti della codificazione. A 200 anni dalla traduzione in italiano del Code Napoléon (1806–2006)* (Atti del Convegno Internazionale di Studi, Mirandola-Modena, 19–20 October 2006 (2009)), 337

G Teubner, *Constitutional Fragments* (Oxford, Oxford University Press, 2012)

——'Legal Irritants: Good Faith in British Law or How Unifying Law Ends Up in New Divergencies' (1998) 61 *Modern Law Review* 1, 11

AFJ Thibaut, *Über die Notwendigkeit eines allgemeinen bürgerlichen Rechts für Deutschland* (Heidelberg, Mohr und Zimmer, 1814), reprinted in Hans Hattenbauer, *Thibaut und Savigny. Ihre Programmatisches Schriften* (Munich, Verlag Franz Vahlen, 1973) 'Trenta giuristi europei sull'idea di codice europeo dei contratti (2012) 1 *Contratto e Impresa/Europa* (special issue)

T Tridimas, 'Fundamental Rights, General Principles of EU Law, and the Charter' in L Niglia (ed), Symposium 'Balancing in European Law' (2013–2014) 16 *CYELS* 362

P Ungari, *L'eta' della codificazione. Lotta per la codificazione e scuole di giurisprudenza nel Risorgimento* (Napoli, Edizioni Scientifiche Italiane, 1967)

RC Van Caenegem, *A Historical Introduction to Private Law*, DEL Johnston (trs) (Cambridge, Cambridge University Press, 1992)

——*Judges, Legislators and Professors: Chapters in European Legal History* (Cambridge, Cambridge University Press, 1987)

C van Dam, *European Tort Law* (Oxford, Oxford University Press, 2006)

W Van Gerven, 'Codifying European Private Law: Top Down and Bottom Up' in S Grundmann and J Stuyck (eds), *An Academic Green Paper on European Contract Law* (The Hague, London, Kluwer Law International, 2002) 405

——'The ECJ Case-law as a Means of Unification of Private Law?' in AS Hartkamp et al (eds), *Towards a European Civil Code* (2nd edn The Hague, Kluwer Law International, 1998) 91

A Vauchez and B de Witte (eds), *Lawyering Europe: European Law as a Transnational Social Field* (Oxford, Hart Publishing, 2013).

C Varga, *Codification as a Socio-historical Phenomenon* (Budapest, Akadémiai Kiadó, 1991)

——'The Contemporaneity of Lukács' Ideas with Modern Social Theoretical Thought' (2013) 99 *Archiv fuer Rechts- und Sozialphilosophie* 42

T Vesting, 'Constitutionalism or Legal Theory' in C Joerges et al (eds), *Transnational Governance and Constitutionalism* (Oxford, Hart Publishing, 2004)

L Vogel, 'Re-codification civile et renouvellement des sources internes' in *Livre Bicentenaire* 159

Ch von Bar, *The Common European Law* of Torts (Oxford, Oxford University Press, Volume I, 1998; Volume II, 2000)

—— et al (eds), *Principles, Definitions and Model Rules of European Private Law: The Draft Common Frame of Reference* (Münich, Sellier, Interim Outline Edition, 2008)

—— and E Clive (eds), *Principles, Definitions and Model Rules of European Private Law. Draft Common Frame of Reference* (Oxford, Oxford University Press, 2009)

—— et al (eds), *Principles, Definitions and Model Rules of European Private Law: The Draft Common Frame of Reference* (Münich, Sellier, Outline Edition, 2009)

——'A CFR for European Private Law – Academic Efforts and Political Realities' (2008) 23 *Tulane European and Civil Law Forum* 37

Ch von Bar, 'Preface' in *The Common European Law of Torts* (Oxford, Oxford University Press, 1998)
N Walker, 'The Idea of Constitutional Pluralism' (2002) 65 *Modern Law Review* 317
——'The Anti-political Polity' (2010) 73(1) *Modern Law Review* 141
A Watson, *The Making of the Civil Law* (Cambridge, MA, Harvard University Press, 1981)
S Weatherill, 'Consumer Protection under EU Law "is not absolute": *yes, but be careful!*' (2012) 2 *European Review of Contract Law* 221
——'The Multi-level Structure of Private Law: Introduction' in R Brownsword, H-W Micklitz, L Niglia and S Weatherill (eds), *The Foundations of European Private Law* (Oxford, Hart Publishing, 2011) 319
——'Competence and European Private Law' in C Twigg-Flesner (ed), *The Cambridge Companion to European Union Private Law* (Cambridge, Cambridge University Press, 2010)
——'An Ever Tighter Grip: The European Court's Pro-consumer Interpretation of the EC's Directives Affecting Contract Law' in M Andenas et al (eds), *Liber Amicorum Guido Alpa. Private Law Beyond the National Systems* (London, British Institute of International and Comparative Law, 2007) 1037
M Weber, *Rechtssoziologie*, J Winckelmann (ed), (Neuwied, Luchthand, 1960) 249
——'Die Drei Typen der legitimen Herrschaft' in M Weber, *Gesalmmelte Aufsäetze zur Wissenschaftslehre* (7th edn Tübingen, JC B Mohr, Johannes Wincklemann ed, 1988) 475–88 (trans by G Roth and C Wittich, M Weber *Economy and Society* 1968, I, 53).
JHH Weiler, *Il sistema comunitario europeo* (Il Mulino, 1985).
—— *The Constitution of Europe; "Do the New Clothes Have an Emperor?" and Other Essays on European Integration* (Cambridge, Cambridge University Press, 1999)
—— *To Be a European Citizen: Eros and Civilization* (Toronto, Toronto University Press, 1998)
F Wieacker, *Das Sozialmodell der klassischen Privatrechtsgesetzbuecher und die Entwicklung der modernen Gesellschaft* (Karlsruhe, CF Mueller, 1953)
——'Aufstieg, Blüte und Krisis der Kodifikationsidee' in *Festschrift für Gustav Boehmer* (Bonn, Röhrscheid, 1954) 34
——*A History of Private Law in Europe* (Oxford, Clarendon Press, 1995)
——*Aufstieg, Bluete und Krisis der Kodifikationsidee in Festschrift fuer Gustav Boerhmer* (Bonn, Roehrsheid, 1954)
T Wilhelmsson, 'The Variety of Welfarism in European Contract Law' (2004) 10 *European Law Journal* 712
H Wüstendörfer, 'Die deutsche Rechtswissenschaft am Wendepunkt' (1913) 110 *Archiv für die civilistische Praxis* 224
F Zenati-Castaing, 'L'avenir de la codification' (2011) 63(2) *Revue Internationale de Droit Comparé* 355
R Zimmermann, 'Codification: History and Present Significance of an Idea' (1995) 3 *European Review of Private Law* 95
—— *Roman Law, Contemporary Law, European Law: The Civilian Tradition Today* (Oxford, Oxford University Press, 2001)
——'The Present State of European Private Law' (2009) 57 *American Journal of Comparative Law* 479
——'Codification: The Civilian Experience Reconsidered on the Eve of a Common European Sales Law' (2012) 8(4) *European Review of Contract Law* 367
KE Zweigert and H Kötz, *An Introduction to Comparative Law*, T Weir (trs) (Oxford, Clarendon Press, 1998)

Index

www.ingramcontent.com/pod-product-compliance
Ingram Content Group UK Ltd.
Pitfield, Milton Keynes, MK11 3LW, UK
UKHW021038150926
475561UK00003B/167